NORTH CAROLINIANA SOCIETY IMPRINTS
NUMBER 14

This edition is limited to
five hundred signed copies
(plus 100 "A" copies for authors)
of which this is number

125

NORTH CAROLINIANA SOCIETY IMPRINTS
H. G. Jones, General Editor

No. 1. *An Evening at Monticello: An Essay in Reflection* (1978)
by Edwin M. Gill

No. 2. *The Paul Green I Know* (1978)
by Elizabeth Lay Green

No. 3. *The Albert Coates I Know* (1979)
by Gladys Hall Coates

No. 4. *The Sam Ervin I Know* (1980)
by Jean Conyers Ervin

No. 5. *Sam Ragan* (1981)
by Neil Morgan

No. 6. *Thomas Wolfe of North Carolina* (1982)
edited by H. G. Jones

No. 7. *Gertrude Sprague Carraway* (1982)
by Sam Ragan

No. 8. *John Fries Blair* (1983)
by Margaret Blair McCuiston

No. 9. *William Clyde Friday and Ida Howell Friday* (1984)
by Georgia Carroll Kyser and William Brantley Aycock

No. 10. *William S. Powell, North Carolina Historian* (1985)
by David Stick and William C. Friday

No. 11. *"Gallantry Unsurpassed"* (1985)
edited by Archie K. Davis

No. 12. *Mary and Jim Semans, North Carolinians* (1986)
by W. Kenneth Goodson

No. 13. *The High Water Mark* (1986)
edited by Archie K. Davis

No. 14. *Raleigh and Quinn* (1987)
edited by H. G. Jones

RALEIGH AND QUINN

The Explorer and His Boswell

Papers Presented at the International Sir Walter Raleigh Conference,
Chapel Hill, North Carolina, 27–28 March 1987,
together with
Papers Read at a Session Titled "The Life and Work of David Beers
Quinn" at a Meeting of the American Historical Association,
Chicago, 29 December 1986

Edited by

H. G. JONES

Chapel Hill

NORTH CAROLINIANA SOCIETY, INC.

AND THE

NORTH CAROLINA COLLECTION

1987

Contents

Preface

Because virtually all of the edited proceedings are printed herein, little needs to be said prefatorily about the International Sir Walter Raleigh Conference (and its associated banquet in honor of David Beers Quinn) held at the University of North Carolina at Chapel Hill on 27–28 March 1987 or the special session titled "The Life and Work of David Beers Quinn" conducted at the annual meeting of the American Historical Association in Chicago on 29 December 1986.

Originally we intended to publish only the papers of the Raleigh Conference, held in connection with the four-hundredth anniversary of the Roanoke colonies, but in recent decades the name Raleigh has become almost inextricably associated with that of a professor at the University of Liverpool whose prodigious research and voluminous writings have peeled away much of the mystery surrounding the Elizabethan courtier and explorer. Consequently, without asking anyone else's opinion, we decided to include in this volume the papers relating to Walter Raleigh and David Quinn given on all three occasions. When our decision was revealed, all of the speakers happily agreed — except, of course, David Quinn, who was kept blissfully unaware of our machinations until it was too late for him to protest effectively. Having gone that far, we took another step by including an updated bibliography of Quinn's professional publications.

Bringing together papers and introductions written by more than two dozen persons with as many personalities, several disciplines, and three nationalities presents a challenge to any editor. Aware of the proclivity of reviewers to dismiss collected essays for their unevenness and disparity of content, style, and format, but wishing neither to pit one discipline against another nor to cause an international incident, in the editing process we allowed considerable latitude to our authors. That permissiveness even extended to the spelling of names — such as those of the courtier (Raleigh, Ralegh) and his science advisor (Harriot, Hariot). We have also been uncharacteristically tolerant of variety in footnoting. Still, we believe that the papers en masse do have commonality in their content, style, and format to warrant inclusion between these covers, and the North Caroliniana Society is pleased to make them available to a wider audience.

Robert G. Anthony, Jr., of the North Carolina Collection assisted in the editing and proofing processes, Jenny Long retyped many of the manuscripts, and the staff of the University of North Carolina's Printing and Duplicating Department exhibited competence, patience, and good humor in our effort to meld the writings of twenty-five speakers into one book. Finally, the staff of the North Carolina Collection, in the midst of moving its rich holdings into spacious and luxuriously renovated facilities, only occasionally muttered about the curator's obvious preference for editing manuscripts over the more physical chore of moving books and artifacts.

H. G. Jones

Chapel Hill, North Carolina
1 September 1987

I

Proceedings
of the
International Sir Walter Raleigh Conference
Held at the
University of North Carolina at Chapel Hill
27-28 March 1987

Cosponsored by

America's Four Hundredth Anniversary Committee
University of North Carolina at Chapel Hill
National Humanities Center
North Caroliniana Society

Most of the speakers at the International Sir Walter Raleigh Conference are pictured in two groups. Left to right, top photo: Kupperman, Canny, Powell, Mills, Wallis, Williamson, Thirsk, Quinn, Warren, Youings, and Thrower; lower photo: Canny, Thrower, Wallis, Youings, Armitage, Kupperman, and Mills. *All photos by North Carolina Collection unless otherwise noted.*

Welcoming Remarks

H. G. Jones
Curator, North Carolina Collection, and
Secretary-Treasurer, North Caroliniana Society

Less than twenty-four hours ago the university campus was treated to a concert by Walter Raleigh Babson and his banjo. Now, I mean no disrespect, and I probably reveal the degree to which my life is sheltered, but I am acquainted with neither Mr. Babson nor his music. His timely appearance, however, entirely coincidental with the opening of this conference, may in the eyes of some students provide a bit of credibility to our two-day study of the man whose name he bears. With or without credibility, we now officially open the International Sir Walter Raleigh Conference. In doing so, I call your attention to the schedule to which we shall rather strictly adhere, for with the exception of civility, perhaps the most precious measure of a society is the efficiency with which it makes use of time. Aside from that admonition, let me make these brief points:

First, during the next thirty-six hours we will hear much about history, but we also will be making history, for the Raleigh Conference is the very first activity in this hallowed Louis Round Wilson Library following its $6 million renovation to accommodate the North Carolina Collection and the other special collections. This is an exciting moment for those of us who have for three years rankled under the proof that the governmental bureaucracy is the embodiment of Murphey's law and who at times lost hope that the project would *ever* be completed. Well, it still is not quite completed, but the long awaited move back into our expanded quarters—the North Carolina Collection will occupy most of this main floor plus four other stack levels—is no more than five months off (we say as we cross our fingers). Sadly, we can show you little of the hollow building during the conference, and, in fact we will be restricted to this floor where only a portion of the new North Caroliniana Gallery, featuring the Sir Walter Raleigh Rooms and a portion of the Raleigh Collection, may be seen. You must come back in the fall to see the transformation of the building.

Second, please wear your badge throughout the conference, for the building is open only to registrants. Besides, those little colored dots on the badge determine to which of the meal functions you will be admitted. Five persons wear red-edged badges—mine plus four members of our staff who will be with us throughout the conference to help solve any problems that arise. They are R. Neil Fulghum, the keeper of the North Caroliniana Gallery; Alice R. Cotten and Robert G. Anthony, Jr., who are handling the registration desk; and Jerry W. Cotten, who will record the conference on tape and film.

Welcomers to the Raleigh Conference were, left to right, top to bottom, H. G. Jones, Samuel R. Williamson, Kent R. Mullikin, and Lindsay C. Warren, Jr.

Third, I must thank several of our library officials for enabling us to pierce the armor of the bureaucracy for permission to hold this unorthodox use of the unfinished building: Joe A. Hewitt, the acting university librarian; Marcella Grendler, associate university librarian for special collections; Larry Alford, assistant university librarian for business and finance; and Michael G. Martin, university archivist and general factotum during the renovation process.

Finally, as the printed program indicates, the conference is sponsored by a private organization, two institutions, and a state agency. As secretary-treasurer of the North Caroliniana Society, I am standing in for our president, Archie K. Davis, who will join us later and speak at the banquet tonight. It has been our pleasure to handle arrangements. With us this morning are representatives of the other sponsors, and each of them will greet you in turn.

Samuel R. Williamson, the provost of the University of North Carolina at Chapel Hill, is author of *The Politics of Grand Strategy* and editor of *Essays on World War I.* As a professor of history with specialization in international affairs, it is appropriate that he welcome this international conference on behalf of the university. It was Provost Williamson who provided resources to bring three of our participants from England.

The prestige of our Research Triangle has been enormously enriched by the presence of the National Humanities Center, whose ties are close with the university for obvious reasons, but also because its assistant director, a member of its staff from the beginning, is one of "ours." To Kent R. Mullikin, I extend our appreciation for his support of the conference and for the delightful reception and dinner given at the center last night for our speakers.

Lindsay C. Warren, Jr., will not only greet you but also preside over the remainder of the morning's program. And properly so, for it is America's Four Hundredth Anniversary Committee that provides the primary support for this entire conference. We are in the final year of a four-year series of commemorative activities that have, under his leadership, educated North Carolinians and other Americans in the significance of the subject that we consider today and tomorrow. Lindsay's father, the former congressman and comptroller general of the United States, as early as 1955 urged preparations for the quadricentennial of the Roanoke voyages, and it was appropriate that in 1980 the Warren name again became associated with the commemoration as chairman of AFHAC.

Samuel R. Williamson
Provost and Professor of History
University of North Carolina at Chapel Hill

I am delighted on behalf of the University of North Carolina at Chapel Hill to welcome you to Wilson Library in its renovated state and to this International Conference on Sir Walter Raleigh. All of us in the university family—faculty, students, staff—welcome you. As a historian, I hope you will permit me some additional remarks.

Historians and universities often think in terms of anniversaries, in terms of traditions, in terms of symbols. The four hundredth anniversary celebrations that have been going on in North Carolina are indicative of that. Thanks to the efforts of Lindsay Warren, John Neville, H. G. Jones, former Governor James B. Hunt, Jr., and Governor James G. Martin, and others, the people of North Carolina have been reminded—and broader audiences even than North Carolinians have been reminded—about the nature of America's link with its British past and of the value of history and of historical activity. We have been reminded of our English heritage, and we have created a lot of work for historians—and of course that's always a good thing. In addition, the university likes anniversaries, and we are beginning to think about how, only two hundred years after the Roanoke voyages of Sir Walter Raleigh, North Carolinians meeting in Fayetteville decided to establish a state university. Now, as this university moves toward its bicentennial celebration, we are reminded again of the importance of anniversaries.

Universities and historians also are interested in traditions. Historians like to refine the past—indeed the past is never over, for each generation reinterprets the past and finds new things of interest about the past. I think this conference and the titles of the papers are perfectly indicative of the fact that what might seem to be a dead past is in fact a live past as we reinterpret and think anew about our history. Universities, in recognizing their traditions, are prone to put together international conferences because this is one of the things we believe the university is about. This is one of the traditions of academic life, bringing together scholars to exchange ideas, occasionally to antagonize and provoke each other, because a little lively controversy, a little dialectical tension, is very useful for generating new sets of perspectives. And so it is particularly fitting, we think, in this renovated library that this should be the very first event—an international conference linking us with the world community of scholars. Helping to put this conference together has been the staff of the North Carolina Collection, as H. G. has mentioned, and I particularly would like to pay homage to Mike Martin, the University Archivist, whose labors in connection with the building renovation have ranged from the mundane to the sublime.

Universities and historians are concerned with a third area of activity—symbols. Historians deal with symbols, and if you go into the Sir Walter Raleigh Rooms you will see a series of symbols—artifacts, parchments, paintings, sculpture. Universities and historians like symbols, and in a sense the Louis Round Wilson Library is a symbol—a symbol of a vision of what we can do for the people of the state, a symbol of how we can relate anew to our fellow North Carolinians. And it is a fitting event that Sir Walter Raleigh, who sponsored new voyages of discovery, should be the topic of the first discussion in this renovated structure. We see this building as a new voyage as the University ventures forth to welcome the people of North Carolina to learn more about their heritage as they see our special collections and pay attention to what we have been able to assemble by the diligent efforts of a lot of people over a long period of time.

So this is a joyful moment for us as a university, and for me as a historian, for it is a grateful chance for us to think about four hundred years of history, to celebrate an anniversary, to think about traditions of intellectual life, and to celebrate the opening of a new symbol. I have to believe that Sir Walter Raleigh would be pleased, perhaps slightly amused, pearl earring and all, by these proceedings, and on behalf of the University of North Carolina, I welcome you to them.

Kent R. Mullikin
Assistant Director, National Humanities Center

I should like to thank H. G. Jones and the others who have had a hand in planning an impressive international conference. A glance through the program suggests that Sir Walter Raleigh retains his power to dispatch adventurers—in this instance scholar adventurers—across the Atlantic. It is an honor for the National Humanities Center to be associated with this intellectual enterprise.

There is no doubt that the National Humanities Center and its company of scholars have found North Carolina a much more hospitable environment than did that small band of English settlers who disappeared from Roanoke Island four hundred years ago. I like to think, however, that Raleigh's colonists have something to do with the Center's location, for among the attractions of North Carolina to the founders of the Center were this state's rich history and, equally important, its deep appreciation of the *value* of history. I might add that the founders of the Center were fortunate to encounter a North Carolinian who embodies that enlightened appreciation of history—the current President of the North Caroliniana Society, Archie K. Davis, who has worked unstintingly in behalf of the Center. His love of North Carolina's past made him a historian in his own right and gave him a sympathetic understanding of scholarly inquiry.

The National Humanities Center has benefited in many instances from its connection with North Carolina, its universities, and its traditions of learning. One very special benefit was the presence at the Center several years ago of David and Alison Quinn; they came over from Liverpool, drawn by the quadricentennial of Raleigh's colony, to complete the book *Set Fair for Roanoke,* which was commissioned by America's Four Hundredth Anniversary Committee and published by the University of North Carolina Press. It is a great pleasure to see the Quinns here again, and it is also gratifying to recognize among our distinguished speakers two current Fellows of the Center, Joan Thirsk and Nicholas Canny, and former Fellow Karen Kupperman.

On behalf of the National Humanities Center, I am happy to welcome all of the participants to a conference that exemplifies the ideals of scholarship which have long characterized this state and which are a powerful reason the National Humanities Center likes calling North Carolina home.

Lindsay C. Warren, Jr.
Chairman, America's Four Hundredth Anniversary Committee

On Behalf of America's Four Hundredth Anniversary Committee, one of the sponsors of this conference, I extend to each of you a warm and cordial welcome. The conference has long been on the agenda of the committee as one of its sponsored programs during this the last year of the commemoration. I want to publicly thank Dr. H. G. Jones for his willingness to assume the responsibility for planning and organizing the conference. As usual, he has done an excellent job, particularly in attracting a distinguished panel of participants, four of whom have come from England and Ireland. I am confident we will enjoy an entertaining as well as educational experience during the next two days.

One of the key goals of America's Four Hundredth Anniversary Committee, during the commemoration of the Roanoke voyages, has been to raise the consciousness of the people of North Carolina, indeed of the nation, to the historical significance of the English beginning in this country. We have done this through a variety of programs, including commemorative events, the construction of the *Elizabeth II* and the Elizabeth II State Historic Site on Roanoke Island, archaeological explorations, and through the publication of books, pamphlets, and folders written and edited by historians familier with the period. This conference is a continuation of that process, with emphasis on the life of Walter Raleigh, whose dreams, ingenuity, and determination made possible the Roanoke voyages. It is good that we pause and reflect upon the life of this interesting man, for he among all Elizabethans did the most to extend English influence to the New World. Although his efforts were frustrated, the dream kindled by his spirit was eventually realized through the permanent colony at Jamestown twenty years later; and from those beginnings, came our English heritage which permeates so many American institutions today. And so it is appropriate during this commemorative year that we salute Walter Raleigh and examine at this conference the man, his times, and his influence on English colonization in the New World.

Raleigh's World

Helen Wallis*

Bishop George Carleton, surveying "the great and mercifull Deliverances of the Church and State" from the reign of Elizabeth to 1624, opened his chronicle with comments on the "weak estate of this Kingdome at Queens Elizabeths entrance": "All the great States about her, were enemies. Friends none." King Philip of Spain, refused in marriage, "grew first into dislike and discontent, after-wardes into hatred, and at last brake out into open warres. The French, King Henry the 2, with whom she sought peace, fell off also into open Warres . . . Spaine, France, and Scotland were enemies. . . . The treasure was exhausted; Calis was lost. Nothing seemed to be left to her, but a weake, and poor State, destitute of meanes and friends."[1]

Such was the outlook in 1558 when young Walter Raleigh was about five years old. The population of England was then 3.16 million as estimated, whereas the population of North Carolina is now 6 million. By 1600 the population of England and Wales was 4.3 million, with a density of 75 per square mile, as compared to 16-18 million for France (the highest in Europe), density 90; and Spain and Portugal, 11 million, density 50. It is believed that by the end of Elizabeth's reign the population of England may have been 35 percent higher than at the start.[2] The increase in population in the earlier years of the reign explains the contemporary belief that England was over populated and therefore needed colonies. Sir Humphrey Gilbert, Raleigh's elder half brother, commented, "England is pestered with people."

If the political situation abroad in 1558 was not encouraging, it must be said that Carleton's picture would have been even gloomier had he raised his eyes beyond the Narrow Seas. The patterns of exploration, discovery, and conquest had been established over more than half a century before, and England as yet had barely entered the race. Two great movements of expansion had commanded the interest and resources of the major European powers, Portugal and Spain.

The first project in execution was the search for the route eastward to the East Indies. By 1520 Portugal had gained control of the route round the Cape of Good Hope and had established a network of commercial and military bases. Intention and achievement went together. She had accomplished what she had set out to do. Her empire was the envy of the world. It is significant that one of the treasures in Raleigh's library was the manuscript Roteiro of the Red Sea, 1541, by João de Castro, fourth Viceroy of India. As Samuel Purchas recorded, Raleigh had purchased the manuscript for £60, and had had it translated into English.[3] Although Raleigh's own activities were directed to the western hemi-sphere, his studies for the *History of the World* (London: 1614) were primarily

Helen Wallis, retired map librarian of the British Library, opened the conference with a slide/lecture on "Raleigh's World."

concerned with old world strategies. He describes the navigation about Africa from east to west by the Phoenicians and the achievement many centuries later by Vasco da Gama in rounding the Cape of Good Hope from west to east in 1497.[4] England was interested in this, the most practicable route to the east, but was hesitant as yet to challenge the Portuguese monopoly.

The second grand aim was the exploration and exploitation of the American continent, following the discovery of its central parts by Columbus for Spain from 1492 to 1504, and of the south (Brazil) by Pedro Alvarez Cabral for Portugal in 1500. Like John Cabot's explorations in the north undertaken for England in 1497 and 1498, these were accidental discoveries made in the search for a western, or (in respect of Cabral) in pursuit of a more convenient southern, route to the Orient.

Contemporaries were disappointed at first with that "other world" of America. Only gradually did Europeans begin to see the continent as valuable in its own right. The discovery of the rich empires of Mexico and Peru accelerated the process. The commercial motive was paramount, whatever explorers conceived as their sense of mission. They sold their projects to the country most interested to back them. Sovereigns and merchants had to be satisfied that they would gain a good return for their money. John Smith, in *A Map of Virginia* (1612), reported that Queen Isabella had pawned her jewels to support Columbus when all the wise men condemned him. (In fact, she proposed to raise the money on her crown jewels, and in the event this was not necessary.)[5]

The pattern of conquest and trade had followed upon the political determinations of Spain and Portugal. The division of the world according to the Treaty of Tordesillas, 1494, gave Spain the western hemisphere and Portugal the eastern. Alberto Cantino's world map of 1502 marks the dividing line. A map of c.1610 (known in a late eighteenth century copy)[6] shows the two empires then united under the sovereignty of Spain, since Philip II had claimed the Portuguese throne in 1580.

Although the Spanish and Portuguese governments enforced strict rules about keeping secret the maps and charts of their imperial domains, emigré map-makers plying their trade abroad could be employed to make maps for well-paying clients. Thus Queen Mary I of England commissioned from the Portuguese Diego Homem in 1558 a fine manuscript atlas of the world, probably intending it for her husband King Philip II of Spain as a New Year's gift.[7] On the chart of Western Europe their joint arms are inscribed over England, of which Philip was titular king. The atlas was still unfinished when Mary died in November 1558, and when the manuscript came into Elizabeth's hands the queen seems petulantly to have scratched out Philip's arms. For the rest, the atlas displays in fine detail Spanish and Portuguese discoveries and settlements.

Nearly twenty years later in 1586 Raleigh was to commission André Homem, Diego's kinsman, to make a map for him, and Richard Hakluyt, referring to the map, described André as "the prince of the Cosmographers of this age."[8] Similarities between Diego's chart of 1558 and André Homem's of 1559[9] (his only work known today) give an idea of what André's chart might have looked like, allowing for the addition of Antonio de Espejo's discoveries in New Mexico in 1583, in which Raleigh had a particular interest.[10] The report of a silver mine aroused hopes of minerals in the hinterland of Virginia.

Queen Mary's atlas was one of many geographical and cartographic works in the royal palaces; others are recorded in the inventory of Henry VIII's possessions at the time of his death in 1547. The little study called "the new Librarye in Whitehall" contained, for example, "a black coffer covered with fustian of Naples full of plattes (maps)" and there was "a great globe of the description of the worlde."[11] Then in 1549, or shortly after, the most important map of its generation was added to the collection, namely Sebastian Cabot's world map. Sebastian had returned to England in 1547 in his old age after 40 years in Spanish service, and had his world map—probably a revised version of his map of 1544—engraved by Clement Adams in 1549.

Cabot's map was hanging in the 1560s in the Queen's privy gallery in Whitehall, as Sir Humphrey Gilbert and Richard Hakluyt record.[12] It provided authoritative evidence for Cabot's claimed discovery of the northwest passage round North

America, c.1508 to 1509. The earlier discoveries of John Cabot, with his son Sebastian as companion, 1497 to 1498, were also documented.

The map remained on display for many years, publicly attesting England's right to northern North America by priority of discovery. Samuel Purchas in about 1618 reports the map as hanging in "His Majesties Gallerie at White Hall, neere the Privie Chamber." He describes it as "that Map (wherein is Cabotas Picture, the first and great Columbus for the Northerne Worlde)," and he names Cabot as "Discoverer for Henry the Seventh, of America," asserting that all the northern coasts of America were discovered by Sebastian Cabot and other Englishmen.[13]

Cabot may be seen as the "eminence grise," who influenced England's overseas activities in Raleigh's early days and for many years to come. His leading reputation in arctic matters and the geopolitics of the day combined to commend northern enterprise. There followed the beginnings of that long search to discover the northern passages to Asia which may be described as the triumph of hope over experience. These arctic exploits illustrate the powerful economic motives operating in the search for an exclusive route to the East. Raleigh's verses in the *History of the World* (1614), translated from the Latin, sum up the driving force of exploration:

> Nor Southerne heate, nor Northerne snow
> That freezing to the ground doth grow,
> The subject Regions can fence,
> And keepe the greedie Merchant thence.
> The subtile Shipmen way will finde,
> Storme neuer so the Seas with Winde.[14]

The first voyages to the northwest were those of Martin Frobisher, 1576, 1577, and 1578. These were very much part of Raleigh's world. There was a family connection through Raleigh's elder half brother Sir Humphrey Gilbert, who in the 1560s was a leading advocate of the discovery of the northwest passage. Gilbert's *Discourse of a Discouerie for a New Passage to Cataia*, written in 1566 and published in London in 1576, sets out the likelihood and the advantages of the discovery. Its woodcut map, notable as the first world map published in England, was drawn on a cordiform projection as a miniature version of Abraham Ortelius's large world map of 1564. The map showed a convenient open route round the North American continent. The publication of the *Discourse* in 1576, ostensibly without Gilbert's permission, was intended as an encouragement for Frobisher's Company of Cathay, which was preparing its first expedition.

The enterprise turned into a treasure hunt, and when Frobisher's supposed mine of 1577 proved worthless, several fortunes were lost. The disappointing results had, however, a wider significance. Disillusioned over the northwest passage, Gilbert turned his interests to colonization in North America. On 11 June 1578 he obtained a royal patent "to discover searche finde out and view such

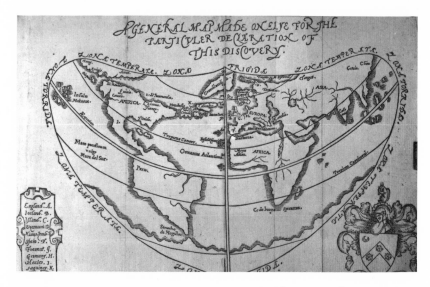

World map by Sir Humphrey Gilbert, from *A Discourse of a Discouerie for a New Passage to Cataia* (London: 1576). *By permission of the British Library.*

remote heathen and barbarous landes . . . not actually possessed of any Christian prince." The expedition that sailed in November 1578 had Walter Raleigh as captain of the *Falcon,* and Raleigh's pilot was the navigator and privateer originally from the Azores, Simão Fernandez, the sinister figure who was to play such an important role for good or ill in the Roanoke enterprises. The expedition proved abortive, its ships returning from a brief Atlantic excursion. Gilbert resumed his plans, and despite the Queen's entreaties set out himself in 1583 on a colonizing voyage to northern North America. He took possession of Newfoundland for the Queen on 5 August 1583, but his ship the *Squirrel* foundered with all hands on the return voyage. "We are as neere to heaven by sea as by land" were his last recorded words.

Gilbert was a true pioneer in England's colonial expansion, and he prepared the way for Raleigh's project. Raleigh's patent for "the discovering and planting of new lands and Countries" was based on Gilbert's, which in this sense had reverted to the younger kinsman; but the new patent excluded Newfoundland, where Gilbert's own family may have claimed rights.[15]

North American projects benefitted also from the interest of the redoubtable Dr. John Dee, lately geographical adviser to Frobisher, now establishing himself as the authority on England's title to northern North America. Gilbert's *Discourse* had gained Dee's attention, and Gilbert was brought into Dee's circle. On receiving his patent, Gilbert granted Dee the right to all discoveries north of 50° north latitude. After Gilbert's death, Dee followed this up in promoting an enterprise with Gilbert's younger brother Adrian and the navigator John Davis.

Dee was active also as a publicist. His *General and rare memorials pertayning to the Perfect Arte of navigation* (London: 1577) foretold the imperial and maritime destiny of England. It was the first volume of a four-volume work on the "British Empire," a term which Dee coined himself. The hieroglyphic frontispiece shows Elizabeth at the helm of the Christian ship of Europe, as mistress of the seas. In 1580 Dee argued the cause to the Queen in person, presenting her with a tract, "Her Majesty's Title Royal to many foreign countries, kingdoms and provinces." He illustrated his thesis with a map of northern regions, endorsed with a summary text of his argument: "Of a great parte of the Sea Coastes of Atlantis (otherwise called America,) next unto us . . . the Title Royall and Christian Supreme Government, is due, and appropriate unto Our Soveraigne Elizabeth . . . No other Prince or Potentate else in the whole world, being hable to allege thereto any Clayme. . . ."[16]

Colonizing projects were thus in the wind in the early 1580s. In 1583 Christopher Carleill, stepson of Sir Francis Walsingham, attempted to promote an English colony in Nova Scotia, Maine, or the St. Lawrence, addressing himself to the Muscovy Company for support in a pamphlet which he reissued in 1584.[17] Richard Hakluyt the younger meanwhile had provided a handbook for the English colonization of North America in his *Divers voyages touching the discouerie of America* (London: 1582), complete with two maps. That by Robert Thorne in 1527 ranks as the first known world map made by an Englishman. A legend off the northeast coast of America, added perhaps by Hakluyt himself, reads (in translation from the Latin), "This land was first discovered by the English." It is, I believe, the first documentation of England's claim on a printed map of wide circulation, as distinct from Cabot's map, which came into the hands of a more privileged few.

Hakluyt's second map, obtained from Michael Lok, the London merchant, was derived from a chart of Gerolamo Verrazzano, c.1527, presented to Henry VIII. It shows the "Mare de Verrazana 1524" as cutting into the American continent in 40° north, a configuration mistakenly deduced from observations of the Carolina Outer Banks by Giovanni Verrazzano, with his brother Gerolamo.[18] This encouraging belief that the Pacific lay close to the continent's eastern shores does not appear to be the reason for the site of Raleigh's first colony. There is no reference to the map or to the ideas behind it in the surviving accounts of the Roanoke Colony. The Verrazzanian concept was to hold sway, nevertheless, for many years.

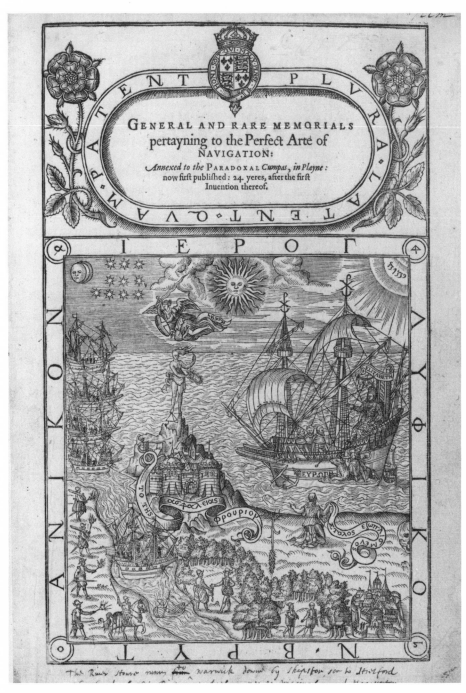

Hieroglyphic frontispiece showing Queen Elizabeth at the helm of the Christian ship of Europe. In John Dee, *General and Rare Memorials pertayning to the Perfect Arte of Navigation* (London: 1577). *By permission of the British Library.*

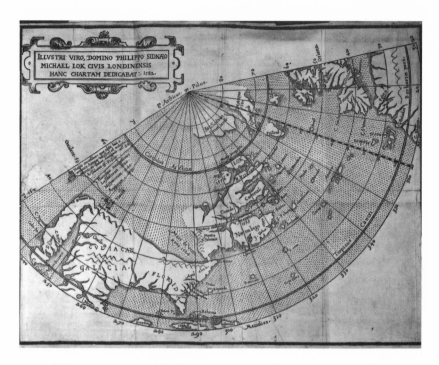

Map of North America by Michael Lok, 1582, from Richard Hakluyt's *Divers voyages touching the discouerie of America* (London: 1582). *By permission of the British Library.*

In the early 1580s American colonization was becoming a serious preoccupation in England. The citizens of London, however, were concerned with a more epoch-making event, the return of Francis Drake from his voyage round the world, 1577 to 1580, later celebrated as "the famous voyage of Sir Francis Drake." He had burst into the closed Spanish sphere of the South Seas, attacking Spanish ports on the western American coasts. He had taken possession of Nova Albion (California) in northwestern America in the name of Elizabeth. Sailing on westward he had confronted the Portuguese at the very heart of their empire, Ternate in the Moluccas. The *Golden Hind* had arrived home laden with gold and silver bullion. Edmond Howes in his continuation (1615) of the *Annales* (1580) of John Stow, wrote that the news of Drake's wealth "so far fetcht was marvelous strange, and of all men held impossible, and incredible, but both prouing true, it fortuned, that many misliked it ... terming him the Master theefe of the unknown world."[19]

If admiration was mixed with unease in certain quarters, Drake had proved, nevertheless, that the Luso-Hispanic world, united in 1580 under Philip II of Spain, was an easy prey. The man in the street and foreigners alike applauded Drake's audacity: "His name (writes Howes) was a terrour to the French, Spaniard, Portugal and Indians. Many Princes of Italy, Germany, and others, as well enemies as friends in his life time desired his Picture. He was the second that ever went through the Straights of Magellan . . . in briefe he was famous in Europe, and America, as Tamburlaine in Asia, and Affrica. In his imperfections hee was ambitious for honor, unconstant in amity, greatly affected to popularity."

Official circles were more circumspect in their reactions. Elizabeth's ministers imposed a rigorous secrecy on all detailed reports of the voyage, securing for themselves the fullest possible records. Early in October 1580 Drake had presented Elizabeth with "a diary of everything that happened during the three years he was away and a very large map." This is the earliest reference to the chart of Drake's voyage which Purchas recorded in 1618 as hanging in "His Majesties Gallerie at White Hall, neere the Privie Chamber," and next to Cabot's map. In the early 1580s Drake's map was not publicly displayed, but surreptitious copies were made. The earliest is that engraved by Nicola van Sype, published probably at Antwerp about 1583. A somewhat later version is the manuscript map now known as the Drake-Mellon map, evidently drawn after 1586 as it marks Drake's West Indian voyage, 1585 to 1586. The third and latest derivative was engraved and perhaps issued in London c.1590 by the Flemish emigré map-maker Jodocus Hondius, who on his return to the continent published it at Amsterdam, c.1595.[20]

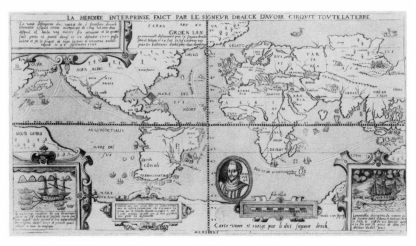

Map of Drake's circumnavigation, 1577–1580. Engraved by Nicola van Sype. (Antwerp? *ca.* 1583.) *By permission of the British Library.*

The full significance of Drake's voyage therefore could not be appreciated at first. Only after the defeat of the Spanish Armada in 1588 was the ban on reports and publication removed. The psychological impact of the achievement, however, was immediate. Many years later, in 1725, Daniel Defoe referred to "that famous old Wives saying, viz. That Sir Francis Drake shot the Gulph; a Saying that was current in England for many Years, I believe near a Hundred after Sir Francis Drake was gone his Long Journey of all. . . ."[21] The saying that Drake shot the gulf, that is, sailed through the Strait of Magellan into the South Sea, became one of the many Drake legends. It is recorded that when the curator at Oxford showed visitors Drake's portrait, with Drake holding a pistol in one hand, he used to say that this was "the very pistol with which Sir Francis shot the gulf." I have identified the picture as the full length portrait which the Bodleian acquired by gift in 1674 and which has recently been revealed as Frobisher's.[22] Thus for many years Frobisher unwittingly masqueraded as Drake with a pistol in his hand shooting the gulf, a symbol of England's challenge to Spanish supremacy in the western world.

Drake was a kinsman of Raleigh's, and about fourteen years his senior. His mother had been the first of the three wives of Raleigh's father. They shared an inveterate hatred of Spain. John Aubrey in his *Brief Lives* (completed by 1696) wrote that Raleigh was "next to Sir Francis Drake, the great Scourge and hate of the Spaniard."[23] Hopes of gaining wealth at the expense of Spain were to feature large in Raleigh's plans, explaining inconstancies of purpose in his colonizing pursuits. Drake was a powerful figure in Raleigh's expanding world. We do not know the full extent of their later collaboration in American initiatives, only the facts of Drake's direct participation in calling at Roanoke in June 1586 and in the event rescuing the colonists.

While Drake's exploit was being celebrated in London and arousing alarm and despondency in Spain, Raleigh was engaged in military service in Ireland from 1580 to 1581. On his recall to England hs embarked in 1582 on his meteoric career as the Queen's favourite at court, receiving many tokens of appreciation, notably the enjoyment of Durham House as his home (1583) and a grant of wines (1584). These favours were crowned on 25 March 1584 by the grant of letters patent for colonization in North America.

In promoting the colonizing venture Raleigh had the advantage of an influential circle of friends and associates. They included Dee, whom he had already consulted in matters of navigation. The map which Raleigh presumably used for planning the voyage of 1584 was a copy of a chart of the Atlantic and North America by Simão Fernandes, who had lent the original to Dee at his house at Mortlake on 20 November 1580.[24] Dee had probably consulted the original in designing his own map for presentation to the Queen in August 1580.[25]

Dee, however, was becoming increasingly interested in the occult, conjuring up through his medium, the notorious Edward Kelley, spirits who were required to advise on various matters, including procedures for colonizing North America. We displayed in our British Library exhibition the magic mirror, a rare Aztec piece, which Dee and Kelley used for their spiritual seances:

Kelly did all his Feats upon
The Devil's Looking-Glass, a stone,
Where playing with him at Bo-peep,
He solv'd all problems ne'er so deep.[26]

When Dee in 1583 took himself off to the continent with Kelley, Raleigh turned to other authorities.

Most notable was Richard Hakluyt. He had hoped to sail to America himself, but instead went to Paris in 1583 as chaplain to the resident ambassador. His "Discourse of Western Planting," as it is now known, was written between July and October 1584 at the request of Raleigh and Sir Thomas Walsingham to encourage the Queen's official support for the American venture. Hakluyt argued persuasively for large-scale imperial expansion, challenging the legality of Spain's claims. He completed the work shortly after the return of Philip Amadas and Arthur Barlowe from their reconnaissance expedition to America, and it was presented to the Queen on 3 October 1584. The only manuscript of the Discourse which survives is a fair copy, probably Sir Francis Walsingham's.[27]

As the colonizing enterprise proceeded Hakluyt also encouraged Raleigh by means of dedications to the books he was sponsoring and editing. In the dedication to Peter Martyr's *De Orbe Novo* (Paris: 1587), he exhorted Raleigh to emulate the "doughty deeds of Ferdinand Cortes, the Castilian, stout conqueror of New Spain."[28] Hakluyt named Raleigh, with Sir John Hawkins and his cousin the elder Richard Hakluyt, as "my cheefest light" for western discoveries. He printed in *The principall navigations* (London: 1589) the narrative of "the beginnings, and proceedings of the two English Colonies planted in Virginia at the charges of Sir Walter Raleigh, whose entrance upon those newe inhabitations had bene happie, if it had ben as seruiously followed, as it was cheerfully undertaken," a shrewd comment on Raleigh's efforts as an entrepreneur.[29]

Fernandes, pilot of the reconnaissance expedition of 1584 and the two colonizing voyages of 1585-86 and 1587, belonged to a very different circle, the privateering fraternity. Since about 1577 he had been in the service of Walsingham, principal secretary of state from 1573, and was known as "Master Secretary Walsingham's man." To the Portuguese and Spaniards he was "a thorough-paced scoundrel," as the Spanish ambassador reported in 1578 to Philip II, writing about Gilbert's expedition and warning the king that Fernandes had given the English "much information about that coast, which he knows very well."[30] This knowledge of American coasts made Fernandes's services invaluable to Raleigh. In 1584 he led the reconnaissance expedition of Amadas and Barlowe to Hatarask, an inlet in the Carolina Outer Banks, which he professed to know from a previous expedition in Spanish service. The harbour at Hatarask was named in his honour

Port Ferdinando. His role, however, became increasingly controversial as the ventures proceeded. His view of the colony as a military outpost intended as a base for attacking galleons of the Spanish silver fleet was in keeping with his predilections as a privateer and his enmity for the Spaniards, which his masters shared.

The conflict of interests became more acute when Fernandes sailed with White in 1587 on the second colonizing venture. Despite the intended destination of Chesapeake Bay, he deposited the settlers at Roanoke. John White, the governor, wrote bitterly of "Fernandes and his wicked pretenses," words reminiscent of comments on Fernandes as "the head and origin of all evil" made by his companions on Edward Fenton's voyage of 1582. Yet he was to be praised, rightly no doubt (to give him his due). Pedro Diaz, pilot of the Spanish ship seized by Sir Richard Grenville, described him "as a great pilot and the person who induced them [the English] to settle there."

Privateering was almost a prerequisite for the success of the first colony owing to the lack of official support. Cautious and equivocal as always, the Queen limited her part in the venture to a gift of gunpowder, the loan of a royal ship, the *Tyger,* and the release of Ralph Lane from military duties in Ireland to serve as governor of the first colony, 1585-86. This meant that Raleigh depended for the most part on merchants in the city. Walsingham, named as an "adventurer," was the most powerful of his backers. As John Smith, governor of the later Virginia colony, was to remark, reliance on "privy men's purses" was no basis for a successful colony.

The conduct of Sir Richard Grenville, who was one of Raleigh's Devonshire cousins and served as "generall" of the 1585 expedition, illustrates the attractions of privateering. On his way home in 1585 to bring out a second expedition under Amias Preston and Bernard Drake, he took a Spanish prize to the value of between 40,000 and 50,000 ducats. The voyage was "made," the adventurers refunded, and profits shared between Raleigh and Grenville. In 1586 on his second Roanoke voyage, having found the colony abandoned, Grenville landed at the Azores, despoiled towns, and took captives. His name comes down in history as "Grenville of the Revenge," who died a hero's death at the Azores in 1591.

Another high ranking adventurer was the young Thomas Cavendish of Suffolk, who served as high marshall and was captain of the *Elizabeth,* which he had furnished himself. His duties were to act as legal authority, and disagreements between him and Grenville as general may have arisen from rivalry as to their respective roles. This was only one of the many dissentions which broke out on the outward voyage and were to beset the company during their stay at Roanoke. Grenville's chastisements of his officers and their attendants called forth from Lane accusations against Grenville of "intolerable pride and insatiable ambitions."

Raleigh himself was destined never to set foot on North American soil. As the Queen's favourite and (from 1587) captain of the guard it was his duty to stay at home. There is no direct evidence, indeed, that he would have planned to go. His role was more effective as the organizer at base. There he received from the Queen signal honours on the return of Amadas and Barlowe. On Twelfth Night in January 1585 she knighted him and allowed the new land of "Winganda-coa" to be named in her honour Virginia. Raleigh was appointed its "Lord and Governor." As David Quinn has pointed out, the name made this a landmark in American history, for it was applied to all the coastlines covered by Raleigh's patent.[31] It set England's seal on a large territory of eastern North America.

Whatever the competence of the officers who carried out Raleigh's undertakings, the first colony suffered the disadvantage of an unsuitable site. It seems clear that under the guidance of Fernandes, Amadas and Barlowe in 1584 had been seeking the "Golfo de Sta Maria," which was in fact Chesapeake Bay; but the area of Pamlico Sound with its numerous islands behind the Carolina Outer Banks could well have been mistaken for the "Gulf."[32] Military preoccupations would also justify a site strategically placed for attacking the galleons of the Spanish silver fleet. The reconnaissance party had chosen, in effect, one of the most dangerous stretches of North American coast. The sketch map (perhaps by Thomas Harriot), sent back probably with Lane's letter of 8 September 1585

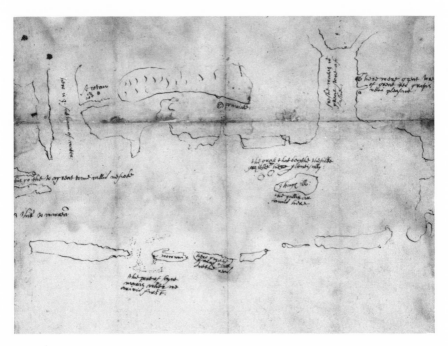

Sketch map of the landing area in Raleigh's "Virginia," September 1585 (looking west). Public Record Office, London, MPG 584. *By permission of the keeper of the records.*

to Walsingham, illustrates the setting.[33] John White's derivative map-view, engraved
by Theodore de Bry, "The arrival of the Englishmen in Virginia," 1590, is decked
with tell-tale shipwrecks.[34] Precarious from the first, the colony was organized
as a military outpost under strict discipline. As to the men, Lane commented
(in a letter to Sir Philip Sydney of 12 August) on having "emungst sauvages,
the chardege of wylde menn of myne owene nacione."

John White's map-view of the site of the Roanoke colony. In Theodor de Bry, *America*,
part 1 (Frankfurt am Main: 1590), pl. II. *By permission of the British Library.*

The end came suddenly and unpredictably. While Grenville's return was still
awaited, Drake called at Roanoke on 9 June 1586 with supplies and reinforcements
collected in the course of the "famous West Indian Voyage" (1585-86). A storm
blew up while Drake was negotiating on land, and the settlers opted for
evacuation.

The venture of 1587 as a colony of settlement was totally different in conception
from the first. Raleigh retained his rights as patentee, but no longer bore the
costs. There were 114 participants, men, women and children, under the governorship of John White, the artist of the first voyage. His twelve assistants included

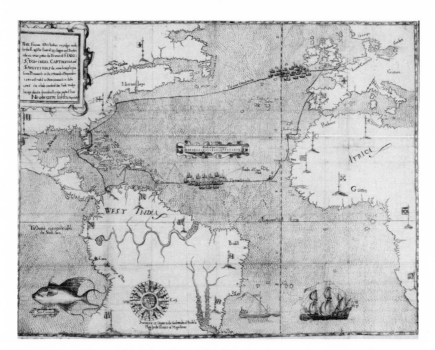

Baptista Boazio's map depicting the track of Drake's West Indian voyage of 1585–86, on which he rescued Lane's colonists. From Walter Bigges, *A summarie and true discourse of Sir Fraunces Drakes West Indian Voyage* (London: 1589). *By permission of the British Library.*

"Simon Ferdinando of London, gentleman." The objective was to establish the "City of Raleigh in Virginia," incorporated on 1 January 1587, and the intended site was on Chesapeake Bay, as recommended by Hakluyt. Fernandes, however, diverted the purpose, and the settlers found themselves at Roanoke.

The final outcome, the story of the Lost Colony, is the first tragic episode of Anglo-American history. White was persuaded to go home for supplies, and his return was delayed by the imminent danger of invasion by Spain. In 1590 when he set foot once more on Roanoke Island, he found the colony deserted. The only clue to its fate was the single word "Croatoan" carved on a wooden post, without the pre-arranged distress signal.

Paradoxically, Virginia was to become famous in the year that White made his discovery of the colonists' disappearance. This was the achievement above all of White himself, and Thomas Harriot, who had joined Raleigh's household in 1583 as tutor in the navigational sciences. They had brought back from Roanoke in 1586 maps and surveys, some hundreds of drawings by White,[35] and manuscripts comprising a full geographical report by Harriot. Together they provided a fine

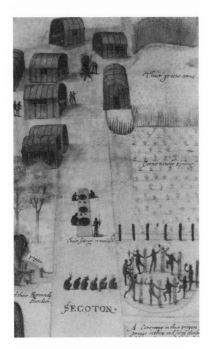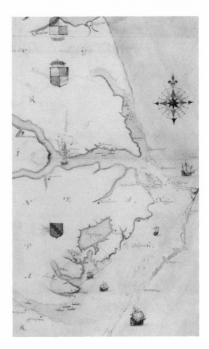

John White's drawing of the village of Secoton (left) and Raleigh's "Virginia" (right). Watercolours. *By permission of the British Museum, Department of Prints & Drawings, 1906-5-9-1(7) and 1906-5-9-1(3), respectively.*

record of the Carolina Algonquian's way of life, and of the resources of the country. Harriot wrote up his notes in summary form for *A brief and true report of the new found land of Virginia* (London: 1588), which was intended to encourage the future development of Virginia.

White's graphic documentation, on the contrary, might never have been published but for the visit to London of Theodor de Bry, the great Flemish printer, He came to engrave Thomas Lant's drawings of Sir Philip Sidney's funeral in February 1586. He became acquainted with Jacques Le Moyne, artist in the Huguenot colony in Florida, 1564-65, of whom Raleigh and Lady Mary Sidney were patrons, and planned to publish Le Moyne's account and drawings. Probably through the good offices of Hakluyt he changed his plan and agreed to publish Virginia first. The reprint of Harriot's text was illustrated by a complete set of drawings provided by White, with captions by Harriot (in the English edition, allegedly by Hakluyt). The result was the first volume of De Bry's *America*, published at Frankfurt in 1590 in a four-language edition. For the first time Europeans could see what life in North America was really like. Raleigh's Virginia became a chapter of world history.

The images created were so powerful that they became the stereotype of the Indian way of life. The villages of Secoton and Pomeioc in what is now North Carolina reappear on maps of America until as late as 1719, migrating west as far as Texas.[36] William Strachey used De Bry's engravings to illustrate his manuscript account of the new Virginia colony, 1610-12. He also showed five pictures of Picts, the early inhabitants of Great Britain, and ventured some enlightened ethnographical comments:

> AEcclesiae et Reipublicae
> Wild as they ar, accept them, so were wee:
> To make them civill, will our honnour be:
> And if good worcks, be the effects of Myndes
> Which like good Angells be, let our Designes
> As wee ar Angli, make us Angells too:
> No better worcke, can state, or church-man doe.
> W. St.[37]

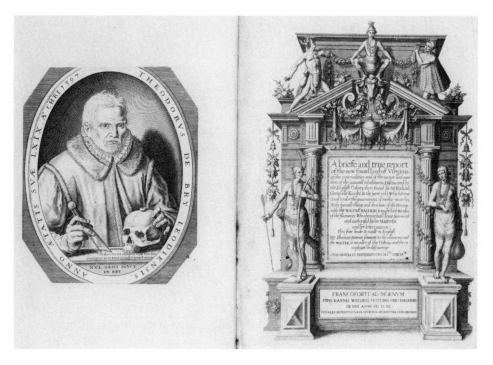

Title page of Thomas Harriot's *A briefe and true report*, with Theodor de Bry's engraved portrait facing. In de Bry, *America*, part 1 (Frankfurt am Main: 1590). *By permission of the British Library.*

Raleigh's Virginia had pointed the way to England's successful settlement of a colony in North America. "I shall yet live to see it an English nation," Raleigh had written prophetically in a letter to Sir Robert Cecil on 21 August 1602. From the Tower he received reports of the Jamestown settlement.

The first Virginia colony, whatever its fate, enabled England to establish her role as a New World power. Elizabeth was now Queen of Virginia, as depicted in the print of the Queen between two columns, perhaps by Crispin van de Passe, commissioned and published by John Woutneel, 1596.[38] "No richer crown in the World" was the motto of Nicholas Hilliard's gold medal, c.1590,[39] countering Philip II's posturing as Hercules,[40] and as commanding the wealth of the Indies.[41]

When Emery Molyneux of Lambeth made the first English terrestrial globe for publication in 1592, he depicted the royal arms surmounting a dedication to the Queen encompassing the North American continent and designed as propaganda for England's imperial destiny in the continent.[42] Evidence from the State Archives in Florence has confirmed this interpretation. Petruccio Ubaldini, writing to the Grand Duke of Tuscany, reports Molyneux's presentation of the first terrestrial globe to the Queen at Greenwich in July 1591: "The Dedication to the Queen has to be printed with the royal arms and its wording suggests that he gave her the globe to let her see at a glance how much of the seas she could control by means of her naval forces. This is a fact well worth knowing."[43]

Elizabeth made play of the symbolism of empire when at a second presentation she received the terrestrial globe with its celestial partner at William Sanderson's house at Newington-Butts. She commented "The whole earth, a present for a Prince, but with the Spanish King's leave"— an ironic reference to King Philip's claim to the whole world, and to his motto, "Non sufficit orbis."[44] A silver medal of c.1585 depicts the motto.[45] The globe was in fact the first geographical work to document the exact site of the Roanoke colony. De Bry's map, like White's, had not marked any degrees of latitude and longitude, presumably to protect the colony from possible discovery and attack by Spain.

Thus England's world expanded across the Atlantic. At the very same time Raleigh's world had contracted to the confines of the Tower where he conferred (in the years from 1603 to 1612) with Prince Henry, and with his fellow prisoner Henry Percy, the ninth Earl of Northumberland, and the Earl's attendants, who included Harriot. To recover his fortunes after his first disgrace of 1592 Raleigh had already been on one overseas adventure to Guiana in search of the lost Inca empire of El Dorado, 1595, and had despatched a second in 1596. A last glimpse of him before his trial and downfall in 1603 is as captain of the guard in Elizabeth's funeral procession. An indication of his moods and pursuits during those years in the Tower is revealed in the autograph commonplace book, written between 1604 and 1608, including historical and geographical notes for *The History of the World*, a list of the books in his library, and a Cynthia poem, one of three surviving autographed poems.[46]

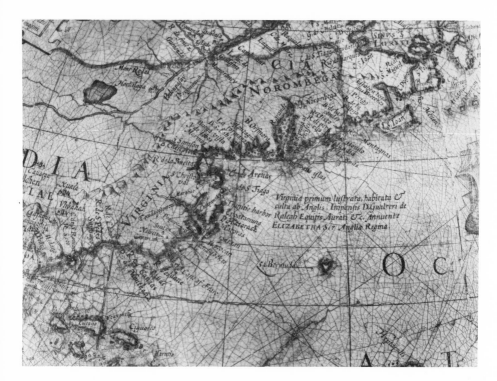

Raleigh's "Virginia" and surrounding region on Emery Molyneux's terrestrial globe, first published in 1592, revised by Jodocus Hondius in 1603. *By permission of the Honourable Society of the Middle Temple.*

The final disastrous expedition to Guiana, 1617-18, culminating in his execution on 19 October 1618, is one of the dark episodes of English history. But just as Drake legends flourished, so did Raleigh's exceed the bounds of ordinary mortals. John Bricknell writes of the Indians in *The Natural History of North Carolina* (Dublin: 1737):

> I hope it will not be unpleasing to the Reader to insert here a pleasant Story which still prevails amongst them; and is attended by the most substantial and credible Planters of this place, which is, "That the Ship that brought the first Colonists, does often appear to them (in Albemarle Sound, near Roanoke) under Sail, in a most gallant Posture," which they call Sir Walter Raliegh's Ship.

The author of *A Short Account of the First Settlement of the Provinces of Virginia,...* (London: 1735), records Grenville's expedition of 1585, and Drake's rescue, and then proceeds to describe Sir Walter's visit in person: "Sir Walter got his ship ready first ... he set sail by himself," two weeks in advance of Grenville.

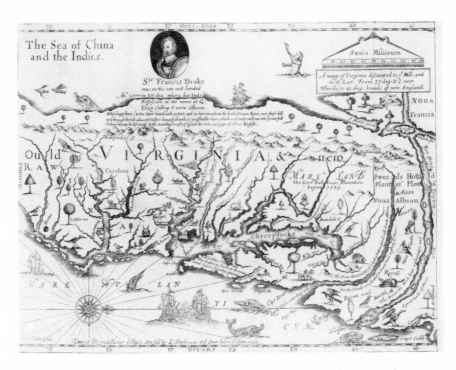

John Farrer's map of Virginia, showing the Pacific ten days' march away, with a portrait of Drake as the discoverer of "Nova Albion." In Edward Bland, *The Discovery of New Brittaine* (London: 1651). *By permission of the British Library.*

The spirit of Sir Walter lives on in North Carolina, despite the remark of James A. Froude in 1895, "of Raleigh, there remains nothing in Virginia [i.e., North Carolina] save the name of the city which is called after him."[47] More to the point is the comment of Richard Biddle (1831), followed by Alexander von Humboldt, that but for Cabot and Raleigh the English language might not be spoken by North Americans today. Raleigh paved the way for the establishment of Anglo-America in the New World.

Notes

*In introducing Helen Wallis, Lindsay C. Warren, Jr., said: "Our first speaker is no stranger to those of us who have been involved in the planning of events associated with the commemoration. Dr. Helen Wallis, who until recently served as the map librarian of the British Library in London, was intimately involved in one of our major projects, the historical exhibition entitled "Raleigh and Roanoke," which initially opened in London in April 1984 then moved to a four-month stand at our own North Carolina Museum of History in March 1985.

"Dr. Wallis was educated at Oxford University, where she received her master's degree and doctorate in philosophy. From 1951 to 1967, she was the assistant keeper in the Map Room of the British Museum. She became deputy keeper in charge of the Map Room in 1967 and served in that capacity until 1973 when the library departments of the British Museum were transferred to the then newly founded British Library. Following the transfer, she became the map librarian of the British Library, serving in that capacity until she retired in 1986. Her vitae says that since 15 November she has served as a "voluntary assistant" in the Map Library. I suspect that means that she is frequently called upon by her former colleagues who value her knowledge and years of experience at that institution. During Dr. Wallis's tenure with the British Library, she was involved in the organization of a number of exhibitions, including one in 1975 on "The American War of Independence," which was transferred to the Museum of Our National Heritage in Lexington, Massachusetts, in 1976. She was also responsible for the organization of an exhibition entitled "The Famous Voyage of Sir Francis Drake," which was later shown in Lexington and the Oakland Museum in California. We know her most fondly for the energy and leadership she exhibited with "Raleigh and Roanoke," which came to Raleigh in 1985. I think I am correct in saying that it was the most successful historical exhibition ever shown at the North Carolina Museum of History.

"Dr. Wallis has contributed to scholarship through her books and articles, many of which are related to Drake and Raleigh. She is a member of various scholarly organizations, currently serving as president of the International Map Collectors Society. In March 1985 she was awarded an honorary degree by our own Davidson College; and in 1986, she was singularly honored by an award of the "Order of the British Empire" (O.B.E.) as part of the Queen's Birthday Honors of that year. We are very pleased to have Dr. Wallis back in North Carolina, and I take pleasure in introducing her to this group which is gathered to hear her paper on 'Raleigh's World.' "

[1]George Carleton, *A Thankfull Remembrance of Gods Mercy* (London: 1624), A.4.2-3.

[2]D.M. Palliser, *The Age of Elizabeth. England under the Later Tudors 1547–1603* (London: 1983), pp. 36-7, 379.

[3]B.L. (British Library) Cotton MS. Tiberius D.IX. Samuel Purchas, *Hakluytus Posthumas or Purchas His Pilgrimes* (London: 1625), II.vii.1122. Purchas prints the translation. Further comments in Armando Cortesão and Avelino Teixeira da Mota, *Portugaliae Monumenta Cartographica* (Lisbon: 1960), I.139–41.

[4]Walter Raleigh, *The History of the World* (London: 1614), I.539.

[5]S.E. Morison, *Admiral of the Ocean Sea* (Boston; 1942), I.137.

[6]B.L. Add. M.S. 17647.A.

[7]B.L. Add. MS. 5415.A.ff.9v-10.

[8]Letter of Richard Hakluyt to Raleigh, Paris, December 30, 1586; the only surviving letter to Raleigh on the Roanoke voyages. Bodleian Library, Oxford, Clarendon MSS Addenda 307, ff.2v-3r. See Helen Wallis, *Raleigh & Roanoke. The First English Colony in America, 1584–1590* (Raleigh: 1985), pp. 23, 45, nos. 4, 33.

[9]André Homem's map is preserved in the Département de Cartes et Plans, Bibliothèque Nationale, Paris.

[10]Helen Wallis, *Raleigh & Roanoke,* pp. 23, 45.

[11]B.L. Harley M.S. 1419A.ff.186-188v.

[12]D.B. Quinn, *The Voyages and Colonising Enterprises of Sir Humphrey Gilbert* (London: 1940),

I.147; Richard Hakluyt, *Principall navigations* (London: 1589), 2.511.

[13]Samuel Purchas, *Purchas His Pilgrimes,* III.iii.461; Maclehose edition (Glasgow: 1906), XIII.3.

[14]Raleigh, *The History of the World,* I.547.

[15]D.B. Quinn et al., *New American World* (New York: 1979), III.267.

[16]B.L. Cotton MS. Augustus I.i.1. See Wallis, *Raleigh & Roanoke,* p. 34.

[17]Christopher Carleill, *A breef and sommarie discourse upon the* extended *Voyage to the hethermoste partes of America* (London: 1583).

[18]Helen Wallis, "Some New Light on Early Maps of North America, 1490–1560," in C. Koeman (ed.), *Land-und Seekarten im Mittelalter und in der frühen Neuzeit,* Wolfenbütteler Forschungen, Bd7 (München: 1980), pp. 101-2.

[19]Edmond Howes, *The Annales, or Generall Chronicle of England begun first by maister Iohn Stowe and . . . continued and augmented . . .* (London: 1615), p. 807.

[20]Helen Wallis, *The Voyage of Sir Francis Drake mapped in silver and gold* (Berkeley: 1979), pp. 19–21; and "The Cartography of Drake's Voyage," in Norman J.W. Thrower (ed.), *Sir Francis Drake and the Famous Voyage, 1577–1580* (Berkeley: 1984), pp. 121–63.

[21][Daniel Defoe], *A New Voyage round the World* (London: 1725), pp. 16–17.

[22]Helen Wallis, "English Enterprise in the Region of the Strait of Magellan," in John Parker (ed.), *Merchants & Scholars* (Minneapolis: 1965), pp. 196–97, 217.

[23]Oliver Lawson Dick (ed.), *Aubrey's Brief Lives* (London: 1950), p. 260.

[24]B.L. Cotton Roll XIII.48.

[25]B.L. Cotton MS. Augustus I.i.1. See Wallis, *Raleigh & Roanoke,* p. 34.

[26]British Museum, Department of Medieval & Lat. Antiquities, 1966, 10-11, 1. See Wallis, *Raleigh & Roanoke,* pp. 29, 33.

[27]New York Public Library, Rare Books and Manuscripts Division; Astor, Lenox and Tilden Foundations. See Wallis, *Raleigh & Roanoke,* p. 41.

[28]E.G.R. Taylor, *The Original Writings & Correspondence of the Two Richard Hakluyts* (London: 1935), 2.366–67. Translation from the Latin by F.C. Francis.

[29]Richard Hakluyt, *The principall navigations voiages and discoveries of the English nation* (London: 1589), sig.*4r.

[30]Cortesão and Teixeira da Mota, 2.130. Quinn, (1940), 1.187.

[31]D.B. Quinn, *Set Fair for Roanoke* (Chapel Hill and London: 1985), p. 51.

[32]William P. Cumming has traced the depiction of the coast on maps in a study now being printed by the University of North Carolina Press.

[33]Public Record Office, London, MPG.584.

[34]Theodor de Bry, *America,* part 1 (Frankfurt am Main: 1590), pl. II.

[35]White's drawings are preserved in one set now in the Department of Prints and Drawings of the British Museum, 1906-9-1. Another set copied from White's originals and discovered in Ireland by Sir Hans Sloane is also in the Department of Prints and Drawings, Sloane MS.5270 (P&D 199.a.3). Unable at first to secure this set, Sloane had them copied, and these are in the Department of Manuscripts of the British Library.

[36]Carte de la Nouvelle France, from *Atlas Historique,* by Henri Abraham Chatelain (Amsterdam: 1719).

[37]William Strachey, "The first Booke of the historie of Trauaile into Virginia Britannia," 1610–1612, B.L. Sloane MS. 1622,f.4v.

[38]B.M. Prints and Drawings, S 114–220. See A.M. Hind, *Engraving in England in the Sixteenth & Seventeenth Centuries.* Pt. 1. The Tudor Period (Cambridge: 1952), p. 285, pl. 144.

[39]B.M. Department of Coins & Medals, 1860-12-18-1.

[40]Reverse of struck silver medal, 1557. B.M. Department of Coins & Medals, George III, Flemish & Dutch 311.

[41]Reverse of silver medal of c.1560. B.M. Department of Coins and Medals, M.1994.

[42]The only known example of the first edition terrestrial globe, 1592, is at Petworth House.

A revised edition of 1603 with its celestial partner is at the London Inn of Court, the Middle Temple.

[43] Archivo di Stato, Florence, Fonde Mediceo, 828, c.477. Ubaldini also reports that Molyneux had sailed with Drake. I am indebed to Anna Maria Crinò for this new source on the Molyneux Globes. See Helen Wallis with Anna Maria Crinò, "New Researches on the Molyneux Globes," in Der *Globusfreund*, no. 35–37 (Vienna: 1987), pp. 11–20.

[44] Sir William Sanderson, *An answer to a scurrilous pamphlet* (London: 1656), sig. A3v.

[45] British Museum, Department of Coins and Medals, George III, Spanish Medals 2.

[46] B.L. Add. MS. 57555. Previously in the collection of Sir Thomas Phillipps, Bart. Phillipps MS. 6339. See also Pierre Lefranc, *Sir Walter Raleigh écrivian, l'oeuvre et les idées* (Paris: 1968); Sir Walter Oakeshott, *The Queen and the Poet* (London: 1970), pp. 17–20.

[47] James A. Froude, *English Seamen in the Sixteenth Century* (London: 1895), p. 156. See also H. G. Jones, "The Americanization of Raleigh," in Joyce Youings (ed.), *Raleigh in Exeter: Privateering and Colonisation in the Reign of Elizabeth I* (Exeter: 1985), p. 73.

Raleigh's England

Joan Thirsk*

My first title for this paper was "The Adventurous Economy of Elizabethan England," and when it was neatened and shortened to match the titles of the other papers, I made no demur. Only later did I realize that it had been turned into a different and more difficult subject. I intended to consider the quite remarkable range and boldness of the new ventures that were launched in Elizabethan England. They set a background against which one can better understand Raleigh's overseas explorations. He was but one of a multitude of people engaged in audacious enterprises. While some sailed across the oceans, others experimented with all kinds of new industrial and agricultural possibilities at home. Bold initiatives were taken and many did not immediately turn out well. But the long-term hopes went along with a great flexibility, so that people seized opportunities that presented in one year, without brooding too much if they abruptly ceased in the next; they turned to something else. And some years later a failed project might well be taken up by others, and succeed. Most of us are out of tune with this world of short-term calculations, but it has to be placed in the background of sixteenth-century life and is, doubtless, inseparable from those other facts of life—short lives and sudden deaths.

The title that has now been given to my paper, "Raleigh's England," has set me thinking along different lines, obliging me to consider England as Raleigh perceived it. His personality is not easily fathomed: an ambitious, audacious, sometimes rough adventurer who was at the same time a reflective, introspective poet is not a very common combination. For me A. L. Rowse has come nearest to explaining the enigma,[1] and I would not compete with him by offering an alternative view. But I also see Raleigh as a typical younger son of the gentry class, in some ways quite remarkably conformist with the rest. I therefore propose to discuss some features of England in the period 1560–1620, as the gentry perceived and exploited them, which may further illuminate the aspirations and career of one of its distinguished sons.

Raleigh shared the circumstances of his time with a multitude of other young men of gentle families born in the middle sixteenth century. As Sir Robert Naunton, James I's Secretary of State, put it when writing a thumbnail sketch of "Rawleigh," he was "well descended, and of good alliance, but poor in his beginnings."[2] A. L. Rowse describes his ancestry more exactly, noticing that in Henry II's reign a Raleigh was sheriff of Devon and that Sir William Raleigh was a judge of the King's Bench.[3] But Walter was the fifth son of a third marriage; he had little prospect of inheriting land from his father.[4]

Joan Thirsk, a specialist on Britain's consumer society, spoke on "Raleigh's England."

Complaints of the plight of younger sons in England became noticeably strident in the course of the century or so after 1540. Some of these young men hung around the houses of their elder brothers, idle, discontented, and deeply resentful of their dependence on their brother's grace and favour. Devon gentlemen may not so readily have submitted to the tyranny of primogeniture as did gentry in some other counties, but the Raleigh family's circumstances could not offer much to a fifth son.[5] A gentleman in a later generation who found his fortune in Virginia designated "learning" as the portion he purposefully allocated to his younger son.[6] That is what Walter Raleigh also received.

With such an endowment multitudes of younger sons had to carve out a career by their own efforts. But in Raleigh's lifetime, each generation found itself obliged to become more and more ingenious or more and more aggressive, since the number of such young gentlemen, all aspiring to remain in the class into which they were born, was rising. All expected to set up a landed estate for themselves, sooner or later, and the consequences of this striving are dramatically portrayed in the increasing numbers of gentry residing in individual counties between 1550 and 1620. Michael Havinden of Exeter University (in an unpublished paper) has counted them in the county of Somerset, next door to Devon. In 1569, 150 gentry lived in the county; in 1623, 352. In other words, the numbers of resident gentry more than doubled in sixty years.

This fact has important implications for an agrarian historian, not all of which are relevant here. But it gives us some sense of the striving for place in Raleigh's lifetime and the effort involved. It explains the deep interest of the gentry in building houses, laying out gardens and orchards, beautifying the landscape and improving the cultivation of farm land. Many of them were creating gentlemen's dwellings and estates where none had been before. I shall return to this theme again in closer connection with Raleigh. At this point enough has been said to indicate the challenges that life presented to younger sons. To carve out a place in gentry society required determined effort in competition with many others, and not all succeeded. Far from ending their days as country gentlemen, some ended their lives as grocers or cheesemongers, many remained landless, many did not marry. Family trees frequently omit younger sons altogether.

Another perception of the sixteenth-century world that was borne in on young gentlemen's sons concerns the conventional stages of a moderately successful career. It could be a monotonous routine with an almost standard pattern; indeed that routine was, I suspect, a boring commonplace of the time, though we only dimly discern it. The familiar path is laid out for us in the life of George Throckmorton in a previous generation. He was the grandfather of Raleigh's wife. The early course of his career was exactly the one taken at the outset by Raleigh himself. George Throckmorton's father, like Raleigh's own father, achieved, in Rowse's words, "nothing much except a good match" (in this case, with a daughter of a lord mayor of London) "and a mass of children." "We find him," continues Rowse, "serving quietly, as we should expect, in the commission of the peace for Warwickshire."[7] George, his eldest son, found his place at Henry VIII's Court as esquire of the body. So did Raleigh at Elizabeth's Court. (It was a piece of fortune for young gentlemen that Henry VIII increased the numbers of his bodyguard from 126 at the beginning of his reign to 200 by 1510. Later he even increased it to 600, but then the cost became alarming, and numbers were reduced.) George Throckmorton duly received, as Rowse puts it, "the rewards of attendance upon the king, in beneficial leases for long periods without fine, in stewardships, keeperships and such advantageous grants."[8] His career was not without setbacks, since he opposed Henry's divorce from Catherine of Aragon, but he made amends and duly became a knight of the shire for Warwickshire, and later on sheriff of Warwickshire and Leicestershire.

Such a career satisfied many. But Raleigh plainly inherited the fiery qualities and a striving energy from his mother. (One wishes that more were known of Katharine Champernowne, remarkable mother of five sons of ability, Sir Humphrey Gilbert, Sir John Gilbert, Adrian Gilbert, Sir Carew Raleigh, and Sir Walter

Raleigh. Rowse recognizes the contribution from the mother to all this, but does not allow her a place in his index.9) For Walter Raleigh careers like that of George Throckmorton were object lessons. To do better than that, it was necessary to break away from the well-trodden path and arrest the attention of an influential patron, best of all the Queeen herself. In this, Raleigh succeeded. His proposals for Ireland, after he had served there, drew him before the Privy Council and attracted the Queen's notice. Sir Robert Naunton counts this as the critical moment in Raleigh's rise to favour. "From thence, he came to be known, and to have access to the queen and to the lords," he wrote.10 But I find the story of the cape thrown on the ground for the Queen to walk over equally credible as a deliberate act to draw attention, in a highly competitive world where Raleigh knew himself to be but one young man among hundreds of others. The story was recorded only by Thomas Fuller, writing later from hearsay. The biographer of Thomas Hariot, Muriel Rukeyser, tells us that it was the Spanish custom to use cloaks in this way. We should also note that while the cloak was made of new plush, we are not told of any expensive ornamentation. The place was "plashy," but the queen "trod gently" on it. We all know that mud when dry brushes off easily. I have heard the story dismissed as apocryphal. I would not be so sure.11

In advancing their fortunes, sixteenth-century gentlemen from Henry VIII's reign onward had one valuable asset of great significance, not possessed by earlier generations—this was their humanist education. It put them in touch with a multitude of fresh and original ideas which clearly inspired them to new and adventurous action. The newly printed books that were put before them included the great classical authors, books imported from the continent of Europe on every conceivable subject, English translations of foreign books, and by the 1560s works by English authors who took pride in writing in English rather than in Latin, so that they put no barriers between themselves and their readers. Young gentlemen were presented in these books with a whole spectrum of possible interests, ranging from the history of nations to astrology, to botany, to navigation. And since humanism called men to action in accordance with their intellectual convictions, gentlemen were urged to be doers as well as readers. Each individual would, of course, choose a different set of interests, but the books were very precise guides to action, and they were often followed to the letter. Historians have not yet squarely faced that fact, though they have long recognised the practical influence of books in limited areas, for example, in architectural design. I perceive it strongly at work in the practice of agriculture.12 I wait to see the gentry's literal imitation of bookish advice recognized over a much broader range of activities. It should not be so difficult for us to comprehend and accept that fact, for do we not all similarly turn to books for instruction in any new pursuit? It meant that well-read young gentlemen carried a fairly standard collection of modish ideas and interests in their mental baggage, ready to bring them into play as circumstances permitted and as their personal interests led them.

In Henry VIII's reign, and continuing through the first half of Elizabeth's, a humanist education also went hand in hand with a political doctrine that cleverly drew young gentlemen into the implementation of government policy. It is true that sometimes this caused them more financial loss than profit. But the gentry's initial efforts to carry out the government's desires often made a positive contribution by launching projects that subsequently were taken up by others with long-term success. Theirs was the responsibility for initiating in their own localities schemes that would serve the nation's needs. For example, when Henry VIII set up in the royal household a corps of gentlemen pensioners—young men whose duties were to ride on ceremonial and military occasions with the king, they were also exhorted to, and did, set up horse studs at home to breed better horses. When the best modes of feeding, housing, and training fine horses were being animatedly discussed, in Elizabeth's reign, influential personages at Court encouraged some of these aspiring young gentlemen pensioners to improve and use their language skills to translate foreign books on the subject into English. Thus Federico Grisone's Italian work on *The Art of Riding* was translated and adapted *circa* 1560.[13] Nor was horsemanship the only fashionable topic. One may speak of a "translation movement" starting in Henry VIII's reign and growing fast in the first ten years of Elizabeth's reign.[14] Counting the classics alone, thirty-six books were translated in Henry VIII's reign, and thirty-nine in the first decade of Elizabeth's reign. The translators were young men, urged on by noblemen and influential politicians to serve their country in this way.[15] Linguistic skills and a wide intellectual curiosity were taken for granted.

Thus young men were given the chance to serve the commonwealth in ways that made greater demands upon them than the strict duties of their office at court dictated or required. Barnaby Googe is one such example, a Gentleman Pensioner in Elizabeth's reign who served in Ireland, and while there translated a comprehensive book of husbandry that had only recently appeared (in Latin) from the pen of a German diplomat. It became a standard agricultural textbook in England for one hundred years. Googe, moreover, had already translated the work of an Italian poet and some Latin verse and later translated the proverbs of a Spaniard.[16]

Young gentlemen were offered many challenges that gave them the chance to show their talents and exercise them for constructive ends. There is, therefore, a wealth of meaning in Sir Robert Naunton's comment on Raleigh that he, being "the youngest brother, and the house diminished in its patrimony, he foresaw his own destiny that he was the first to roll through want and disability to subsist, before he came to a repose." Naunton continued, he was "the first that exposed himself into the land service of Ireland." Moreover, "he took pains," he was not "pulled up by chance," he "had the adjunct of some general learning, which, by diligence, he enforced to a great augmentation and perfection; for he was an indefatigable reader, whether by sea or land. . . ."[17]

In short, here was an ambitious young gentleman who throve in the exhilarating atmosphere of the first two decades of Elizabeth's reign. The aspirations of educated humanists, both men and women, that had wrought such impressive effects in Henry VIII's reign, were still upheld, inspiring belief in one's ability to contribute to the commonweal. Raleigh was just in time—but only just—to catch that mood in the early stages of his career.

Other more mundane features in the background of these expansive decades between the 1560s and 1580s built up confidence in the future. Elizabeth's reform of the coinage in 1560–62 helped to stabilize prices after the soaring inflation of the 1540s.[18] More reassuring still was the long period of plentiful grain supplies, beginning in 1558 and lasting until 1585. Shortages were so brief and local that by 1585 some complacency had crept in. It prompted William Cecil to condemn the wicked use of wheat to make starch for stiffening ruffs. For the past twenty-seven years, he said, Englishmen had enjoyed peace and plenty of grain, but they should not assume that shortages would never come again.[19]

Thus one may describe the first two decades of Elizabeth's reign as a new start in many different senses. It saw the effective beginnings of many audacious undertakings, apart from those exploring territories overseas. Industrial enterprises were of lasting importance, encouraged by the use of that ingenious device, the grant of a patent of monopoly. This gave the recipients the sole right of manufacturing, mining, engineering, or otherwise using processes of which they were the first inventors. By the end of the century monopolies stood for everything that was unjust in the government's meddlings with the economy, but the original idea was innocent of corruption. It was a device borrowed from Continental countries who had been using it since the 1460s. By granting inventors the sole rights to use their own new processes, the Crown gave them hope of recovering their due reward for enterprise and investment. This European idea was first adopted in England in 1552, in a patent for making glass, and secondly in 1554 in a patent to search for and work metals in England.[20] The 1560s saw the launching of a large number of highly original industrial ventures. In contrast with the two patents granted in the 1550s, twenty-two were issued in the 1560s.[21]

Through the grant of monopolies was started the making of hard white soap of Spanish type, of saltpetre, of ovens and furnaces that were economical of fuel, of sulphur, of oil, Spanish leather, white salt, drainage engines, and a whole miscellany of other goods. In all but four cases in the 1560s the patentees were foreigners; and some of the most influential men in government, William Cecil, above all, made strenuous efforts to welcome foreigners and introduce them into high places. Privy Councillors assisted large towns under their influence to recruit foreign craftsmen who might, and in several cases did, rescue their economies from decay. William Cecil, living just outside Stamford in Lincolnshire, brought foreigners with the required skills into that town.

This kind of individual endeavour in the 1560s was then carried forward under fresh momentum in the 1570s when religious refugees streamed into England, bringing their skills with them and setting up in business without waiting for any patent of monopoly. The patent system had set wheels in motion that were thereafter propelled by other sources of energy. Some twenty-three patents were granted between 1561 and 1570 but only twelve were issued between 1571 and 1580.[22] This did not mean that economic enterprise was fading; only that the methods by which it was launched were changing. It was an encouraging sign in some respects, for Englishmen in the 1570s were now in the majority as recipients of patents (seven Englishmen against four foreigners). In certain cases it meant that foreign inventors who needed financial backing had found English nobility and gentry willing to take financial shares.[23]

The financial arrangements of such enterprises, moreover, were being manipulated to spread the risks more widely. This may, indeed, contribute towards the answer to John Shirley's question concerning "Sir Walter Raleigh's Guiana Finances." How, he asked, could "a Devonshire sailor of a good family but no apparent wealth ... equip, outfit, provision and man expedition after expedition ... ?" About £60,000 was needed for Raleigh's Guiana expedition alone.[24] In enterprises involving the planting of new and potentially profitable agricultural crops, it was the practice to divide the shares that named large sums into much smaller units, thereby spreading the burden between many more kin and friends. Such practices do not emerge in the official accounts and are only accidentally brought to light, usually in the course of subsequent disputes. For example, when George Bedford held a one-third share in a madder-growing project in Kent in the 1620s, he did not expect to find all the money for that third from his own pocket. He expected to break down his share of the responsibility into many smaller shares to which his family and friends subscribed. A similar subdivision of one share into eight parts was contrived in a tobacco-growing project in Gloucestershire *circa* 1619, which at first appearance looked like a partnership of only three people.[25]

Financial manoeuvres with regard to patents of monopoly, and partnerships formed outside the patent system, enabled more and more gentry to contribute, though in a less active way than the foreign innovators, to the diversification of the economy. In the second half of Elizabeth's reign, however, this development led the gentry in entirely the wrong direction. Patents of monopoly were degraded into mere profit-seeking devices, requiring no effort from the monopolist beyond the collection of a rent. Raleigh's career mirrors the change of mood exactly, for what Professor David Quinn calls the spring and summer of his career from May 1583 to July 1592 were launched by the grants to him of two of those monopoly patents which brought the whole system into disrepute. "The impoverished gentleman," he writes, "became the wealthy and magnificent courtier,"[26] because Raleigh received the monopoly right to issue licenses for the sale of wines, which brought him £700–800 p.a. at least. (A. L. Rowse says £1100 p.a., an income larger than that of some peers.) Then in March 1584 he secured the monopoly of licenses to export cloth free of statutory restrictions.[27]

The healthy economic vigour of the kingdom in Elizabeth's early years, to which the gentry had made a positive contribution, was now sapped as abuses crept in. At the same time, confidence was checked from another direction. A bad harvest in 1585 was followed by two more in 1586 and 1587.[28] The year 1586 also brought a crisis in the cloth trade with the Low Countries and an outburst of violence against foreigners.[29] Thus, while Raleigh's economic circumstances were improving, for the nation as a whole economic trends in the 1580s were unhealthy and augured ill for the future. Foreigners, who had done much to diversify and strengthen England's industrial and agricultural base in the previous twenty years, were reviled and attacked, and Raleigh himself joined in the chorus. When he lost his influential place close to the Queen and transferred his energies into speeches in the House of Commons, he expressed a deep antipathy to foreigners. His words were incisive and left no room for another opinion. "Whereas it is presented that for strangers it is against charity, against honour, against profit to expel them; in my opinion it is no matter of charity to relieve them. . . . I see no reason that so much respect should be given unto them."[30] Such sentiments mingled only too readily with the jealousies and feudings at Court and the sense of disenchantment that hung over the last two decades of Elizabeth's reign. The depressing years of the 1590s were depressed further by yet another sequence of disastrous harvests and epidemics which historians now mark as a watershed throughout western Europe. Population growth slowed down for a century and a half, and another economic era with different problems opened out after 1600.[31]

The gentleman's portmanteau of intellectual interests and ideas, to which I referred earlier, contained more than enough variety to divert gentlemen as the mood of the age changed, and particularly if they tired of the courtly round. Among other challenges, the gentry had been invited to set themselves up in the country, and books had given them practical instructions and intellectual reasons for enjoying that life. Raleigh turned his thoughts in this direction in the 1580s. He lived in Durham House in the Strand in London but conceived the idea of returning to his childhood home at Hayes Farm in Devon and wrote to the owner asking him to sell the house to him.[32] He was cheated of his hopes and had to wait until 1592 before he achieved his desire for a different and grander estate at Sherborne, Dorset, prised by the queen for him from a reluctant bishop of Salisbury. It proved to be the source to Raleigh of endless troubles, disagreements with the bishop, and with John Meere, the man whom he chose to manage the estate.[33] But for us special interest lies in the way, as soon as he acquired Sherborne, he followed the accepted routine prescribed by the books and by the fashions of the day—laying out orchards and gardens, bringing water to the site, and ultimately building a new house.

Earlier than this, however, we have evidence of Raleigh's interest and vigour bestowed in the same direction when setting up his plantation in Ireland. This is Professor Canny's territory, and I do not wish to transgress the boundaries laid between us. But the intellectual baggage of the gentry is my theme, and it was full of stimulating notions about land and its potential, which individuals carried all over England and some of them to Ireland as well. In this baggage were stored first and foremost readings from the classical writers like Cato, Varro, and Columella, to which practical experience was added, teaching gentlemen a highly professional attitude towards farming as a rewarding, honourable occupation, and inspiring high optimism in man's capacity to improve barren or neglected soils. Many young gentry, of course, had not the means to set up an estate unless they chose neglected land which was cheap. Thus they moved into pastoral country, fenlands, marshlands, and woodlands, where their houses were likely to be in hamlets, rather than villages. But in course of time they would gentrify that countryside, which had not been so tamed before. We see the transformation most clearly in the Arden forest of Warwickshire between the mid-sixteenth and mid-seventeenth century; also in the Lincolnshire fenlands, where by the 1650s some truly model farms had been set up.[34] Young men were helped by the fact that techniques for draining wet land were being improved, and many new crops were being introduced that were recommended for less fertile, or overcropped, arable. Sons of the gentry, therefore, became active rather than passive owners of land, while some went further still, chose farming as a career, specialized in some of its newest branches, such as hop-growing and fruit growing, and then wrote books that described their experience and encouraged their fellows to follow suit.[35]

Against this background of contemporary bookish knowledge and intellectual argument concerning the noble life of the countryman, the agrarian historian approaches the evidence of Raleigh's plantation in Ireland with certain expectations. Gentlemen were being urged to try new plants from Europe and overseas, especially on barren land. One or another crop, so the argument ran, might be just the one that would miraculously turn poor land to good account.[36] Such were the hopes lying behind the gentry's many trials with new plants in the sixteenth century. They make it wholly credible that potatoes were tried on Raleigh's estate in Youghal. He may not personally have been the one most responsible, but portions of his land were being taken up by many gentlemen and esquires, with the same intellectual baggage. Thomas Hariot, gentleman, was one of his tenants. He was an indefatigable investigator in many branches of knowledge. It is difficult to imagine that he was not interested in trying new plants. Thomas Hill, gentleman, was also a tenant.[37] Is that name of significance? A Thomas Hill of London was the author of the first book on gardening in 1563.[38] That Thomas Hill cannot have been the planter in Ireland since he died somewhere between 1572 and 1575. Thomas Hill is a comparatively common name, moreover. But it is worth considering the possibility that he had a son, Thomas Hill, who followed his father's interests and was the planter in Ireland. So often in this period sons had the same names as their fathers and followed the same careers, as did Walter Raleigh's son, Walter.

Thomas Hill's book on gardening was thoroughly practical, using an unusually wide range of classical authors critically and adding the observations of his experienced gardening friends, as well as his own. It was concerned first and foremost with the most useful aspects of gardening, the sowing of vegetables and herbs for food and medicine. A man with such enthusiasms would certainly have been interested in new lands to cultivate. For other reasons too an association of the Hill family with Thomas Hariot is not an absurd guesss, knowing as we do how like-minded gentlemen formed cliques and turned up in each other's company in many different situations. Thomas Hill, writer on gardening, was a citizen of London, with a lively interest in many other branches of learning. He was a considerable translator of foreign works, translating *A Brief Epitomy of the Whole Art of Physiognomy gathered out of Aristotle and Others* (London, 1550?) and an Italian work on measures against plague. He practised astrology (i.e., astronomy); he translated a book on comets (published after his death, 1590?) and another on the stars (1599). He wrote a book on vulgar arithmetic. With such interests, coinciding so remarkably with those of Thomas Hariot, one may conceive of some acquaintance between Hariot and the Hill family, though Hariot arrived in London (1580) too late to meet the writer and translator, Thomas Hill. But Hill wrote so eloquently and sensibly on the planting of vegetable gardens, one in 1563, another in 1568, and a new edition with an additional section on the grafting of trees in 1574, we need not summarily dismiss the notion of a son alongside Hariot in Ireland who would not have neglected potatoes if they had come his way.[39]

The keen interest of many Londoners in gardening encourages the suggestion that one or another of the tenants on Raleigh's plantation, if not Raleigh himself, made a contribution to the planting of the potato in Ireland.[40] Professor Hawkes, the botanical authority on the potato, has described the conditions which were required for its success in Europe—notably twelve hours of daylight but not more, to enable it to develop tubers rather than stalk and leaf. These conditions from the very beginning were present in southwestern Ireland but not in England, for tubering could start in autumn when the days shorten to twelve hours while the temperature continues mild. In Ireland, potatoes could have given a reasonable yield from the outset.[41] Trials by any one of the gentlemen tenants on Raleigh's estate would then explain why soldiers of Cromwell's army arriving in Ireland in the 1650s saw potatoes growing in the fields.[42] Not until later, in the 1660s and 1670s, were they reintroduced into England, this time with more success. They appeared first in Lancashire, which had a regular trade with Ireland; and by that time potatoes in Ireland would have been selected and made suitable for the English climate.[43]

Finally, another of the fairly common items in a gentleman's mental baggage, which Raleigh certainly carried and in which he found great solace in his latter days, was an interest in the distilling of essences from herbs. These essences were distilled principally as medicines, though they were also prized as perfumes and cooking ingredients. Hieronymus von Braunschweig had published in German in 1519 a treatise on distillation, in order to help the poor to cure their own illnesses. This had been translated into English in 1527, and more books on distillation followed thereafter. Among the early devotees of this particular interest were the Percys, earls of Northumberland.[44] Raleigh picked up the same enthusiasm, and when he was imprisoned in the Tower in 1604 distilling was one of his principal occupations. Indeed, he turned a former henhouse into a stillhouse. Then he was joined by Henry Percy, the ninth Earl, who was imprisoned for his alleged complicity in the Gunpowder Plot. He had inherited his family's consuming interest in the same subject—indeed, he was called the Wizard Earl—and produced the much-needed money to buy more equipment.[45]

It is anachronistic to turn these activities, as some historians have done, into a precocious interest in the science of chemistry. To contemporaries they were far more immediately important; the essences were the essential medicines that would save, and prolong, life. As Sir Thomas Smith, another enthusiastic distiller and Elizabeth's principal secretary between 1572 and 1576, expressed it, "I must needs make much of that [i.e., his stills] to the which, next God, I perceive I owe my life and health, as this winter."[46] Raleigh acquired such a high reputation for his medicinal cordials that, despite the charges of treason against him, James I countenanced the use of his special distillation to save the life of the dying Prince Henry, his heir. Unfortunately, it did not work the miraculous cure that was hoped for. But the cordial continued into the later seventeenth century to find an honoured place among the medicines in great men's households.[47]

If Raleigh had escaped the scaffold, A. L. Rowse is unable to imagine him enjoying the contentment of the country life. I have no such difficulty. Gentlemen knew the intellectual arguments in its favour, and these gave them plenty to do on their land. Circumstances at James's Court powerfully strengthened the desire to retire from Court. In the very year of Raleigh's death they were reiterated yet again. The lively debate on the Court versus the country life had been initiated in 1548 when the Spanish humanist and companion of the Emperor Charles V, Antonio de Guevara, published a *Dispraise of the Life of a Courtier and a Commendation of the Life of the Labouring Man*. Antonio de Guevara was one of the most widely read authors in sixteenth-century Europe (though he is now totally neglected). This essay was translated into English in 1574, reissued in 1575 and 1579. Something was evidently happening in the seventies to awaken a yearning for the peace and contentment of country life. It is not difficult to guess at the reason for a reissue of the same debate in 1618. This time Nicholas

The Country-man.   *The Courtier.*

The debate between courtiers and country gentlemen, discussed by the sixteenth-century Spanish humorist Antonio de Guevara in *Dispraise of the Life of a Courtier...*, appeared again in 1618 under the name of Nicholas Breton in *The Court and Country.*

Breton claimed to be the author, giving his essay the title *The Court and Country or a Brief Discourse Dialoguewise.*[48] But Nicholas Breton's point of view was already stowed away in our gentlemen's baggage of current notions on the world around them. Antonio de Guevara's essay had been widely read. He had also written of "we courtiers much cumbered with tediousness," and of the many men at court "loitering, superfluous, idle, vagrant, and evil-tongued." Raleigh had already turned such thoughts into the far more melodious, gleaming, but bitter lines:

> Say to the court it glows
> and shines like rotten wood.[49]

That viewpoint won increasing support from gentlemen towards the end of James I's reign, as onlookers expressed with candour their distaste at the sight of their king—"this monster in excess"—and his Court. The chaplain to the Venetian ambassador in 1618, describing a series of banquets, comedies, and masques which he attended in London after Christmas that year, finished his account thus: "Should your lordships writhe on reading or listening to this document, you may imagine the weariness I feel in relating it."[50] Raleigh did not get the chance to retire to the country. But his brother-in-law, Arthur Throckmorton, wisely had long since done so and was kept fully occupied. We may learn more in the future about early seventeenth-century Court and country by identifying other gentry who followed the same path. In a later generation such men were responsible for some quite notable model farms.[51]

Notes

*Joan Thirsk was introduced by Lindsay C. Warren as follows: "Our next speaker also comes to us from England, although she has been in North Carolina for several months as a fellow at the National Humanities Center in the Research Triangle Park.

"Dr. Joan Thirsk was educated at the Camden School for Girls and Westfield College of the University of London, where she received her B.A. and doctoral degrees. She received her master's degree from Oxford. During World War II, she served as a subaltern in the Intelligence Corps. Until her retirement approximately three years ago, Dr. Thirsk was a reader in economic history at the University of Oxford and professorial fellow of St. Hilda's College at Oxford. She has specialized in English agricultural history, especially of the sixteenth to eighteenth centuries, and is general editor and substantial contributor to *The Agrarian History of England and Wales,* published by the Cambridge University Press. She has written much on rural industries and on the consumer society of the period 1500-1700. She is a fellow of the British Academy and has an honorary degree from Leicester University, where she was the senior research fellow from 1962 to 1965. Dr. Thirsk is also a member of the Royal Commission on the Historical Monuments of England and a foreign member of the American Philosophical Society. She now resides at Hadlow Castle, Tonbridge, Kent. Her vitae says that her recreations include gardening and sewing. I want to extend a special welcome to Dr. Thirsk at this time, and we look forward to hearing her paper on the subject of 'Raleigh's England.' "

[1] A.L. Rowse, *Sir Walter Raleigh, his Family and Private Life* (New York: 1962).

[2] Sir Robert Naunton, *Fragmenta Regalia. Memoirs of Elizabeth, Her Court and Favourites* (London: 1824), p. 103.

[3] Rowse, *op. cit.,* p. 129.

[4] Norman Lloyd Williams, *Sir Walter Raleigh* (London: 1962), p. 1.

[5] For the pamphlet literature on younger sons, see Joan Thirsk, "Younger Sons in the Seventeenth Century," in idem, *The Rural Economy of England. Collected Essays* (London: 1984), pp. 335–57, especially pp. 338, 351.

[6] Louis B. Wright, "The 'Gentleman's Library' in Early Virginia: The Literary Interests of the First Carters," *Huntington Library Quarterly,* I (1937–8): 19.

[7] Rowse, *op. cit.,* p. 2.

[8] *Ibid.,* pp. 2–9. The King's bodyguard was first permanently established in Henry VII's reign. Col. Sir Reginald Hennell, *The History of the King's Bodyguard of the Yeomen of the Guard* (London: 1904), pp. 12, 23–5, 60, 78.

[9] Rowse, *op. cit.,* p. 130.

[10] Naunton, *op. cit.,* p. 109.

[11] Williams, *op. cit.,* p. 46; Muriel Rukeyser, *The Traces of Thomas Hariot* (New York: n.d. but 1971), p. 67. The author also says of the episode "it is true to his nature. . . . It is in character for Ralegh." On Raleigh's "stage play world," see also Stephen J. Greenblatt, *Sir Walter Raleigh. The Renaissance Man and His Roles* (New Haven: 1973), p. 22.

[12] I developed this theme in my Neale lecture at University College London, in 1983, to be published in *Alternative Agriculture. A Seventeenth-Century Perspective on Past and Present.* Some illustrative examples of bookish advice in practice are given in Thirsk, "Plough and Pen," in T.H. Aston *et alii, Social Relations and Ideas: Essays in Honour of R.H. Hilton* (Cambridge: 1983), pp. 303–306. For the care given to the reading of books on architectural design, see the evidence of Henry Percy's annotated text of Vitruvius, in G.R. Batho, "The Library of the 'Wizard' Earl: Henry Percy, ninth Earl of Northumberland (1564–1632)," *The Library,* 15 (1960): 255.

[13] Joan Thirsk, "Horses in Early Modern England: For Service, for Pleasure, for Power," in idem, *The Rural Economy of England, op. cit.,* pp. 385–91.

[14] As does C. H. Conley in *The First English Translators of the Classics* (New York: 1927), pp. 18 ff.

[15]Conley, *op. cit.*, pp. 18, 23–31, 35–41.

[16]*Dictionary of National Biography, sub nomine*. A disappointingly incomplete account of Googe's career also appears in Richard C. Barnett, *Place, Profit and Power. A Study of the Servants of William Cecil, Elizabethan Statesman*, James Sprunt Studies in History and Political Science, 51 (1969): 65–7.

[17]Naunton, *op. cit.*, pp. 104–05, 108–09. See also John Aubrey's account of Raleigh, studying most while at sea, always carrying a trunk of books on his voyages. Oldys and Birch, eds., *The Works of Sir Walter Ralegh* (Oxford: 2 vols., 1829), VIII, p. 739.

[18]CSPD 1547–80, pp. 159, 161, 193.

[19]Joan Thirsk, *Economic Policy and Projects. The Development of a Consumer Society in Early Modern England* (Oxford: 1978), p. 88.

[20]*Ibid.*, p. 52.

[21]In listing them Wyndham Hulme took pains to point out that this number could be incomplete since it rests on the entries printed in the Calendars of the Patent Rolls. E. Wyndham Hulme, "The History of the Patent System under the Prerogative and at Common Law," *Law Quarterly Review*, 46 (1896): 145. For the negotiations with foreigners, see CSPD 1547–80, *passim*.

[22]Wyndham E. Hulme, "The History of the Patent System under the Prerogative and at Common Law. A Sequel," *Law Quarterly Review*, 61 (1900): 52.

[23]*Ibid.*, p. 52.

[24]John W. Shirley, "Sir Walter Raleigh's Guiana Finances," *Huntington Library Quarterly*, 13 (1949): 55, 59.

[25]Thirsk, *Alternative Agriculture*, to be published.

[26]David B. Quinn, *Raleigh and the British Empire* (London: 1947), p. 37.

[27]*Ibid.*, p. 37; Rowse, *op cit.*, p. 140.

[28]Anxiety about grain shortages is mirrored in the State Papers in government-solicited reports on measures to restrain grain export and keep the markets furnished. They begin in May 1585 and continue until December 1588. CSPD 1581–90, passim.

[29]J.D. Gould, "The Crisis in the Export Trade, 1586-7," *English Historical Review*, 71 (1956): 212-22.

[30]Eleanor Grace Clark, *Ralegh and Marlowe. A Study in Elizabethan Fustian* (New York: 1941), p. 31.

[31]Peter Clark, ed., *The European Crisis of the 1590s. Essays in Comparative History* (London, 1985), pp. 4–5.

[32]Oldys and Birch, eds., *Works of Ralegh, op. cit.*, vol. VIII, pp. 744–5.

[33]Rowse, *op. cit.*, pp. 148–9; J. B., "Sir Walter Raleigh at Sherborne," *Gentleman's Magazine*, 1853, part II, pp. 435 ff., and 1854, part I, pp. 19 ff.

[34]Joan Thirsk, ed., *The Agrarian History of England and Wales, V, 1640–1750* (Cambridge: 1986), Part II, p. 323; Victor Skipp, *Crisis and Development. An Ecological Case Study of the Forest of Arden, 1570–1674* (Cambridge: 1978), *passim*; H. C. Darby, *The Draining of the Fens* (Cambridge: 1956), pp. 275, 279.

[35]See, for example, Reynolde Scot, *A Perfect Platforme of a Hoppe-garden* (London: 1576); Leonard Mascall, *The Husbandrie, Ordering and Government of Poultrie* (London: 1581?); *idem., The First Book of Cattel* (London: 1596). For a fuller list, see G. E. Fussell, *The Old English Farming Books from Fitzherbert to Tull* (London: 1947).

[36]Thirsk, *Alternative Agriculture*, to be published.

[37]PRO SP63/144.

[38]*Dictionary of National Biography, sub nomine*; Francis R. Johnson, "Thomas Hill: An Elizabethan Huxley," *Huntington Library Quarterly*, 4 (1944): 329–51.

[39]On Hill, see Johnson, *op cit*. On Hariot, see DNB, *sub nomine*; Muriel Rukeyser, op. cit; and John W. Shirley, *Thomas Harriot: a Biography* (Oxford: 1983), pp. 51, 67, 70. For one of Hill's gardening books, in a modern reprint, see Dydymus Mountain, *The Gardener's Labyrinth* (New York: 1982).

[40]In discussion at the Raleigh conference Professor David Quinn correctly pointed out that potato cultivation could have developed in the time of Robert Boyle, Earl of Cork, who bought Raleigh's estate from him; he was extremely interested in farming and gardening.

[41]J.G. Hawkes, "The History of the Potato, Part III," *Journal of the Royal Horticultural Society*, 6–7 (1967): 290–91.

[42]W. Coles, *Adam in Eden* (London: 1657), p. 33.

[43]Joan Thirsk, ed., *The Agrarian History of England and Wales* (Cambridge: 1986), V, part I, p. 64; Hawkes, *op. cit.*, p. 292.

[44]Joan Thirsk, "Forest, Field and Garden: Landscapes and Economies in Shakespeare's England," in John F. Andrews, ed., *William Shakespeare: His World, His Work, His Influence* (New York: 1985), vol. I, pp. 265–6.

[45]Williams, *op. cit.*, pp. 212, 214–5; Rowse, *op. cit.*, pp. 242–3.

[46]Mary Dewar, *Sir Thomas Smith. A Tudor Intellectual in Office* (London: 1964), p. 143.

[47]Rowse, *op. cit.*, pp. 242–3.

[48]Rowse, *op. cit.*, p. 262; Joan Thirsk, "Forest, Field, and Garden," *op. cit.*, pp. 258–9.

[49]Oldys and Birch, eds., *Works of Ralegh, op. cit.*, vol. VIII, p. 725.

[50]Robert Ashton, ed., *James I by his Contemporaries* (London: 1969), pp. 232, 238–42.

[51]Many glimpses of this tension between the Court and the country life are seen in contemporary correspondence. See, for example, Ashton, *op. cit.*, pp. 237 (Lord Thomas Howard to Sir John Harington, 1611: "God speed your ploughing at the court: I know you do it rarely at home"), 244 (Sir John Harington describing drunken frolics at Court when the King of Denmark visited James I, 1606: "I wish I was at home: *O rus, quando te aspiciam?*" Raleigh himself, when in the Tower, wrote "There is no course more comely, nor any resolution so well beseeming a wise man . . . as to retire himself from court and company." Rowse, *op. cit.*, p. 262. See also Arthur Throckmorton's preoccupations in Northamptonshire, when he withdrew from Court. Rowse, *op. cit.*, pp. 218, 273, 190–1, 275, 281.

Who Were the Roanoke Colonists?

William S. Powell*

Walter Raleigh secured his charter from Queen Elizabeth in the spring of 1584, taking up where his half-brother, Sir Humphrey Gilbert, was unfortunately obliged to end his efforts at colonization in America. As it turned out, Raleigh was little if any more successful, yet over the next three years he was responsible for sending a reconnaissance expedition to America in 1584; something of a military expedition in 1585–86; and a colonizing expedition—consisting of men, women, and boys—in 1587. And finally, in 1590 a futile attempt was made to locate the settlers left in 1587.

We know who some of the leaders were of each of these groups making their way to Roanoke Island. Philip Amadas and Arthur Barlowe of the first are perhaps not as well known as some of the others, but more and more is being discovered about even these two young men who were still in their twenties. Of those involved with the second voyage, Ralph Lane, Thomas Harriot, Simon Fernándes, Sir Francis Drake, and Sir Richard Grenville among them, we know more. John White, governor of the 1587 colony, is still a shadowy figure, but his reputation has been growing of late, and we have the names of more than a hundred of his colonists.

Among the Roanoke Colonists during these three years were several other men who were not actually leaders but with whom we have more than a passing acquaintance. Among them are Thomas Buckner, mercer, at whose house in London Harriot died; Thomas Cavendish, who later sailed around the world; Joachim Ganz, native of Prague, a mineral expert, and the first American Jewish colonist; Edward Gorges, relative of both Gilbert and Raleigh, and member of a family prominent in both old and New England; Daniel Höchstetter, German mineral specialist; Abraham Kendall, veteran navigator, noted for his mathematical skill, and who afterwards was with Raleigh in South America; Martin Laurentson, a Dane who was in England to study maritime warfare and navigation; and George Raymond, who subsequently had a notable career at sea but was killed in 1625 by the last shot fired in the taking of the castle at Cadiz. These were all men in whom Raleigh (or his advisors) must have had confidence and who, indeed, proved themselves a little later.

Before trying to suggest who some of the ordinary people may have been, let me alert you to what I am about to do. The *names* of the people among the Roanoke Colonists have been something of a hobby with me that I have enjoyed for more than forty years. Having collected notes about them on both sides of the Atlantic, I have come to consider some of these people, who really are no more than names in lists, to be *real* people, and in the "next world"

William S. Powell, professor emeritus at UNC-CH, spoke at the Saturday luncheon on "Who Were the Roanoke Colonists?"

I expect to recognize them! To say that I have some questions for them is an understatement.

My sources have been county and local histories, biographies, parish registers, lists of university alumni, reports of the Historical Manuscripts Commission, finding aids and documents at the London Guildhall, the Public Record Office, Somerset House (before the wills were moved), and at many county record offices, but one of the best tools has been the Burnett-Morris Index in the public library at Exeter. I have looked for needles in every haystack I encountered.

H. G. Jones instructed me not to be scholarly this afternoon even if I could. In a moment you will conclude that I took his advice. For one thing, I have usually omitted the customary weaseling (but often necessary) words such as "perhaps," "undoubtedly," and "quite likely." But you must understand that what I tell you this afternoon about the Roanoke Colonists applies not necessarily to a particular *colonist* but only to someone with the same *name* as a colonist—

living at the same time and of roughly the right age. Nevertheless, in the case of the 1587 colonists, what I shall say pertains only to people for whom I have found nothing to suggest that they survived beyond that date. Rarely am I confident beyond doubt that what I have turned up actually applies to a Roanoke Colonist, much as I would like for it to.

There is good evidence, however, of five men who came to Roanoke whose names do not appear in the contemporary lists. One THOMAS BAYLY, according to the Historical Manuscripts Commission report on the papers of the Marquess of Bath, wrote a letter to the Earl of Shrewsbury about the return of Drake to Portsmouth which indicates that Bayly had been with Drake. An 1868 biography of Raleigh cites a Spanish deposition at Simancas by RICHARD BUTLER saying that he went to America with Captain Amadas. The sketch of Sir THOMAS GATES in the *Dictionary of National Biography* says that he was with Drake at Roanoke when the colonists were picked up. The inscription on the tomb of ROBERT MASTERS at Burghill, Herefordshire, records that he was in Virginia with Cavendish. And according to the list of graduates of Cambridge, Sir MARTIN STUTEVILLE was also in America with Drake.

There are several general statements that can be made which can be substantiated. (1) Around a dozen of the Roanoke Colonists had been at Oxford or Cambridge a year or two before they set out on Raleigh's second or third expedition. Such a voyage, they must have hoped, would offer excitement, a challenge, or an opportunity to get rich. (2) Fathers, or other relatives with the same family name, pledged generously towards the defense of the country against the Spanish Armada. I imagine that one reason they did this was in the hope of speeding relief to the Roanoke Colonists. (3) It seems quite apparent that there were many French Huguenots among the Roanoke venturers. (4) Many colonists bore typical West Country names, but there were some from Essex, Lincolnshire, and Yorkshire. Others clearly originated in Ireland and in London. A number of Welsh and a few Scottish names also appear, while a few seem to be German or Dutch. (5) If I could definitely connect the Roanoke Colonist with the person about whom I have found some facts, I could tell you that there was a priest, a doctor, a lawyer, a basketmaker, some Thames watermen, and practitioners of other professions and occupations. (6) I would say that some of the 1587 colonists were wives, sisters, brothers, fathers, sons, or otherwise related to some of the 1585–86 colonists and suggest that we might thereby have a clue as to the surnames of a few of those abandoned by Lane or left by Drake. (7) Some of the earliest settlers at Jamestown bore the names of Roanoke Colonists, and while I realize that most of them were common English names (including three which appear in my own family), I would suggest that they came to America in hope of finding relatives left at Roanoke in 1587. (8) From Governor John White's journal we know that two of the women in his colony were pregnant and gave birth soon after their arrival. Another was the mother of a nursing child. (9) The crossing took just ten days short of three months. When I think of the conditions under which these people reached Roanoke, I feel a great deal of admiration for their courage and imagine them to have been people of great determination. I like to think that they might have felt rewarded if they could have known the ultimate result of their sacrifice in laying the foundation of English culture in America.

Fourteen of the Roanoke Colonists crossed the Atlantic more than once. John White came the maximum number of times—four. Simon Fernándes came three times, while Philip Amadas made the voyage twice. Two of the 1587—or "Lost Colonists"—had been over previously. Six men who returned with White in 1590 had been among Ralph Lane's company.

But who might these brave, or perhaps foolhardy, people have been? As time permits I will share with you some hints from my random notes—and encourage you to take up the challenge, if you like, to match hints and facts.

JOHN ACTON had attended Balliol College, became a captain, and was eventually knighted. While he may well have been the colonist, don't forget that I really don't know.

JOHN ARUNDELL was colonel of horse when Raleigh was lieutenant general. Three other members of the same Roanoke colony, JOHN HARRIS, ROTTENBURY, and ROWSE also served in the same unit, so I am willing to conclude that this is a bit of "new" information about four of Ralph Lane's men. That four friends from the same military unit decided to go to Roanoke would not be surprising.

VALENTINE BEALE was with the Lane colony for a year. Surely this name was unusual enough that he can be identified as the father of baby Valentine Beale baptized at St. Matthew, Friday Street, on 19 February 1597.

JOHN BEDFORD is identified by David Quinn as master of the *Moonlight* on the 1590 expedition. Papers at Hatfield House show, among other things, that he was also master of the *Roebuck* in 1592.

WILLIAM BERDE of the "Lost Colony" was involved in some correspondence pertaining to coastal defense in 1586—just the year before going to Roanoke. His knowledge certainly would have been valuable at Fort Raleigh in America. One Christopher Marshall, who had been at Roanoke Island with Ralph Lane in 1585–86, was married to Elizabeth Byrde, so the possibility exists that Christopher persuaded his brother-in-law, William, to go to America.

RICHARD BERRYE, also of the "Lost Colony," was a muster captain in 1572, and identified in 1579 as being the son of James and his wife, Jeane, daughter and heir of Thomas Lane. This, of course, suggests some connection with Ralph Lane. He might have been a cousin.

JOHN BROCKE was a shoemaker and certainly would have been a useful member of the Ralph Lane expedition when shoes must have been worn out on treks along the Chesapeake Bay and down to Lake Mattamuskeet.

FRANCIS BROOKE is identified by Quinn as treasurer of the 1585 expedition. The 12th Report of the Historical Manuscripts Commission has several letters from one of this name from Portsmouth about shipping affairs, all of which tie together very nicely.

THOMAS BUTLER was one of the "Lost Colonists." Ten years previously one of this name had been in court in Essex because "a red petycote" had been stolen from his house.

ANTHONY CAGE. Harley manuscript 1483, fol. 17b, has a rough sketch of arms granted Anthony Cage of London. Several children of a man of this name were baptized at St. Matthew's, Friday Street. Remember that Valentine Beale's name also appears in the same register. This Anthony, I suggest, was a brother of John Cage. John came over in 1584 and Anthony in 1587. John may have convinced Anthony to join up.

JOHN CHANDLER of the Lane colony was the father of several children baptized at another church in Friday Street in the 1570s. It might be possible to make a case for Friday Street as a recruiting center for the Roanoke voyages.

JOHN CHAPMAN entered Trinity College, Cambridge, in 1568 and was rector of a church in Suffolk in 1577, but there was another man of the same name who was a grocer in 1566, while many John Chapmans show up in documents in the Essex Record Office. Take your pick—priest, grocer, or litigant. He was one of the Lost Colonists and so was ALIS CHAPMAN, perhaps the wife of John. Or she may well have been the wife of the Chapman (for whom no Christian name is recorded) who may have been left in charge of the men who remained on Roanoke Island in 1586 when the Lane colony departed—or perhaps he was one of the unfortunate men out on reconnaissance at the time the fleet sailed, and Alis had come over seeking him. Or perhaps Alis Chapman was a widow seeking a lost son. The unnamed Chapman may have been Robert, as one Robert married Ales Pouker at St. Mary the Virgin, Aldmanbury, London, in 1579. It may merely have been a coincidence, but at the same church and in the same year, a William Millerd married Dorothy Booth, and William Millard was also one of Lane's colonists.

JOHN CLARKE is a name that occurs at about the right time in both Cambridge and Oxford lists, and he may well be one of them, as he was described as one of the "principall Gentlemen" of the 1585 voyage. One of this name contributed to the defense against the Armada, while another, conceivably the son of the colonist, was captured by the Spanish at Point Comfort, Va., in 1611.

WILLIAM CLEMENT and JAMES HYNDE, both "Lost Colonists," were imprisoned at Colchester Castle at the same time in 1582; apparently the two were guilty of stealing forty sheep.

ABRAHAM COCKE was captain of one of the ships on the 1590 crossing intended to relieve the colonists. It rather clearly was he who later achieved fame as a privateer. On one occasion in 1581, however, while only a seaman, he fell out with the captain over victuals and went ashore at Bahia, Brazil, where he married and settled down. In 1587 he was captured by an English ship as he was piloting a small Portuguese ship, but he afterwards commanded English ships sailing to Brazil.

MARMADUKE CONSTABLE is one of the few heretofore obscure colonists whom I think I have positively identified. He matriculated at Caius College, Cambridge, in 1581 at the age of 16, was the son of Marmaduke of Yorkshire, died in 1607, and is buried in York Minster.

CHRISTOPHER COOPER, a member of the Lost Colony of 1587, was one of the Assistants in the government and it was he who initially volunteered to return to England with the fleet that brought them over to expedite the shipment of supplies. He changed his mind the following day, however, and Governor White returned. It is possible that Cooper was White's brother-in-law or his nephew, as White was married in 1566 to Tomasyn Cooper.

ANANIAS DARE is best remembered as the father of Virginia Dare, the first English child born in America. He was a tiler and bricklayer and was the father of a "natural son," John Dare, in London. A member of the Dare family living in England now thinks he is a descendant of John Dare. In Australia, a pilot named Dare, who flies sightseers from Alice Springs to Ayers Rock, tells me that his father, a native of England, was aware of the role of the Dares in early American history, but he does not know whether this was based on family tradition or simply from his reading.

This year in London, Lebame Houston of Manteo was doing some research in the Guildhall where she consulted the register of St. Martin's Parish, Ludgate, and found that ELINOR WHITE (DARE) was baptized on 9 May 1568. She was, therefore, 19 years of age when Virginia, her daughter by Ananias Dare, was born.

ROGER DEANE was from Devon and married to Elizabeth Wood — and there were four Woods, including Agnes, among the colonists. He was described as a gentleman in 1573 when he purchased a part of Frithelstock Manor. He was still living in 1616 and recorded as a resident of Newton Petrock. Deane was with Lane's colony; THOMAS ELLIS, a warden of St. Petrock, Exeter, was a "Lost Colonist." The place-name suggests that they may have been acquainted and naturally raises a question about the role of Deane in the decision of Ellis to go to Roanoke. But a bit more about Ellis in a few minutes.

EDMOND ENGLISH was a "Lost Colonist," and someone named Edmund English had entered Magdalene College, Cambridge, in 1565. The same? Maybe so.

SIMON FERNÁNDES, identified then simply as a mariner, was licensed by Raleigh in 1582 to keep a tavern and sell wine in Plymouth. We remember him now as the pilot of Raleigh's expeditions, and because he refused to follow his employer's directions to take the 1587 colony to the Chesapeake Bay.

THOMAS FOXE was with Ralph Lane at Roanoke in 1585–86. In 1559 he was described as being 12 years old and the son of Thomas Foxe, a clothworker. He was taken in by a Mr. Quarles "for his lewdness." One of this name was married in 1567 and died in 1603, but another one—or perhaps the same one—in 1594 was part owner of the cargo of a ship of Teignmouth.

JOHN GIBBES is an example of a "Lost Colonist" for whom a number of scattered facts fit. One of this name entered St. John's College, Cambridge, in 1564; the same or another married a widow in 1575; and a John, "Gentleman," who may have been his father or a relative, contributed £25 towards the country's defense at the time of the Armada. According to a genealogy of the Gibbs family by Herbert C. Gibbs, this family as well as the Cheyne and Wotton families were all related. Another source reports that the Wooton family was related by marriage to the Courtney family. If these sources are correct and the Roanoke colonists were members of this branch of the family, it is likely that VINCENT CHEYNE and RISE COURTNEY of the Lane colony and this John Gibbes and LEWES WOTTON of the 1587 colony were all related.

RICHARD GILBERT of Lane's colony and WILLIAM GRENVILLE of 1584, because of the possibility of a relationship to both Raleigh and Sir Richard Grenville, should, in time, be identified. One secondary source suggests that William Grenville's experience with Amadas and Barlowe may have influenced Sir Richard in taking charge of Raleigh's large expedition of 1585. Another example of possible persuasion exists between JOHN and THOMAS HARRIS; John came first and Thomas then joined John White's 1587 colony. If this is the case, I can imagine that poor John was tormented by the thought that he had sent Thomas off to be swallowed up in the wilderness of America. This just might account for the fact that one William Harris contributed the handsome sum of £50 towards the defeat of the Armada.

HENRIE GREENE is one of only eight names known of members of the 1584 expedition. One was graduated from Corpus Christi, Cambridge, in 1577. There is a 1685 genealogy of the Greene family of Dorset with information on those who came to America, and in time it may be possible to figure out how the Roanoke Colonist fits in.

I have already suggested that two colonists may have spent time together in the same prison. ROWLAND GRIFFYN, probably Welsh judging by his name, returned from having spent nearly a year with the Lane colony. A man of this name in August 1594 was convicted of robbery and sent to the same prison as Clement and Hynde, but he escaped in September. But just to suggest how impossible it is to identify the Roanoke Colonists, a 16-year-old youth named Rowland Griff*ith*, of County Caernarvon, entered Exeter College in December 1587 and was a student at Lincoln's Inn in 1594.

There probably was some connection between THOMAS HEWET of the Lost Colony and JACOB WHIDDON, captain of Raleigh's ship the *Roebuck*.

Since both Hewet and one Joan Whiddon are mentioned in the 1586 will of Joan Woulston there must have been some relationship.

GEORGE HOWE, the Lost Colonist who was killed by the Indians soon after his arrival, may have been the brother-in-law of Thomas Rottenbury of Lane's colony. Rottenbury's wife was Elizabeth Howe. And more about Howe next.

RICHARD HUMFREY was one of Lane's colonists. There are numerous clues as to his identity, but an unusual fact is that in 1589, Elizabeth, the daughter of one Richard Humfrey, ran in the way of workmen at a mill and was crushed by the millstone. There was a boy named Thomas Humfrey with the Lost Colonists but no adult of that name. I think a good guess would be that he came with his uncle, George Howe, to verify for himself the reports his father made of America, and after Howe's early death he surely was some comfort to his cousin, young George Howe, Jr.

JOHN JONES is clearly a common name, but it will help me make a point. This was the name of one of the 1587 colonists, and there were two others Joneses in the group—a man and a woman, GRIFFEN and JANE. Strange to say, in my research I have not been overwhelmed by John as a Christian name in the Jones family. There was one, however, of the right dates who was licensed to practice medicine and was patronized by the Earl of Pembroke and the Earl of Shrewsbury. However, another (at least I assume it was not the doctor!) was charged in 1581 with "violent and outrageous behaviour, breaking the peace, beating the constables and other officers, abusing the clergy, drinking, dicing, brawling, quarrelling, scoffing, loitering, swearing, &c." I would not be surprised if his neighbors urged him to try his luck in America. But I am left to contend with still another John Jones, one who was a gold and silversmith in Exeter between 1569 and 1584. There is some slight suggestion that Jane Pierce, of the 1587 colony, may have been related to the Joneses.

EDWARD KELLEY and THOMAS WISSE were both members of Ralph Lane's colony. The homes of the Kelley and the Wisse families in Devon were only about 2½ miles apart, and so far as I can determine both are still standing. I have quite a few notes on people of these names and hope eventually to be able to sort them out.

RICHARD KEMME, a Lost Colonist, has a name that has turned up only once, even if in a slightly different form, so it may be he. On 13 May 1582 it was suggested to the Privy Council by a former mayor of Thetford that "Mr. Richard Kempe" be nominated for the office of Recorder, the chief legal officer of the city. Now Thetford is in Lincolnshire not far from the home of John Pory, a Jamestown official a few years hence. Pory's sister married a man name Ellis, and there was an Ellis man and a boy also with the Lost Colony. Pory, in 1622, was one of the earliest explorers from Virginia to visit and report on the northeastern part of North Carolina—looking, I wouldn't be surprised, for his brother-in-law and nephew. Tempting bits of evidence (even more than I have just cited) suggest that a few other Lincolnshire folks were on Roanoke Island.

EDWARD KETTELL, is not a common name, since I have found only one reference to it. In the Essex Record Office there is a 1602 document in which a maimed soldier, then in the Low Country, seeks the aid of Edward Kyttlye in getting a pension. Since the pension was granted, we may conclude that Kettell was a man of some influence.

RALPH LANE is too well known to require more comment than to add a few facts. He was a cousin of Sir Christopher Hatton, lord chancellor to Queen Elizabeth. William Cecil, Baron Burghley, was responsible for bringing Lane to the attention of the Queen. Lane participated in Drake's Portuguese expedition of 1589 during which he was critical of Drake and described by one historian as "a captious critic, with a genius for grumbling at his superior officers." Although not a new fact, it is not widely known that Lane was knighted in 1593.

Captain WILLIAM LANE, who was with John White on his 1590 search for the Lost Colony, may have been the one of this name who married Jane Mattacott in Barnstaple, Devon, in 1579 and whose will and inventory, dated 1632, are in the Cornwall Record Office.

One MARGARET LAWRENCE, the name of a Lost Colonist, was christened at St. Thomas the Apostle church, London, in January 1569.

JOHN LINSEY was with the Lane colony in 1585–86. A John Linsey entered Peterhouse College, Cambridge, in 1578 and was graduated in 1581 from Clare College; he was a schoolmaster in Cambridgeshire in 1582 and ordained to the priesthood in Norwich in 1584. In 1591 he was vicar of a parish in South Creake, Norfolk.

ROBERT LITTLE was one of the Lost Colonists of 1587. A document in the Essex Record Office contains the testimony of a man of the same name about a death resulting from an accident at a football game in 1567 in which he apparently participated.

WILLIAM LUCAS appears in the roster of 1587 colonists. A yeoman of this name of London in 1568 married Alice Bill. In the course of time Thomas Lucas of Middlesex contributed £25 towards the defeat of the Spanish Armada.

The name of THOMAS LUDDINGTON, although it has no title accompanying it, appears fifth in the list of Ralph Lane's colonists among the "Masters" and "Captains." There may well have been some connection between—or, indeed, he may have been the same person—with Thomas Lodington, fellow of Lincoln College, Oxford, from 1582 to 1605. He became a noted preacher in the last decade of the sixteenth century and afterwards. This Thomas Lodington was from the County of Lincoln, entered St. Mary Hall, Oxford, at the age of 14 in 1579, was graduated in 1582, awarded a master's degree in 1585, a divinity degree in 1594, and licensed to preach in 1597. The question naturally arises, why the lapse of time between the master's and the divinity degree? A year in American might account for some it.

JANE MANNERING, a Lost Colonist, undoubtedly was a Mainwaring, a common family name, and Jane often appears in it as a given name. Jane, the colonist, may have been a cousin of HUMFREY NEWTON, another Lost Colonist, as his grandmother was Katherine Mainwaring.

CHRISTOPHER MARSHALL, one of the Lane colonists, bears a name common in Yorkshire as well as in London. A man of this name was married at St. Martin, Ludgate, London, to Elizabeth Byrde of Essex in 1572, and, as we have just seen, William Berde came over the following year. Or Colonist Marshall may be identified with a younger man of the same name, as a "Xpofer" Marshall and Margaret Robinson were married in 1597, in Rotherham, Yorkshire, where a Christopher Marshall was buried in 1632. It is of further interest that one Christopher Marshall of Berkshire contributed £25 towards the defeat of the Spanish Armada. Was he perhaps the Lane colonist who was concerned about the safety of his brother-in-law?

JAMES MASON, a Lane colonist, might have been the young man of the same name who entered St. John's College, Cambridge, in 1579, was graduated from Trinity in 1583, received the M. A. degree in 1586, and was licensed to teach grammar in 1583. He may be the one who died in 1638.

The name of ROBERT MASTERS does not appear among those recorded by Richard Hakluyt or known to and mentioned by John White. Nevertheless, he remembered his voyage the rest of his life and the facts were engraved on the brass plaque attached to his tomb:

> Here lyeth the bodye of Robert Masters
> Gent: Late Lord of this Mannour, who travelled with Thomas Candish
> Esqr: to Virginia and afterward aboute the globe of ye whole worlde
> & after his returne marryed Winefrid ye daught^r of Thoms: Cornwall
> of Buckland Gent. By whom he hath 2 sones & 7 daughters. He departed
> this life the .3. of Iune A^o. 1619.

WALTER MILL, a Lane colonist, likely was a member of the Mill family whose home, Traymill, built about 1400, still stands on the River Exe between Thorverton and Bickleigh, north of Exeter. It is now a farmhouse. The Cornwall Record Office has the inventory of the estate of Walter Mill dated 1625 consisting mostly of cattle.

WILLIAM MILLARD, as we have already seen, was married to Dorothy Booth in the same church and in the same year as Robert and Alis Chapman, and there were Chapmans involved in both the Lane and the John White colonies. Millard was with Lane. One of this name, later knighted, was sheriff of Bedford-shire, while still another was a preacher in 1592 in Worcester.

HENRY MILLETT, who was with John White on the 1590 search for the Lost Colony, surely was the Henry Millett, whose son, Thomas, was baptized in the Parish of St. Thomas the Apostle, London, in 1587. He may have hoped that his presence on Roanoke Island would help him find MICHAEL MYLLET who was perhaps his brother or father.

HUMFREY NEWTON of the Lost Colony may well have been the baby of this name christened at Wilmslow Parish, Cheshire, in 1569. The Newton family lived at Pownall Hall. He was the grandson of Katherine Mainwaring, and it was noted in a local history that he died without children and unmarried, facts which would make his identity as an 18-year-old Lost Colonist reasonable.

WILLIAM NICHOLES and JOHN NICHOLLS were both associated with John White's 1587 colony although John did not sail; he was one of the Assistants and probably one of those who remained in London to represent the colony there. Both men may have been related to Philip Amadas whose mother was Jane Nichols. In 1581 one William Nicholas petitioned Sir Francis Walsingham for letters to the King of Scotland for the restoration of a ship and cargo seized by one Lachlan McLane "of the Out-Isles of Scotland." Some of the crew had been slain "and cast to the dogs to be devoured." William in 1590 may have been the father of the minor, George, associated with "the trade of a clothier."

FRAUNCIS NORRIS of the Lane colony may have been a member of the noted Norris family some of whose members held high positions during this time. One Francis Norris became the first Earl of Berkshire while another, of Brentwood, was a musician and one of the "recognizances for alehouse-keeping" for Richard Sommers, suggesting a connection with Sir Walter Raleigh. Raleigh issued a license to the wife of George Sommers (discoverer of Bermuda) to keep a tavern, so there may have been some relationship between George and Richard Sommers and Norris, the colonist.

GABRIELL NORTH, who was at Roanoke in 1585–86, possibly was the father of Robert North (1585?–1652?), grandson of Roger, second Lord North, and who sailed with Raleigh on his voyage to Guiana in 1617.

EDWARD NUGENT is described as an Irishman serving Ralph Lane. Later sources refer to him as a gentlemen and a man to whom extensive grants of land were made in County Cavan, Ulster.

HENRY and ROSE PAYNE, undoubtedly husband and wife, were members of White's 1587 colony. Henry Paynes who may have been this one appears in contemporary records in Suffolk and Devon.

Several possibilities exist to suggest the identity of Lost Colonist IANE [JANE] PIERCE, but none of them are positive. One Henry Piers, who died in 1623, had married Jane Jones, and this is a hint that Jane Pierce may have been a cousin or some other relationship to Lost Colonists Griffen, Jane, and John Jones, a cozy family group. An equally interesting puzzle might exist in the fact that a study of aliens in London notes that Jone Pierse was Portuguese, daughter of Balthasar Pierse, merchant. She was the sister of Fornando and Simon, which certainly suggests that they might have known the pilot, Simon Fernándes. But a further coincidence is that their landlord was one Frauncis White.

MICHAEL POLISON was referred to as "Master" in the list of Lane colonists, suggesting that he was a cut above the average man, at least in rank. He may have been the Mihill, son of Thomas Pullison of St. Antholin Parish christened in 1562, but more certainly he was the Alderman Pollison who in 1581 reported the number of aliens living in Vintry Ward of London.

STEVEN POMARIE, of Lane's colony, must have been a member of the extensive Pomeroy family of Devon and Cornwall. Records of administration for the estate of Stephen Pomery were registered in 1598, but at the time of the last search they could not be found.

A clue to the identify of Lane's RICHARD POORE may be found in County Tipperary where Richard Poore of Poores Town in 1592 was authorized a lease for as much of the Queen's land as was valued at about fifty pounds a year, or it may exist in Dublin where the will of Richard Poore, a husbandman of Ballyfermot, was recorded in 1616. To complicate the determination, however, it appears that a man of this name was married to Margarett Buttler in St. Andrew's Church, Plymouth, in 1592 and that one of the same name was buried at St. Martin's in the Field, London, in 1603.

Among Lane's colonists was HENRY POTKIN, and a list of aliens in London notes that Henry Potkyn of Southwarke was over the age of 12 but not a householder in 1549; in 1572 a man of the same name was married to Sicely Argentine at St. Peter's, Westcheap.

EDWARD and WENEFRID POWELL, Lost Colonists, were probably husband and wife. One Edward Powell was christened at St. Martin's in the Field, London, in 1569, and at the time of the threatened invasion by the Spanish Armada both Robert and Thomas Powell of Shropshire contributed £25 towards the defense of England.

It is known that Ananias Dare was a tiler and bricklayer and that John White was a painter; we may also now know the occupation of another Lost Colonist. ROGER PRATT in 1571 was described as being 38 years old, a native of Flanders who had lived in London for three years, who went to England for religious reasons but was member of no church, and that his occupation was that of a cooper.

GEORGE RAYMOND, captain of the *Red Lion* with Drake in 1585, was called a "gentleman captain and privateer promoter." He was with Drake at Cadiz in 1587, was captain of the *Elizabeth Bonaventure* in the Royal Navy at the time of the Spanish Armada attack, and went on an expedition to the West Indies in 1591; he was captain and owner or part owner of several other ships and engaged in a number of expeditions. In 1625 on the Cadiz voyage he was captain of the *Great Sapphire.* Just as the castle was about to yield, he embraced the master of his ship by way of congratulation for a good day's fighting when a bullet, the last shot fired by the enemy, killed both him and Sir John Bruce, the master.

The parish register of Widecombe-in-the-Moor, Exeter, records the burial in 1596 of Heugh Rogers, perhaps the HUGH ROGERS who spent the year 1585–86 at Roanoke Island.

THOMAS ROTTENBURY, one of Lane's colonists, must have been a member of the Rattenbury family of Okehampton, Devon, as Thomas was a name appearing frequently among its members. Marriage and birth records as well as references to military service for them are numerous, and Sir Francis Drake's will in 1595 mentions Thomas Rattenburie as "my servant."

ANTHONY ROWSE, a Lane colonist, was a member of Parliament from East Looe, Cornwall, in 1584. A friend and finally an executor of the estate of Drake, Rowse once commanded a regiment under Raleigh. He was knighted at Whitehall in 1603 just prior to King James's coronation. He was married three times and had six children. He died in 1620 and is buried in the church of St. Dominick near his home, Halton, on the Tamar River below Cotehele.

HENRY RUFOOTE, a Lost Colonist, may have been the son, or surely a relative, of Christopher Ruffote of Devon, a tailor who was described in naturalization records as having been born in Brittany in 1524. The name of one John Ruffoote, who may have been Henry's brother, appears in documents in the Essex Record Office dated 1592 and 1593.

The names of JOHN SAMPSON, an adult and a boy, appear among the Lost Colonists as well as frequently in parish registers in the City of London at dates which make them candidates to be these people. Yet the John Sampson who contributed £25 towards the defense against the Armada was from the county of Durham.

The RICHARD SARE with Lane could have been the Richard Sayer who entered Jesus College, Cambridge, in 1576 and was ordained deacon in London in 1585 at the age of 24. It is possible that he did not survive long after returning home as one Richard Sara of Ludgvan, Cornwall, was dead in 1587 when his will was entered for probate—but this may have been a different person. Further, between 1591 and 1608 there are records in Essex of one or more persons of the same name who were fined for refusing to work on the roads and for stealing sheep.

In trying to identify THOMAS STEVENS, one of the Lost Colonists, there are two likely candidates to consider. One entered Magdalene College, Oxford, in 1575, was graduated in 1578, and became a lawyer in 1585. It would certainly have been logical to have a lawyer in a permanent colony composed of men, women, and children. Another entered St. John's College, Oxford, in the same year, 1575, and was graduated in 1577. A Thomas Stevens (the father of one of these?) contributed £25 towards the country's defense against the Spanish Armada. It is quite likely that another colonist, RICHARD TOMKINS, was Stevens's brother-in-law, as a Richard Tompkyns was married to Margaret Stevens in St. Sepulchre's Church, London, in 1566. It may well have been Tomkins's father, also named Richard and entitled to bear heraldic arms, who contributed £25 towards defense against the Armada.

JOHN STUKELY, who came over with Lane, appears to have been the brother of Sir Richard Grenville's brother-in-law. It is certain that he was the father of Sir Lewis Stukely, vice-admiral of Devon and Raleigh's keeper while he was in the Tower. That the elder Stukely's interest in Roanoke and in the New World continued probably is reflected in two facts: He contributed £25 towards the defeat of the Armada, and in 1610 he was one of the incorporators of the New-foundland Company.

MARTYN SUTTON, a Lost Colonist, has eluded my best efforts to identify him, but I have an interesting assumption concerning him. I would guess that he was a young man, an only son, and likely to inherit some valuable property. Why do I think this? Thomas Sutton of Essex, a man entitled to bear heraldic arms, contributed the large sum of £100 to the nation's defense against the Armada while two other Sutton men each contributed £25. I can imagine a distressed father, a grandfather, and perhaps a childless uncle all deeply concerned about the future of the family.

NICHOLAS SWABBER, who stayed a year with Lane, must have been a member of the family of that name associated with St. Martin's in the Field, London, in the early seventeenth century. Of German extraction, they settled in Lambeth about 1584, and Nicholas perhaps had some special talent that would have been useful in a new colony. In the summer of 1622 the newsletter writer, John Pory, mentioned that one Swabber had made some false accusations against Sir Francis Wyatt, governor of Virginia. My curiosity makes me wonder whether Swabber had been one of those who spent the winter on the Chesapeake, and had the governor of Virginia made some claim that Swabber disputed?

The names of AUDRY TAPPAN and THOMAS TOPAN appear in the roster of 1587 colonists. Considering the vagaries of spelling in those days, to say nothing of the carelessness of typesetters, we may assume that they were husband and wife. There is a possibility that they were related to AGNES WOOD of the same colony. Although BENJAMIN and JOHN WOOD had been with Amadas and Barlowe in 1584, Agnes was the only Wood with the Lost Colony. In 1549 in St. Bride's Church, Fleet Street, London (where Elinor White and Ananias Dare were also married), Robert Woode was married to Johanna Toppam. Was Agnes Wood the cousin, or some other relative, of Thomas Topan or Audry Tappan?

The TAYLOR family appears to have had an unusually strong interest in Raleigh's ventures. JOHN and THOMAS were among Lane's colonists, and John returned in 1590 with John White to search for the Lost Colonists. Both John and Thomas Taylor appear frequently in records of the time — in Cambridge-shire, Devon, Essex, and Kent for John and in Devon, Cornwall, Lincolnshire, and Sussex for Thomas. Two men named John each contributed £25 towards the defeat of the Armada. CLEMENT and HUGH were Lost Colonists. Several

Clements, whose dates are roughly right for the latter two, appear in Kent. One Hugh (Hewe de Tailour) was described in 1571 as a native of Flanders who had lived in London for two years, was "a twister of silk," and who had one son. Hugh possibly was the father of Clement; perhaps it was anticipated that their knowledge of silk production would be useful in America. The boy WILLIAM WYTHERS may also have been at least acquainted with the Taylor family as a Robert Taylor in 1592 married the widow Elizabeth Wythers.

A Lane colonist, JOHN TWYT, may have been an apothecary as that was the occupation of a man of this name who was married in St. Alphage's Church, London, in 1580.

There has been a great deal of speculation about the name HAUNCE WALTERS which appears among the list of Lane's colonists and simply HANCE as a person accompanying White in 1590. The latter was described by White as a surgeon, and he was drowned at Port Ferdinando in 1590. Hance does appear as a surname in England. One William Hance entered Trinity College, Cambridge, in 1570, while he or another of the same name was questioned in 1583 concerning his ecclesiastical and civil obedience to the Queen. Hance Walters appears frequently in various records. He was described once as "of Brissels, the Kinge of Spaines subiecte," who lived in London after 1567, belonged to no church, and had his meals at a boarding house kept by a widow. A year later it was reported that he and his servant were going "to the Douche churche," that is, the Dutch Reformed Church. He was listed as a "merchaunt" in "Candlewykestreete Warde" in 1567, but in 1590 he was described as one of the "merchants of Antwerp" living in London. Initially it was said that he contributed £100 towards the defeat of the Spanish Armada, but a later accounting noted that he had made a loan of £500, apparently in addition to the earlier amount. There also was a WILLIAM WALTERS with the Lane colony, but what his relationship might have been to Haunce is not revealed.

There is no evidence to connect Lost Colonist JOAN WARREN with a case reported in the Essex Record Office but the names. A single woman, Joan Warren of Wetherfield, was found not guilty on 4 July 1560 of stealing £5.13s.4d. "from a leathern pouch on his [Tho. Cranford] person." Richard Warren, of Myleande, Middlesex, armiger, gave £100 to the Armada defense fund.

Three unrelated facts may pertain to Lost Colonist WILLIAM WATERS as easily as to others of the same name: one was admitted to the Merchant Taylors School in 1565; one was christened at St. Mary Somerset Church, London, in 1561; and one was a mariner of Plymouth in 1579.

JOHN WHITE, the artist and the governor of the 1587 colony, was a member of the painter-stainers company. He has been studied and reported upon a number of times. It is partly from his journal that we know so much about the various Roanoke voyages, but Lebame Houston of Manteo has recently discovered in the parish register of St. Martin's, Ludgate, London, that White was married on 7 June 1566 to Tomasyn Cooper. Their son Thomas was born 27 April 1567 and buried 26 December 1568. Their daughter, Elinor, was born 9 May 1568. We do not know what relationship, if any, existed between John White and CUTHBERT WHITE of the Lost Colony and WILLIAM WHITE of the Lane colony. The latter, however, may have been Governor White's son as one of this name was described as a member of the painter-stainers company in 1597 when he received a license to marry Agnes Richardson in St. Sepulchre's Church, London. There are some surviving copies of John White drawings believed to have been made by a member of his family, so perhaps it was this William.

RICHARD WILDYE, Lost Colonist, illustrates the difficulty of identifying the Roanoke Colonists from no further evidence than a name. One Richard Wilde or Wylde was graduated from Brasenose College, Oxford, in 1576; another one entered Cambridge in 1561 and was a physician in 1583; another entered Cambridge in 1561 at the age of 18; one inherited Nettleworth manor in Nottinghamshire; another one was at Eton, 1556–61; one was married in January 1587; one contributed two sets of verses to Queen Elizabeth in 1560; and finally in 1580 one was "judged and punished as a vagabond"—and these were all contemporary Richard Wildes, any one of whom (or none of them) might have been the colonist.

It is quite likely that THOMAS WISSE, a member of the Lane Colony, and JOHN HARRIS of the same colony were cousins or uncle and nephew. Harris was provost marshal when Raleigh was lord lieutenant general of Cornwall. Wisse's mother's maiden name was Harris. Wisse inherited Sydenham, owned by the family since the time of Henry IV, and he built "the faire mansion house" that was occupied by the family until 1937, when its contents, accumulated by the family over three hundred years, were sold. The house is now a school.

DAVID WILLIAMS, a Lane colonist, entered Jesus College, Cambridge, in 1573, became a distinguished jurist, and was knighted in 1603. A portrait of him is preserved at the manor house, Nether Winchendon, Buckinghamshire.

BENJAMIN WOOD, an Amadas and Barlowe explorer, and ABRAHAM KENDALL, who was one of the settlers who came with Lane, were on a 1590 expedition to the Straits of Magellan.

The reader, having worked his way through this mass of facts and supposition, will conclude that it is still impossible to answer with any degree of certainty the question *Who WERE the Roanoke Colonists?* There are more clues on this point, however, than to the persistent query as to the fate of the Lost Colony. We know neither their origin nor their fate, but the events that occurred between 1584 and 1590, and their relationship to the subsequent permanent settlement of America are most important. It was these events that determined that the United States would be a nation patterned after an English model. Democratic self-government, religious liberty, the English language, and the heritage of Magna

Carta are ours in great measure because of the sacrifice of the men, women, and children who went to Roanoke. A lively tradition may have survived in the families of the 278 people who were at Roanoke Island between 1584 and 1590. Among them 235 different family names were represented. Between 1607 and 1625 at Jamestown, England's first permanent settlement in America, there were 74 families with the same surnames as those that had been at Roanoke Island.[1] Although we cannot be certain of their identity, their names are a precious part of our heritage.

Notes

*In presenting Professor Powell, H. G. Jones, secretary-treasurer of the North Caroliniana Society and first chairman of America's Four Hundredth Anniversary Committee (1978-80), said: "To provide a lengthy introduction for William S. Powell in North Carolina would be the extreme of superfluity, for few names are so well known to our citizens who read and study their history. Furthermore, his name is in the forefront of those on the international scene who have been intrigued by the earliest English attempts to colonize North America. A native Tar Heel—a nickname that under all circumstances he insists must be spelled as two words—Bill Powell from childhood was fascinated by history. As a librarian, he contributed significantly in the growth of the North Carolina Collection, including its incomparable Sir Walter Raleigh Collection; as a professor, he has taught his state's history to more than six thousand students at the University of North Carolina at Chapel Hill; as a professional writer, his entries measure nearly an inch and a half in the card catalog; and as a journalist, he has disseminated the story of the past with such exactitude and flowing prose that he passes equally as a popular historian and a historian's historian.

"In addition to the usual works on specialized subjects, Bill Powell compiled the indispensable *North Carolina Gazetteer* and is now preparing the third volume of his massive *Dictionary of North Carolina Biography.* He also is working on two textbooks for North Carolina history courses, one for universities, one for public schools. The longtime historian of the Roanoke Island Historical Association, Professor Powell has had an abiding interest in the early English explorers and settlers, and today's paper on 'Who Were the Roanoke Settlers?' reflects thirty years of research on both sides of the Atlantic."

[1]The names of the Jamestown colonists will be found in Annie Lash Jester (ed.), *Adventurers of Purse and Person, Virginia, 1607–1625* ([Richmond? Order of First Families of Virginia], 1964).

Raleigh's Devon

Joyce Youings*

In October 1551 Walter Raleigh, Esquire, with his second son John, who had recently come of age, obtained from Richard Duke, Esquire, a lease of the capital messuage of the barton of Hayes in the parish of East Budleigh in east Devon. Walter had probably lived at Hayes for over twenty years, but he and John now had the security of a typical west country lease for a theoretical eighty years but terminable by the death of whichever of them lived the longer.[1] For this they had probably paid a substantial entry fine. Walter had recently married for the third time, the new Mrs. Raleigh being Katherine, née Champernowne, the widow, since 1547, of Otho Gilbert of Compton. It was at Hayes farm, probably in 1554, that Katherine gave birth to her and Walter's youngest son, Walter junior.

The kingdom of England, part only of an island off the mainland of Europe, which was first reasonably accurately mapped by Christopher Saxton in the 1570s, has at its southwest extremity a peninsula reaching out towards the Atlantic and comprising Cornwall, Devon, and parts of Somerset and Dorset. Devon alone, measuring some sixty-five miles from west to east and barely seventy-five miles from north to south, in North Carolina could almost be squeezed in between Raleigh and Greensboro. By English standards it was, and is, a large county, with a very distinctive physical geography. Its magistrates were organised into three "divisions," north, south, and east, but for such matters as the militia or taxation the all-important units were still the county's ancient "hundreds," thirty-two of them in all. The hundred of East Budleigh comprised the twenty parishes, including that of East Budleigh itself, east of the estuary of the river Exe and its tributary the river Clyst, some fifty thousand acres in all, with a population, calculated from the muster rolls of 1569, of about five thousand.[2] This meant that there were about a thousand households, or about thirteen to the square mile, considerably more if the uninhabited heathland is excluded.

Hayes farm lay about a mile from the village of East Budleigh and is as isolated today as it was in 1551. A barton at that time was usually a large compact and enclosed rural estate. The Raleighs occupied the house but not all the land, Richard Duke's lease reserving to himself valuable meadows called "Hay Mede," "Clap Mede," and "Little Mede." The farmhouse was not the neat building you see today, which has been authoritatively dated to the end of the century, possibly as late as the year 1627 carved by the rear entry, but probably a long, low medieval house with shuttered, unglazed windows. There may still be parts of the earlier house hidden behind plaster, but there are no telltale early roof timbers. Nor is there any sign of the chapel dedicated to St. James, which is mentioned in a lease of 1525.[3] The firmly Protestant Raleighs would have had no use for a

The county of Devon in 1575 by Christopher Saxton, from a copy of his *Atlas* in the library of the University of Exeter. Arrow at top points to the hamlet of Raley [Raleigh] in north Devon; the one at lower right points to Hayes Farm, where Walter Raleigh was born.

private chapel, and probably used it as a barn. The lease of 1551 mentions only "shippens," that is, stables or cowhouses. There were extensive common pasture rights on heathland stretching as far as the "towns," that is, villages, of Woodbury and Lympstone.

How much arable land appertained to Hayes is not on record. It would appear to have been a predominately pastoral and dairy holding, which would have suited Walter Raleigh senior with his many other preoccupations. But when at home

Aerial view of part of the parish of East Budleigh, Devon. The village is at extreme lower right. Hayes Farm (now Hayes Barton), Raleigh's birthplace, lies in the fields just to the left of the centre of the photograph. Woodbury Common is on the far left. *Photograph O 132/3, 39/RAF/3700, 15 July 1971, Crown copyright.*

he and his boys, like some 90 percent of their fellow Devonians, will have known all the sights and smells of the farmyard. They were required by their landlord to keep Hay Wood fenced against "destruction and biting of beasts" following any treefelling by him. The great timber was his, and also the hawking, hunting, fishing, and fowling, but his tenants could help themselves to wood for fuel and carpentry. The rent was £12 a year, payable quarterly, with 4d. a year payable to the lord of Woodbury for the pasture, and one of the Raleighs had to act as tithing man for Hayes. They owed suit, probably no more than occasional attendance, at the hundred court of East Budleigh, an ancient tribunal which, if it met at all, probably confined itself to small debts. Such obligations on the part of tenants varied from place to place, but were attached to the land, not to the occupier.

The Hayes tenancy is interesting in that the Raleighs were undoubtedly gentlemen, undoubtedly armigerous, with a lineage far superior to that of their landlord. They themselves owned a modest but scattered estate in the parishes of Withycombe Raleigh and Colaton Raleigh, all of it, presumably, occupied by tenants.[4] The Dukes had acquired Hayes in about 1500 by marriage with its heiress, and members of the family had been successful merchants and held civic office in Exeter. Richard Duke had done very well for himself in government service and had bought a great deal of former monastic property in Otterton, on the other side of the river. Gentlemen, of course, whether of ancient or recent lineage, were rarely soley rentiers: most occupied some of their land, supplying not only their own households but also the markets. Up in north Devon in the parish of Pilton, near Barnstaple, was seated one of the many branches of the Chichester family. When Sir John Chichester, one of the deputy-lieutenants of the county, lay dying in Exeter in 1586 of gaol fever caught from prisoners awaiting trial at the Assizes, he left to his wife Ann not only £500, a good deal of silver, no less than 16 feather beds, fully furnished, and all his butter, cheese, and wool, but also 12 kine (cows), 12 oxen with their gear, 450 sheep, and all his pigs, both those at his farm at Youlston in the neighboring parish of Shirwell and those at his barton of Raleigh.[5] This last lay in a hamlet in Pilton parish which had been part of the estate the Chichesters had acquired in about 1400 by marriage with the heiress of the senior branch of the Raleigh family. Our Walter's immediate forbears had lived at Fardel in the parish of Cornwood near Plymouth.

Having moved as a young man from Fardel to East Budleigh, Walter Raleigh senior was to move again in comparative old age, this time to the city of Exeter. In 1555 he became a freeman, which cost him £4.[6] His original intention may well have been to take advantage of the trading privileges enjoyed by freemen. At any rate by 1569 Walter was missing from the muster roll for East Budleigh, his place being taken by his eldest son George, while John had moved to Newton Abbot.[7] Young Walter had probably already left home, in the company of his

Gilbert half brothers and his Champernowne cousin.

Quite a few Elizabethan gentlemen did move from the country into town, usually, it was said, in order to economise on servants, the country gentlemen being expected to keep a great many. In Exeter the Raleighs would not have lacked good company. The city, with its Rougemont Castle and its ancient cathedral, towered both physically and figuratively over the Exe valley. Some nine thousand people were crammed into the ninety-three acres within the walls. The Raleighs lived near the bishop's Palace Gate, not far from the fashionable High Street where most of the city's wealthier merchants had their houses, but actually in the parish of St. Mary Major, which sprawled down the hill over one of the poorest parts of the city, inhabited by cloth makers and unskilled labourers. They will have seen a good deal of both extremes of Exeter society. They will no doubt have made common cause with the minority of Exeter citizens who were militantly Protestant, including the busy city chamberlain, John Hooker. The elder Raleighs died and were buried in Exeter in 1581 and 1594 respectively.

Only Plymouth approached Exeter in terms of population, but there was a handful of other essentially urban communities, notably the twin ports of Barnstaple and Bideford in north Devon, both with facilities for large ships, and Totnes and Dartmouth on the river Dart in the south. Far more numerous were the country towns, basically large villages with a variety of full-time craftsmen, a few shopkeepers, and, of course, weekly markets. In east Devon the largest were Tiverton, Cullompton, Ottery St. Mary, Honiton, and Axminster, with Bradninch and Colyton not far behind, each of them strategically placed, on a busy road, usually near a river crossing. Devon was notorious for its number of what were only technically boroughs: the population of each of these superficially urbanised villages barely reached one thousand, even including the residents of the large parishes of which, in terms of acreage, the country towns occupied only a very small core.

Besides these larger country towns there were throughout the country, except on Dartmoor, and Exmoor, dozens of villages where about thirty homesteads lay tightly clustered together—the word is "nucleated"—some strung out along the highway but mostly in a glorious jumble of interlocking tenements, gardens, orchards, closes, and alleyways, all under the shadow of a parish church. Although in many cases rebuilt in the fifteenth century, a time of generally low population, most parish churches could still comfortably accommodate the 150 or so inhabitants expected to attend regularly. No one in Raleigh's Devon needed to travel far to a church. There were seventeen in the city of Exeter, and elsewhere they ranged from the splendid church at Cullompton extended in the 1520s by the munificence of John Lane, a local clothier, to the little early medieval church in the middle of the fields at Upton Hellions in mid-Devon, or its neighbor at Shobrooke, all of them as sentinel then as they are today.

The parish of Upton Hellions represented a complete contrast to the country town or nucleated village. Here there was only a scatter of single farms or hamlets, the latter mere huddles of three or four farms. Such dispersion was to be found not only on the thinner soils of west Devon and on the fringes of Dartmoor but also here and there on the rich clays of the river valleys. Thousands of farmhouses are still there today, still as isolated as Hayes (or more so), usually tucked away in sheltered valley bottoms at the end of long lanes, their inhabitants still snug within cob walls and beneath roof timbers heaved into place well before Raleigh's day.

There were in Elizabethan Devon very few landed magnates and, even after the dispersal of the former monastic lands, none who really dominated any part of the county. The Courtenay family, earls of Devon since the thirteenth century, had come nearest to doing so, especially in the Exe valley below their castle at Tiverton, their principal residence. But they had ended on the executioner's block in 1538 and their political successors, the Russells, later earls of Bedford, though endowed by Henry VIII with an estate to match their status, were only occasional visitors. They were entirely rentiers and not aggressive landlords. The death of the second earl in 1585 leaving as his heir a fourteen-year-old grandson, effectively ended their political ascendancy, and indeed put into reverse their accumulation of land. Bedford's successor as Lord Lieutenant of Devon, the earl of Bath, possessed only a modest estate in the county. Unlike Russell in 1539, neither he, nor his opposite number in Cornwall, Sir Walter Raleigh, was provided by the Queen with any augmentation of his landed estate.

By contrast mere gentlemen were fairly thick on the ground, upwards of three hundred heads of households by the 1580s, the majority entitled to be called esquire. Dozens of them lie in uncomfortable but lifelike effigies in parish churches all over Devon, as if awaiting to be visited as in their day they visited their many relations. Christopher and Christina Chudleigh not only visited her parents, William and Ann Stratchley, at Ermington in south Devon but, no doubt because she was their sole heiress, are commemorated there although they lived all of twenty-five miles away at the Chudleigh's ancient seat in the parish of Ashton. Indeed Christina also appears on her parents' fine brass memorial and the eldest Chudleigh boy was christened Stratchley. With a name like that he could hardly survive, and he died, aged ten, in 1572; only two years after his father. It was his younger brother, John, who inherited the substantial addition to the Chudleigh family property at William Stratchley's death in 1583, only to dispose of much of it to pay for his luckless privateering ventures. He was drowned in the Magellan Straits in 1589, but not before, aged only twenty, he had accompanied Sir Walter Raleigh to Westminster in 1585 as knight of the shire for Devon. Stratchleys, Chudleighs, and Raleighs: they could all present to the visiting heralds authentic ancestries stretching back many centuries.

About a dozen or so of the country's gentlemen at any one time were knights, not necessarily on account of their military experience and reputation but selected as those thought best able to serve the Queen as civilian administrators. Indeed the knights were not always the wealthiest gentlemen as witness Walter Raleigh in 1585. Allowing for absentees, including the considerable number of Devonians who followed successful careers as lawyers in London, not all the 450 parishes had a gentleman resident. Nor was the territorial scatter at all even. In selecting them to be named as JPs the powers-that-be faced considerable difficulties. There was always more choice near Exeter than in the vicinity of Plymouth. Only the ownership of one or more manors conferred real prestige and while many knights and gentlemen were in the feudal sense landlords, others possessed only a scatter of small freeholdings from which to derive their cash income. The almost universal lack of identity between manor and parish in any case meant that few gentlemen had a monopoly of local lordship. Few had had the capital to invest substantially in the land market unlocked in the early part of the century by the dissolution of the monasteries, but there had been plenty of scope for careful timing of small sales and purchases in the interests of rationalisation.[8] Marriage with an heiress, or its corollary, death without male heirs, was still the biggest factor in determining the pattern of landownership. But some of the Devon gentry were pretty successful in rearing at least one son generation after generation. In the Exe valley there is still a squire who can trace the ownership of his estate back over seven hundred years in the direct male line. His family had already survived for three centuries when Raleigh lived, but for all their lineage the Elizabethan Fursdons kept a very low profile. Not so the majority of gentlemen, even those of modest substance being at pains to advertise their status by building ostentatious gatehouses at the approaches to their unpretentious mansions, not to speak of grotesquely ornate fireplaces in their newly ceiled halls.

But their prime concern was to conserve and if possible augment their ancestral estates, to ensure the continuity of their line. Primogeniture was the rule in Devon, but gentlemen were under some pressure to endow their younger sons. William Amadas of Plymouth (calling himself merely "gentleman" although his father, John Amadas, had bequeathed to his younger son a silver-gilt goblet bearing the family arms) died in 1561 possessed of a considerable amount of property in and around Plymouth and Tavistock. He left all the land he had purchased, including the former Carmelite or White Friary near the waterfront in Plymouth, to be equally divided among his four sons. His eldest, John, who alone inherited the ancestral land, was only eighteen and a half years old. The Amadases did not make old bones and when John died, aged thirty-nine, in 1581, but not before he had been mayor of Plymouth in 1574–75, he left everything to his widow Jane for her lifetime, though naming Philip, the eldest of his three sons, aged only sixteen, as his sole heir. How long Mrs. Amadas lived I have not yet been able to discover—she almost certainly married again into the Plymouth civic establishment—but Philip will not be unknown to North Carolinians as the ship's captain, still only nineteen, who came with Arthur Barlow to these shores in 1584.

Although the earlier John Amadas, Philip's great-grandfather, who lived in Tavistock, referred to William Hawkins of Plymouth as his "cousin," it is clear that Amadases had been gentlemen when Hawkinses, and certainly Drakes, had been mere tradesmen and farmers. As one reads their wills something not only of their lifestyle but also of the changes which only a decade or two had wrought in their lives comes across the centuries. John of Tavistock, when he made his will in 1546, although, like all good Protestants, he committed his soul to God alone, made provision for an elaborate and conventional funeral, and for the distribution of an enormous number of doles to the poor of a circle of parishes in both Devon and Cornwall. One of his many bequests was that of his furred black camlet gown, his best tawney satin doublet, a feather bed with bolster, pillow, and a pair of sheets to his stepson William Trevesper, who also got a cow. John's own younger son, Robert, was to be kept at school until he had mastered his grammar and the Latin tongue and was then to proceed to such other "science" as should be thought by the executors meet for his living. When William (Robert's elder brother) made his will in 1553, though fortunately in view of his very definite commitment to Protestantism he did not die until 1561, he provided for the reading, in an audible voice, on the Sunday following his death, of the homily of the salvation of mankind by Christ alone. He nevertheless left money for a "competent dinner" for the Mayor and Council of Plymouth, to be followed a week later by a "drinking" for the common people. Nor were the poor of Plymouth forgotten, but he had clearly established himself as a town gentleman and there were no doubt others like him in the port. Young Philip came of no mean parentage in any sense of the term.[9]

As active farmers there was little to distinguish gentlemen from yeomen, except that the former, if they could afford to do so, employed bailiffs, and were addressed as "Master" rather than simply by their forenames. But yeomen were far more numerous than gentlemen, there being usually around a dozen of them in any large parish, "manuring," that is cultivating, upwards of fifty acres of arable land, besides keeping stock.[10] They were the main suppliers of the urban markets — and hence the principal targets of popular and official displeasure when poor harvests sent the price of their grain rocketing. They nourished, it was said, no envy of the gentlemen, to whom they were often economically superior, having fewer expenses and, unless in a village without gentlemen, fewer public responsibilities. They were the greatest buyers of long leases.

The investigation of surviving Devon yeomen's farmhouses, both those in nucleated villages and those in hamlets or in complete isolation, has progressed a long way archaeologically in the last thirty years or so. But the identification of their owners or occupiers lags way behind.[11] There is, for example, a house called Boycombe in the parish of Farway in east Devon, still today in its setting very much the farmhouse. Even its basic layout is like that of the typical farm, with a cross passage more than halfway down the slope. But its detailed fabric

Sanders, Lettaford, in the parish of North Bovey, Devon, is pictured at top. Bottom photograph shows the shippen at the lower end of the building with its original central drain. *Both photos by the author.*

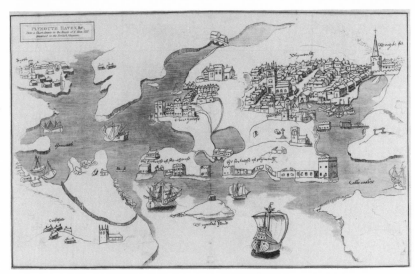

Parts of the "barton" below the parish church of Shobrooke date from the sixteenth century. The large yard below the farmhouse is enclosed by "linhays," solid cob externally and open fronted on the inside. At bottom is the town of Plymouth about 1540. British Library, Cotton MSS, Augustus I i, 35–9, from engraving in D. and S. Lysons, *Topographical and Historical Account of Devonshire* (London: 1822). *Both photos furnished by the author.*

has certain unmistakeable refinements, the external worked stone, the upper storeys, the upstairs fireplaces, and the neat and extraordinarily sanitary gardrobes. If it had been the residence of a gentleman we should almost certainly know his identity. Was it perhaps the unusually sophisticated house of a yeoman farmer? Compare this with another stone house, a traditional "long house" on the fringes of Dartmoor. Sanders, at Lettaford, a hamlet in North Bovey, also has a cross passage, and on the lower side there still survives intact the shippen for the stock. Across the passage is the family's accommodation, each side helping no doubt to keep the other warm. The upper storey was not added until the seventeenth century. Its survival is a miracle, but whether it was originally built in the early sixteenth century as a yeoman's house or, as it later became, that of a modest husbandman, we still have to find out.[12]

Building materials varied, of course, according to what was most readily available locally. In east Devon there was an ample supply of flint, and near Dartmoor plenty of granite, but on the clay soils elsewhere everything was of cob, that is, earth bound by straw, and, if available, hair, always, however, set on stone footings. Cob produces timeless walls, very difficult to date: hence the importance of roof timbers. Equally suitable for small homesteads or large mansions, it could also be used for really large buildings such as the great linhays or open-fronted barns arcaded around vast internal yards, which gave, and still give, so many large Devon farmhouses the outward look of fortresses.

By and large Elizabethan farming in Devon was on a small scale. Why this should be is difficult to explain except in terms of the natural inertia of Devonians. Even the plentiful supply of good pasture did not produce large-scale graziers. The Spencers of the Midlands or the Bacons of East Anglia had no counterparts in Devon. There was indeed little scope for agrarian aggression. Open fields, that is, strip patterns, with or without communal management, were not unknown, especially in those parishes with large nucleated settlement, but much land which had earlier been open fields had been peaceably enclosed long before 1500 and far more had been enclosed from the beginning. The correlation with scattered farms is, of course, very close. The enclosed fields of Devon were, and to a large extent still are, bounded by massive hedgebanks, many feet high and wide. Until the advent of Dutch elm disease, most were topped by great timber trees, and until modern machinery took its toll, by much sapling growth. Main roads and lanes were not only banked on either side, but being rarely level for any distance, soil and traffic combined to reduce them to the narrow hollow ways still very typical of Devon's more remote countryside.[13]

Farming practice in Elizabethan Devon was, however, by contemporary standards, advanced. Sand and seaweed were widely used for dressing the soil—and indeed the former carried long distances—and also a technique known as "De[vo]nshiring." This entailed paring off a thin layer of turf, leaving it to dry, burning it in heaps and finally spreading the ashes. John Hooker of Exeter, writing in about 1600, not only admired the ditches which the Devon farmers dug, both for drainage and irrigation, but he also described how the country people "dress, prune and trim" their apple trees "by opening the roots, by paring away the watery [weak] boughs and by grafting." He commended enclosure which, he said, promoted the growth of valuable timber and also enabled stock to be moved at appropriate intervals to "new springing grass."[14]

There was still much "waste," that is, land not yet "manured" but better than mere upland grazing, some of it in fact used for the growing of gorse for fuel. "Outfield" was occasionally made to yield a crop or two, and in most parishes there were still possibilities of adding permanent "intakes" to the "infield." On the large manor of Hartfield in northwest Devon in 1566 hardly more than half the land was cultivated as compared with the situation in 1842. On Dartmoor the occupiers of the "ancient tenements" were allowed by the Duchy of Cornwall, at each change of tenancy, to take an extra eight acres, but in 1600 it was reported that new tenants usually took possession of far more, calling it "forest measure"! In theory everyone in Devon, except the inhabitants of Barnstaple and Totnes, could for a modest payment put animals on Dartmoor, and we hear no complaints (as we do today) of overstocking.[15]

For all that, and allowing for the fact that large parts of Devon, especially Dartmoor, were uninhabitable, the county was, by national standards, heavily populated. A map showing the number of householders assessed for tax in the early sixteenth century shows that the valleys of the Exe and its tributaries, and also of the rivers Teign and Dart, and the great southern wedge known as the South Hams, were among the most densely populated parts of England, with over twenty households to the square mile.[16] Since then, in Devon as throughout England, population had risen substantially and whether as a result there were more or only larger households, by the mid-1580s there may well have been some young men over whom loomed the possibility of being without regular employment, and young women waiting impatiently for marriage. The price of food, too, although erratic, was moving steadily upwards. In the 1590s wheat prices in Exeter averaged over thirty shillings per quarter compared with under twenty in the 1560s. By comparison wages had hardly moved, the maximum permissible for non-resident farm labourers from 6d. to 8d. a day without food and drink in 1564 to 7d. to 8d. in 1594. Even harvest rates had risen from 10d. to only 12d. Living-in bailiffs, however, had progressed from 40s. a year to 53s.4d.[17] There are no quarter sessions records for Devon until the 1590s, but even then the magistrates seem to have been chiefly occupied in sorting out claims for relief from wounded soldiers and sailors. The only serious case of riot seems to have emanated from the household of the earl of Bath, the Lord Lieutenant. Earlier the county had sent as many as possible of its rogues and vagabonds to Ireland: now it was Brittany.

Unemployment, or what was equally serious, underemployment, was probably never a major problem in Devon. Even for those with minimal land, there had always been ample opportunities for supplementing income by part-time or seasonal industrial occupations. In terms of numbers employed, the most important was the manufacture of woollen cloth, in particular spinning, which was almost entirely a rural occupation. There were weavers and fullers who were full-time, but they were usually to be found in the larger villages and country towns, and of course in Exeter. Most clothmakers, whether full- or part-time, were self-employed, buying and selling from week to week in the multiplicity of markets all over Devon. As in farming so in cloth-making there were few entrepreneurs, except for the merchant exporters. Devon specialised in kerseys, usually called "dozens" because they were half the standard length and breadth. Tools such as the teasel-frame and cloth shears appear on many early-sixteenth century bench ends, including those at East Budleigh, and there is a pair of shears to be seen, clasped by an angel, in the Lane aisle at Cullompton.

Next in importance numerically were the tinners, also largely part-time, but in their case seasonal workers. Tin was only to be found on Dartmoor and the working tinners would leave their valley farms and live in rough dug-outs near the mines and blowing houses. By the late sixteenth century the industry had passed its peak but the highly privileged tinners, gentlemen employers as well as labouring men, were not easily discouraged. Profits were modest, except for those of the tin merchants, but presumably sufficient to make the incredibly hard living conditions worthwhile.[18] Raleigh claimed that, as Lord Warden of the Stannaries, he had increased the working tinners' livelihood. He also persuaded many of them to go to Ireland.

Devon's fourth "commodity," to use John Hooker's term, was the sea which lapped, and ofter battered, the county's long coastline, both north and south. A survey made in 1560 credits Devon, without Exeter, not only with more ships of 100 tons and over than anywhere else except London, but with 1,268 mariners—that is, men skilled in their handling. This does not sound many but even then it was over one sixth of the total in the whole of England. Another survey of 1583, this time excluding Plymouth and Dartmouth, puts the whole number at 2,016, plus 150 master mariners.[19] Probably as many again were fishermen, using only rowing boats. The principal catch in coastal waters, especially west of Start Point, was pilchards, of which sufficient were brought into Plymouth in the 1590s to be worth taxing to pay for the town's defences. But the really spectacular maritime growth point, the one which probably went furthest to mop up Devon's surplus manpower, was the annual voyage to the Newfoundland Banks for cod. Here, both in terms of total catch and of number of ships and seamen involved, Dartmouth probably had the edge over Plymouth. Far more seamen were involved (and in the process learned to sail in deep waters out of sight of land) than were ever engaged in privateering. Most of the catch was brought over dried and sold directly to the largely Catholic continent of Europe.[20]

This again was a seasonal occupation, which may explain why the seamen were principally resident, not in either Plymouth or Dartmouth but spread along the coastal parishes and in some cases some way inland. A survey made in 1570 locates the largest number, 123, in the parish of Stokenham which, although it has several miles of coastline had no haven suitable for anything but small fishing boats. Seamen from this area adjacent to the strip of sandbank and freshwater lagoon known as Slapton Ley will have felt very much at home on the Outer Banks, though no doubt awed by the latter's extent. To return to seamen and their homes, Plymouth, even with its neighbours, Stonehouse and Saltash, produced in 1570 only 122. Salcombe, with its splendid estuarine harbour, was home for 56 mariners but there were also 55 in Blackawton to the east, which had a very tenuous connection with the sea. The inclusion in the 1583 survey of 24 named ships' masters living in Kenton, and ten in Topsham, reminds us of the continuing importance of the Exe estuary. Lympstone, the reputed birthplace of Ralph Lane, had four masters and 22 others who were either mariners or fishermen. In north Devon the greatest comcentration of masters was not in Barnstaple or Bideford, each with six, but in Northam, the large parish at the meeting of the rivers Taw and Torridge, which contained the growing maritime community of Appledore.[21]

Two decades later Clovelly, for long only a cliff-top village to the west of Barnstaple Bay, would no doubt have produced more than the three mariners noted in 1583, and certainly more fishermen, for by then the local landlord, George Cary, at his own expense, some £2,000 according to his will, had built the quay and harbour which still serves its original commercial purpose as well as providing a promenade for summer visitors.[22] Cary's fish cellars and his tenants' stout little stone cottages still cling to the steep hillside on either side of the cobbled street. Clovelly, he claimed, was no longer a place of no importance. He had married, incidentally, the widow of John Chudleigh.

Efforts to develop havens on the coast of east Devon, though strenuously pursued, were not so successful. Here the problem was to undo the late-medieval silting up of the narrow inlets. Sandbanks were a problem at Plymouth, too, before the building of the Breakwater, and also in Barnstaple Bay, where they still are, but in both cases they were passable at high tide. Energetic efforts were made by the men of the small inland town of Colyton in the 1570s to raise money, in their case to excavate the former upper estuary of the river Axe. They were sufficiently percipient not only to have noticed but to draw to the Queen's attention the fact that "sundry anchors and ships' timbers [are] daily found in the land, meadows and marshes thereabout." The Queen not only agreed to recommend all her clergy to mention Colyton's project to "wealthy persons in time of sickness" but sanctioned the compulsory purchase of stone and timber and the impressment of workmen, the latter hardly suggesting that there was much local unemployment. Within two years there are hints that some of the money raised had disappeared before it reached Colyton, and the work itself was probably never started.[23]

But in Raleigh's very own country efforts to reopen the river Otter to shipping had a longer history. Richard Duke had already been attempting something in the 1540s, but presumably to no effect for a splendid map in the British Library must be part of a later attempt to interest Lord Burghley.[24] This depicts the Devon and Dorset coast from Dartmouth to Portland with a great expanse of deep water inside the mouth of the Otter below the twin village of East Budleigh and Otterton which the promoters promised would be "very good for savegarde of shippes." Entry was to be between two projecting piers and the introduction of elaborate compass bearings was possibly intended to suggest that this was the centre of the universe. Whether Raleigh's support was ever sought or given is not recorded, but the dream of a new Otterton haven was never realised.

Some initiatives, however fruitless, do at least indicate a growing interest in developing the county's maritime potential. They need to be viewed against the background on the one hand of conventional coastal and overseas trade and, of course, on the other of privateering and even of piracy. In north Devon all four of them were deliberately and inextricably complementary. At Exeter the emphasis was on the longstanding legitimate and safe trade with France, while the men of Plymouth and Dartmouth, especially the former, were far more adventurous. Plymouth owed much to the Hawkins dynasty, which had, of course, an abiding interest in legitimate overseas trade, but when the trade of the Devon ports in the late sixteenth century has been fully investigated it may emerge that substantial fortunes were made by those who have not yet attracted the limelight. As for privateering, it is only too obvious from the Roanoke story what a large part was played by the insatiable appetite for prizes in the failure to sustain the colony. How are we to explain why Raleigh and some at least of his fellow Devonians, normally civilised and law-abiding at home, content with a modest income and what luxuries it would buy, regarded the oceans not as common land where all could work their own passage in peace and harmony, but as a sort of waste which all could plunder? Privateering, and indeed naked piracy, was for too long the expensive sport of gentlemen. Few made it pay. With the notable exception of Buckland Abbey, there is scant material evidence of their success in Devon's heritage today.

Notes

*Introducing Joyce Youings, John D. Neville, executive director of America's Four Hundredth Anniversary, said: "This afternoon we continue our look at Sir Walter Raleigh through two papers about areas important to him. Our first paper, 'Raleigh's Devon,' is by a fellow Devonian, Joyce Youings, a native of Barnstaple on the northwestern coast of the county. There she attended Barnstaple Girls' Grammar School. She then earned her bachelor's and doctoral degrees from the University of London. For many years she has been professor of English social history at the University of Exeter; she has also been a visiting professor in New Zealand universities and at the University of Kansas. The author of *Devon Monastic Lands* (1955), *Tuckers Hall Exeter* (1968), *The Dissolution of Monasteries* (1971), and *Sixteenth Century England* (1984), Dr. Youings also wrote for America's Four Hundredth Anniversary Committee the booklet, *Ralegh's Country: The South West of England in the Reign of Queen Elizabeth I* (1986). A year earlier, she organized the Raleigh conference at her university and published the papers under the title *Raleigh in Exeter 1985: Privateering and Colonisation in the Reign of Elizabeth I.*

"Professor Youings is a fellow of the Royal Historical Society and serves as, or has served as, president of the Devon History Society, president of the Devon and Exeter Institution, chairman of the Council of the Devonshire Association, co-director of the Leverhulme Research Project on the maritime history of Devon, and since 1953 has been honorary general editor of the Devon and Cornwall Record Society."

[1]T.N. Brushfield, "Raleghana," *Transactions of the Devonshire Association*, 28 (1896): 274–76.

[2]A.J. Howard and T. L. Stoate, *Devon Muster Roll for 1569* (Almondsbury, Bristol: 1977), pp. 3–13.

[3]Devon Record Office, Rolle MSS, 96/M/32/10.

[4]For details see Joyce Youings, *Ralegh's Country: The South West of England in the Reign of Queen Elizabeth I* (Raleigh: 1986) pp. 1–2.

[5]Public Record Office, Wills, PROB 11/69/19.

[6]M.M. Rowe and A. Jackson (editors), *Exeter Freeman 1266–1967* (Exeter: Devon and Cornwall Record Society, Extra Series I, 1973), p. 81.

[7]Howard and Stoate, *op. cit.*, pp. 9, 234.

[8]J.A. Youings, *Devon Monastic Lands* (Exeter: Devon and Cornwall Record Society, New Series I, 1954), pp. xx-xxix.

[9]Public Record Office, Chancery, Inquisitions Post Mortem, C 142/135/126; 201/79, and Wills, PROB 11/37/31 and 44/35. The discovery that John Amadas was mayor of Plymouth I owe to Peter Cornford.

[10]M. Campbell, *The English Yeomen* (New Haven: 1942), which draws a good deal on Devon evidence, was a pioneer work of its time, but a new book on the subject is badly needed.

[11]The best work on the subject is M. W. Barley, *The English Farmhouse and Cottage* (London: 1961).

[12]N.W. Alcock, P.C. Child, and J.M.W. Laithwaite, "Sanders, Lettaford: a Devon Longhouse," *Proceedings of the Devon Archaeological Society*, 30 (1972): 227–33.

[13]Almost everything that can be said about the history of the Devon landscape derives from the pioneering work of W. G. Hoskins, especially his *Devon* (London: 1954 and 1972).

[14]John Hooker, "Synopsis Chorographical of Devonshire," British Library, Harl. MS 5827, fo. 8.

[15]H.S.A. Fox, "Outfield Cultivation in Devon and Cornwall," in M. Havinden (editor), *Husbandry and Marketing in the South West* (Exeter: 1973), and M. Havinden and Freda Wilkinson, "Farming," in Crispin Gill (editor), *Dartmoor* (Newton Abbey: 1970), pp. 139–82.

[16]J. Sheaill, "The Distribution of Taxable Population and Wealth in England during the Early Sixteenth Century," *Transactions of the Institute of British Geographers*, 55 (1972): 119.

[17]W.G. Hoskins and H.P.R. Finberg, *Devonshire Studies* [a collection of essays], (London: 1952): 420–21.

[18]For a brief account with references, see Joyce Youings, *Ralegh's Country*, chapter IV.

[19]Public Record Office, SP 12/11/27; 156/45.

[20]H.A. Innis, *The Cod Fisheries* (Toronto: 1954).

[21]Public Record Office, SP 12/71/75; 156/45.

[22]Public Record Office, PROB 11/100/40.

[23]P.L. Hughes and J.F. Larkin, *Tudor Royal Proclamations* (New Haven and London: 1964–69), pp. 387–89.

[24]British Library, Royal MSS, 18 D III, fos. 9v.–10.

John D. Neville (top), director of America's Four Hundredth Anniversary Committee, introduced Joyce Youings (bottom right) and Nicholas Canny. They spoke respectively on "Raleigh's Devon" and "Raleigh's Ireland."

Raleigh's Ireland

*Nicholas Canny**

Walter Raleigh had dealings with Ireland at three separate junctures in his career. His first direct association with Ireland was as a soldier-adventurer during the years 1580–82; his second association, which spanned the years 1586–1602, was related to his attempt to establish himself as a proprietor in the plantation of Munster; and his third association occurred in 1617 when he was desperately attempting to finance his last Guiana expedition.

Insofar as Raleigh's engagement in 1580 with the interminable Elizabethan wars in Ireland evinces any surprise, it is because he had not become involved there at an earlier stage. Most English gentlemen adventurers of his generation who wished to make a career or reputation for themselves had found their way to Ireland before 1580, and Raleigh's close relatives Humphrey Gilbert, Richard Grenville, and Peter Carew had been prominently involved in Irish military affairs since the mid–1560s.[1] The fact that Raleigh had not joined his relatives when they first went to Ireland was probably explained by his youth (he was only eleven in 1565), and his absence from there provided him with the opportunity to become briefly involved with the French wars of religion and to further advance his education at Oriel College and the Middle Temple as well as in a privateering venture of 1578.[2] Such a varied training and experience was quite typical of those English captains who had preceded him to Ireland, and Raleigh might be said to have been rounding off his education as a soldier adventurer while at the same time he was becoming involved in a fresh theatre of activity which some hoped would provide the opportunity of fame and fortune for the venturesome.

This portrayal of Raleigh's motivation when he did go to Ireland in 1580 indicates that he, like so many other younger sons who had preceded him there,[3] was grasping about for any employment that might eventually lead to his elevation to a social position appropriate to his birth and education. Military employment in itself was unlikely to lead to this elevation, but the successful conduct of a campaign could bring a captain to the attention of his superiors which, in turn, might lead to his being appointed to a permanent position on the civil or military establishment. This would have meant being put in charge of a permanent garrison in one of the outlying provinces or being placed in a quasi-civil position on one of the provincial councils that had recently been established in Ireland.[4] Successful service in the provinces could then lead to advancement to a senior office in the Dublin administration, and it always placed one in a position to identify and advance claim to any property in the provinces to which Crown title might be established.[5] It was necessary that one should be appropriately qualified before one was thus favored but it was even more important that one should enjoy the support of those who were in a position to dispense patronage. This was the case because there were always more qualified candidates than there were positions to be filled in the permanent establishment and the honors went invariably to those who were best connected. We can take it that Raleigh was seeking to establish just such a connection when he hung about the Court in the months before his departure for Ireland in July 1580, and the patron that he then found was Arthur Lord Grey de Wilton[6] who had been appointed to serve as lord deputy of Ireland and who was assigned to deal with the rebellion that had recently broken out in Munster and that threatened the very security of the state in Dublin.

Lord Grey was as suitable a patron for Raleigh as he was a suitable client for the nobleman. They were both fervent Protestants who were enthusiastically in favor of resisting the threat of Catholicism whether it presented itself at sea or on land, whether on the Continent or in Ireland. Moreover, Grey had been selected for appointment in Ireland only after the position of governor there had been declined by Sir Henry Sidney and after he had taken advice from Sidney on what policies to pursue there.[7] This meant that those clients of Sidney who already served in Ireland, including Raleigh's own kinsmen, would enjoy the favor of Lord Grey as they had enjoyed that of Sidney who had brought them to the country during his first period of government in Dublin.[8] And most important of all, Grey was given the command of an army of 8,000 men, a force far in excess of that commanded by Sidney, and a force that was considered sufficient both to suppress the current revolt and to prepare the way for a comprehensive scheme of colonization such as had been adumbrated by Sidney when, during the years 1569–71, Ireland had also been disturbed by revolt.[9]

It seemed therefore that Raleigh had been particularly fortunate in winning appointment as a captain under Lord Grey. The possibility that a comprehensive reform of Ireland would be undertaken by this force seemed even better in 1581 because by then a second revolt had erupted in Ireland this time under the leadership of James Eustace, Viscount Baltinglass.[10] Lord Baltinglass was a landowner of Anglo-Norman descent who held his property within the English Pale, which was the most anglicized part of Ireland incorporating most of the four counties closest to the city of Dublin. Political and social grievance contributed to the dissatisfaction that led to revolt but the reason that was articulated by Baltinglass was that he could no longer owe allegiance to a monarch who had been excommunicated by the Pope. His call did not, as it happened, evoke much response within the Pale, and his action became dangerous only when he joined forces with some Gaelic chieftains of the mountainous region south of Dublin. Nonetheless, the revolt of Baltinglass, coinciding as it did with that of the earl of Desmond in Munster, presented the serving English officials and captains in Ireland with the opportunity to impress upon the Queen that only convinced

Protestants born in England should be entrusted with positions of responsibility in Ireland.[11] Then, it was argued, with reliable people in place it would be possible to proceed with a systematic course of action that would bring the Gaelic Irish from their erstwhile barbarism to an acceptance of civility, and that would bring all elements of the Irish population into conformity with the Protestant state religion.

Those who argued this case with the Queen were conscious that extensive confiscation of property was likely to result from the rebellions that had occurred, and they wanted to make sure that these lands would be assigned to some of themselves. There were none more conscious of the possibilities than Raleigh's kinsmen who were already stationed in Munster, and Raleigh quickly made his way to the Munster theatre of action so that he could join with them in the conduct of a war they hoped would lead to their own enrichment. Raleigh was no sooner there than he identified Thomas Butler, earl of Ormond, as the person most likely to frustrate these ambitions, and Raleigh comes to our attention in the documents principally when he is engaged upon an assault against the person of Ormond.[12]

This earl was, like the earl of Desmond and Viscount Baltinglass, of Anglo-Norman descent and he held enormous estates in the northeastern part of Munster as well as in south Leinster. Unlike the rebelling lords, however, Ormond was a Protestant, he was a cousin of Queen Elizabeth through the Boleyn family and he had spent most of his early years at Court before retiring to his family estates in 1569. Moreover he was an inveterate foe of the earl of Desmond, despite the fact that Desmond was married to his widowed mother, and he had been given responsibility by the Queen to bring Desmond and his adherents to justice. In accepting appointment as Lord General of the government forces in Munster, Ormond was determined that no quarter should be given to Desmond or his immediate relatives, but he did favor the offer of pardon to the less prominent confederates, and he hoped to win support from the quiescent landowners in Munster by suggesting that they would become the beneficiaries of the confiscation of the Desmond family estates.[13]

The adoption by the Queen of this advice would have put paid to whatever hopes the English captains and officials might have fostered of profiting from the war in Ireland. It was for this reason that a vendetta against Ormond had been organized before Raleigh's arrival in the province and why he, together with all other English captains and officials in Munster, stood firmly behind Lord Grey when he moved into the province with his fresh army to take over the military command from Ormond. The war that was now waged was a total war, aimed at bringing a quick conclusion to the revolt by the elimination of the Catholic expeditionary force of 600 men that had been sent from the Continent in support of the rebels and by the forced unconditional surrender of all native landowners who were known to be involved in the rebellion.[14]

The first of these objectives was attained when the continental force was tracked down in its fortified position at Smerwick on the Atlantic coast of the south-west. Once a surrender had been forced the garrison was put to the sword, and Raleigh and his company were particularly energetic in that bloody enter-prise.[15] Then he and his fellow captains, under the command of Lord Grey, devoted their attention to the local rebels, and each captain was assigned control over a particular area of the province while Grey himself returned to Dublin. The area assigned to Raleigh's control was the fertile area to the south and east of Cork city, and Raleigh, like his associates, was not only determined to over-throw those who were in actual rebellion but was also anxious to arrest those native landowners whom they suspected of being sympathetic towards the rebels. The particular target of Raleigh's attack was Lord David Barry of Barryscourt, whose castle and lands he coveted, and it was certainly Raleigh's ill-concealed animosity towards Barry which forced the latter into open rebellion.[16] What occurred in this instance occurred elsewhere throughout the province so that the scope of the Munster rebellion was increasing rather than contracting as the winter of 1580–81 proceeded. This was as the English captains of the province would have wished it because they were fully confident of the support of Lord Grey in their endeavors, and they were convinced that only persistence with their scheme would lead to a lasting settlement of the province.

What these soldier-adventurers did not count on was the determination of Ormond to oppose their efforts and his continued influence with the Queen. It was Ormond who championed the cause of David Barry against the intrusions of Raleigh upon his property, and it was Ormond who now contended that it was Grey's unwillingness to accept any of the rebels to mercy which explained why the conflict in Munster was becoming too prolonged and expensive for the Crown to bear. Furthermore, he, as well as some of the supporters in the Pale, criticized the bloody methods that were being employed by Lord Grey and his subordinates and suggested that these reflected poorly upon the Queen's cherished reputation as a clement ruler.[17]

Such arguments made a deep impression upon the Queen, especially when they were combined with charges of dishonesty. These latter were advanced by some Old English officials in the Pale who contended that the land which had come into Crown possession following the overthrow of the Leinster rebel-lion had been disposed of by Grey to a small group of personal followers and at rents prejudicial to the Crown's interests.[18] Queen Elizabeth harkened to these charges, and Grey was duly recalled in disgrace in August 1582, and Ormond was restored to command of the military enterprise.[19]

This turn of events proved devastating for those English captians and officials who had pinned their hopes on Lord Grey being able to proceed with a consis-tent policy. They had further reason to be alarmed when they saw much of the land in Munster which might have been declared forfeit to the Crown being frittered away by Ormond who, they believed, proved excessively generous in granting pardon to the lesser rebels. Their hopes for a coherent plantation in Munster, which would advance the cause of civility while enriching themselves, were also set back by Ormond's insistence that the "English by blood" (by which he meant the Old English population of Ireland) should receive equal consideration with the "English by birth" when the land of the outstanding rebels came to be confiscated.[20] This wish of Ormond was in fact not followed and Ormond himself was the only member of the Old English community to benefit directly from the confiscation of property in Munster. However, the death in rebellion of the earl of Desmond in the winter of 1583 did prove anti-climactic for those who had endured the travails of war on the Crown's behalf because the decision was then taken to have a committee in London, rather than in Dublin or Munster, deal with the disposition of the forfeited property.[21] Such a committee could be counted on to favor those who were well connected at Court over those who had served in Ireland. The frustration of the latter group was put most effectively by Geoffrey Fenton, a consistent advocate of plantation, who had been so confident of a grant of some of Desmond's estates in North Kerry that he had brought "tenants and cattle out of England" to populate and stock the property. All to no avail, however, because the lands on which Fenton had set his sights were granted to the English courtier Denzil Holles, and Fenton's six or seven years of service "spent in the suppression of that rebellion" were completely disregarded.[22]

This outcome had apparently been anticipated by Walter Raleigh even before the forced resignation of Lord Grey, and Raleigh had abandoned Ireland in fury once his claims on Barry's land had been denied him because of Ormond's obstruction. His early departure from Ireland placed Raleigh in a position to offer advice at Court when the subject of Ireland came under discussion among those who had to adjudicate between the strategies favored respectively by Ormond and Lord Grey. The fact that Grey was dismissed in 1582 indicates that Raleigh's advice was ineffectual, but the occasion which he then had to attend at Court on official business also presented him with the opportunity to bring himself to the attention of the Queen and her closest advisers. The eagerness with which Raleigh seized on this opportunity is legendary, and the favor which he then found with Queen Elizabeth suddenly and permanently changed the course of his career. "True it is," averred one contemporary, "he had gotten the queen's ear in a trice; and she began to be taken with his elocution, and loved to hear his reasons to her demands; and truth is, she took him for a kind of oracle, which nettled them all; yea those that he relied on began to take this his sudden favour for an alarm, and to be sensible of their own supplantation."[23]

The ones who appeared most nettled were Robert Dudley, earl of Leicester, and Sir Christopher Hatton, whose clients Raleigh and his associates in Ireland had previously been. But while losing their support he had acquired that of

the Queen and it was through her munificence that Raleigh was appointed to
a series of positions that provided him with a regular income and enabled him
to become the maker of his own fortune. Furthermore, he was now able to
remain in virtual permanent residence at court and in close proximity to the
Queen, and was thus able to look out for his own interest whenever patronage
came within the Queen's gift. The new interests which Raleigh then developed,
including his heavy involvement with the Roanoke expedition, meant that Ireland faded from his mind, but an interest quickly revived in 1585 when plans
were afoot to establish a formal plantation on the confiscated property of the
deceased earl of Desmond.

We now know from the research of recent scholars, led by our honored David
Quinn, that this scheme of plantation in Munster was worked out on paper
in advance like no previous English plantation effort had been. This advance
planning was done primarily by Lord Burghley and Sir Francis Walsingham
together with Thomas Egerton, the English solicitor general, and Sir Christopher Hatton, the English lord chancellor. These had decided that the confiscated estates should be divided up into twenty seignories each of 12,000 English
acres and that grants of these blocks of land should be confined to English men
of substance who had the resources necessary for the development of their estates.
To facilitate the plantation effort it was required of the lord deputy in Dublin,
who was now Sir John Perrott, that he should have a bill passed through the
Irish parliament declaring Desmond's estates to be forfeited to the Crown. At
the same time, three skilled men were appointed to survey the confiscated property and plot out a plantation on paper.[24]

Scarcity of manpower and shortage of time explain why this preliminary work
was never completed. However, the organizers of the plantation made their task
easier for themselves by drawing upon the project for a plantation in Munster
that had been devised over a decade earlier by a group of adventurers from the
English west country and which had since lain dormant among the papers of
Lord Burghley.[25] The ideas contained in that project were now given official
form when it was stipulated that those who undertook to plant these several
blocks of 12,000 acres should each accept responsibility for placing six freeholders,
six farmers, forty-two copyholders, and thirty cottagers on the seignory by the
end of seven years. The estate itself was to be held in common soccage from
the crown in return for an annual rent which ranged from £200 per seignory
in County Kerry to £66-13s-4d per seignory in County Cork. The freeholders
were to be given grants in fee simple from the principal undertakers to whom
they would pay a specified rent, and they in turn were to be obliged to introduce
farmers, copyholders, and cottagers on their estates. All were prohibited from
accepting Irish tenants on their estates, and stringent conditions were laid down
in relation to the construction of defensible buildings, the pursuit of English-style
agriculture, and the maintenance of trained men and weapons to provide for

their security. What was envisaged therefore in the formal plantation conditions of the 1580s, as in the project of 1569–71, was the erection of a self-sufficient English community comprised of six nucleated settlements on each seignory of land. Moreover, we can assume that the designers of the 1585 scheme were guided by their predecessors into thinking that this English community would flourish through the efficient cultivation of the land after the most advanced English fashion; through the exploitation of the natural produce of the country such as timber and fish; through the introduction of new experimental crops such as woad and madder which were considered wasteful of good tillage land in England; and through the development of manufacturing employment that was related to these agricultural products.[26]

There is nothing to suggest that Walter Raleigh played any part in the formulation of this scheme for plantation in Munster, and we can take it that he did not do so because he was preoccupied with the Roanoke expedition when the scheme was being devised. He was, however, keenly aware of the supposed economic potential of Munster, both because he had spent two years there and because it was Raleigh's Munster associates, most notably Warham St. Leger and Richard Grenville, who had been responsible for the earlier project. These two, as well as most prominent captains and officials who had served in Munster during the recent wars, expected that their long-cherished hopes would finally be realized. In this they were to be generally disappointed, and Grenville and St. Leger managed to have themselves included in the Munster plantation only by surrendering to the Crown the property which previously they had acquired from the earl of Desmond through mortgage transactions with the request that this should be regranted to them under plantation conditions and augmented to bring it up the size of a full seignory.[27]

The main beneficiaries of the grants made of Munster land were not therefore those who had previous experience of the province but rather those who happened to be in favor at Court when the grants were being made. It was in this capacity that Walter Raleigh became involved as a planter and his influence with the Queen was such that he not only did better than anybody whose claims were based on Irish experience, but he received a grant which was far in excess of the maximum stipulated in the plantation conditions and which was in the best location in the province. The grant was for three and a half seignories of land, when the plantation conditions stated that nobody should have more than one seignory, and the land lay along the banks of the River Blackwater waterway which flowed into the sea through the navigable port of Youghal. The seignory granted to Lord Chancellor Hatton lay astride that of Raleigh, and these were not only the most fertile and the most strategically placed lands in the province in economic terms, but they were also the first to be measured and surveyed and granted with clear title to the recipients.[28] The fact that Raleigh's grant was in contravention of the plantation regulations themselves did not escape the attention of his contemporaries, but when Lord Deputy Perrott would have objected he was advised by Burghley against doing so because Raleigh "is able to do you more harm in one hour than we are all able to do you good in a year."[29]

Perrott took advice from Burghley on that occasion, but both he and his successor Sir William Fitzwilliam continued to resent his plantation project which was effected with scant reference to themselves as chief governors in Ireland.[30] But if they had occasion to be resentful because of the treatment accorded them by the government in London they were given much more occasion by individual grantees in the plantation. Some of the soldier settlers behaved as if they were subject to no superior authority in Ireland while some courtiers referred all their problems to London as if no government existed in Dublin. Nobody behaved with more arrogance in this respect than Sir Walter Raleigh, and, while this earned him the enduring hatred of both Perrott and Fitzwilliam, it did ensure that his grant was not subject to diminution because of the legal claims advanced against the settlers by the dispossessed landowners. The recognition by the government of such claims and their successful pursuit by Old English lawyers meant that what had originally been a carefully planned settlement became in the words of MacCarthy Morrogh "a mosaic" which rarely provided "any unified blocks of land."[31] This development caused consternation among the settlers, and Sir Warham St. Leger spoke for many when he complained how the Queen by her leniency had bestowed land which was rightfully hers "upon a company of hollow-hearted papistical wretches and disinherited her loving and natural English subjects."[32]

Such problems were not shared by Raleigh, or for that matter by Sir Christopher Hatton, because they were secure in the Queen's favor. This meant that they were able to proceed more energetically than the others in the matter of developing their estates, and Raleigh would also have been better than most as a planter because he would have known from his American experience how to set about providing for a settler community during the first phase of settlement. The details of how Raleigh set about populating and developing his estate are not known, but the principal responsibility was placed in the hands of Andrew Colthurst, a captain in the government's pay, and Robert Mawle, but Raleigh himself visited his lands in the autumn of 1588 and in the late summer of 1589. It is clear that he never intended his residence there to be a permanent one, and we know from the surviving leases for his estate that he intended that the primary investment should be made by his freeholders rather than by himself.[33] The names of the fourteen freeholders that had been introduced there by 1589 are known to us from Raleigh's own listing of that year.[34]

The fact that these freeholders included some who went by the description of merchant indicates Raleigh's intention of establishing a commercial dimension to the plantation. The first priority was, however, the introduction of tenants, livestock, and agricultural equipment, as well as the delineation of tenancies and the construction of houses. In this respect Raleigh, or his agents, proved more enterprising than most settlers, and he was able to name 128 English tenants on his estate in 1598 of whom sixty-four were listed as having had wives, and sometimes children, with them. These figures he claimed in a postscript to his report of 1589 were an underestimate of his total achievement because there were "more over there and diverse others not here set down which are gone into England to fetch their families and many of these have diverse persons in their families not here nominated besides mariners, fishermen and Irish tenants inhabiting upon some of the escheated or seignory lands of the said Sir Walter Raleigh, knight."[35] Whatever of this claim we know that he continued after 1589 to introduce still more English settlers to his lands, and these arrivals included the artist John White who went there after his last Roanoke voyage to join Thomas Hariot who was already listed in 1589 among the settlers on Raleigh's Irish estate.[36] These settlers were declared in 1589 to be in possession of 1,430 cattle, 1,160 sheep, 28 ploughs, 10 teams of horses, and 310 small Irish horses, stud mares, hackneys, goats and swine. It is not clear what proportion of these animals had been imported from England but most of the ploughs were deep cutting ploughs of English origin which would be drawn by a team of animals, and the acres of fallow land ready for ploughing were enumerated.[37] The freeholders had by this time occupied some ruined castles on the estates and were presumably repairing them, and Raleigh himself acquired a comfortable residence in the port of Youghal as well as Lismore castle which he intended as his seat. The tenants were as yet living in hastily constructed timber houses but they were required by their terms of lease to build houses after "the English manner" within a specified time, and they were also usually required to enclose their property into fields using white-thorn quicksets and ditches after the manner of the southwest of England.[38]

These were exacting terms by any standards but they were matched by relatively low rents and usually long-term leases extending in some instances to a hundred years. Such a rent structure was clearly designed to promote a high level of investment by the tenants which indicates that Raleigh intended his profit to come either from commercial activity or from the eventual sale of the property. The postscript to his report of 1589 indicates that he recognized the potential offered by the fishing ground off the southwest of Ireland, but the immediate cash crop was the rich supply of hard timber that grew upon his lands. This he set about felling for the purpose of making pipe and barrel staves which were exported through his agent Henry Pyne to the wine islands in the Atlantic where timber was at a premium. It appears that Raleigh also contemplated the development of iron smelting on his lands, and he or his agents experimented with the growing of hops.[39] Legend has it that Raleigh introduced the potato on his lands, and it is possible that he did so because climatic conditions in Ireland were suited to the development of the tuber, and potato growing was certainly widespread in the southern half of Ireland a half-century later.[40] We know from the researches of Joan Thirsk that Raleigh's planter neighbor, Sir Christopher Hatton, encouraged woad growing on his Irish estate,[41] and it is likely that Raleigh followed his example because two small manufacturing villages had come into being on the Raleigh lands previous to 1598.[42] Even more dramatic was the physical transformation of the countryside which resulted from the systematic felling of trees and the gradual enclosure of the land. We get a visual impression of what had been achieved from the 1598 map of the farm of Mogeley granted in lease by Raleigh to Henry Pyne. This splendid map, which some attribute to John White of Roanoke fame, presents a picture of a countryside resembling that of southwest England with neatly divided and fenced fields organized about a settled community and displaying a rabbit warren as a symbol of civility.[43]

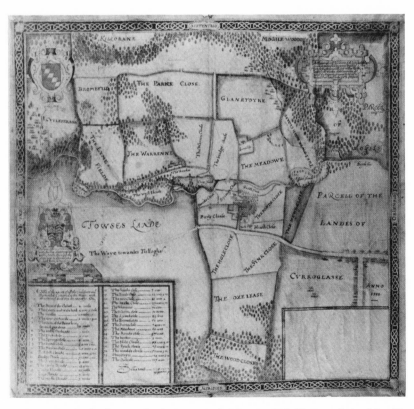

Walter Raleigh's lands in Ireland. From *Irish Maps* in *Irish Heritage Series*, No. 18 (Dublin: Eason and Son, 1978).

Whether this map represented the actuality of 1598 or the ideal that was being striven after is not clear, but we are certain that this section as well as most of the original Raleigh estate was enclosed in this fashion from the early decades of the seventeenth century. The estate was also made more compact through the systematic acquisition by Raleigh of neighboring church property, and we also learn from the seventeenth century sources that a sizeable number of the families who had settled on the Raleigh lands in the 1580s were still represented among the tenants of thirty years later.[44] Their persistence is the best evidence there is that Raleigh had created the conditions that were best suited to settlement in Ireland, but even his best efforts did not preserve the lands free from the consequences of the native uprising that occurred in 1598, just after the estate map had been made.

Native resentment over loss of property was the factor that most contributed to this uprising, and those who had been dispossessed had an opportunity to reoccupy what had been lost once government authority was paralyzed by the early military successes of Hugh O'Neill, earl of Tyrone, who had risen in revolt against the crown. The houses of the principal Munster settlers were pillaged, their manufacturing towns, such as Raleigh's town of Tallow in County Waterford, were destroyed, and their tenants were chased off the land and forced to flee back to England.[45] This turn of events represented ruin for many of the planters in Munster but hardly so for Raleigh, who had invested upwards of £1,000 in the experiment but who had already recouped much of his investment by leasing his entire estate from 1594 forward for £200 per annum. The fact that he did so indicates that his interest in the Munster plantation was already waning by that date, and this loss of interest may be explained as much by the difficulty he experienced in controlling his agents at a distance as it had been by the pessimistic view of the plantation that was fostered by some of his fellow planters in Munster. We know that Raleigh during his brief sojourns in Ireland as a planter established a close friendship with Edmund Spenser, who was one of those pessimists and who predicted that the entire plantation would fail because the planned settlement had lost its coherence as a result of the restoration of so much land to the native proprietors.[46]

But if Raleigh and Spenser shared a premonition that a revolt would occur in Munster, their reactions to that revolt were strikingly different. Where Spenser, whose livelihood depended on the success of the plantation, called upon the Queen to wreak vengeance on those who had been responsible for the revolt, Raleigh, the courtier, accepted the inevitable and sought to salvage what he could from the wreck by putting up his Irish lands for sale.[47] He had already been considering a sale for £2,000 in 1596 before the revolt occurred, so he seemingly considered himself fortunate to dispose of the property in 1602, when peace had been restored to Munster, for an agreed price of £1,500 of which only £1,000 had been paid to Raleigh before he was committed to prison by King James.[48]

This transaction would probably have ended Raleigh's connection with Ireland were it not that the purchaser, the calculating Richard Boyle (subsequently earl of Cork), advanced to dazzling economic and social success on the basis of his shrewd investment. As Raleigh languished in prison he must have regretted his sale and he must have particularly resented Boyle's defaulting on the final payment when reports reached him of the income that Boyle (a knight since 1603) enjoyed from the property. Already by 1613, Boyle's rental income was £4,000 per annum and most of this came from the Raleigh estates which he had freed from incumberance by breaking the long-term leases that Raleigh had entered into with his tenants.[49] The benefit of the original investment in the development of the property thus became Boyle's, while the Raleigh house in Youghal and the castle at Lismore were now developed to become suitable residents for the future earl of Cork.

All of the achievements of Richard Boyle are as much a tribute to the initial colonization efforts of Raleigh as they are to the energy and astuteness of Richard Boyle. It is hardly surprising therefore that when Raleigh was finally released from prison in 1617 and was engaging upon his last fateful voyage to Guiana he should stop off the coast of Munster and make contact with Richard Boyle who was now Baron of Youghal. The baron received him cheerfully, entertained him well, and obviously settled the debt to Raleigh's satisfaction because he took Boyle's part in bearing witness against Henry Pyne to the effect that the lease by which Pyne held his lands had been forged. By this means Boyle and Raleigh took revenge on Raleigh's erstwhile agent who had proven as much a thorn in Boyle's side as he had in that of Walter Raleigh.[50] What the terms of the settlement were between Boyle and Raleigh are not clear, but they were hardly as generous as those depicted by Boyle of their last encounter. He had, he claimed, given Raleigh 1,000 marks towards the cost of fitting him out for his voyage and proffered him a further £100 in French crowns as a free gift which was allegedly refused by Raleigh. Then in full view of a company Raleigh supposedly took his son by the hand and professed:[51]

> Watt you see how nobly my Lord Boyle has entertained and supplied me and my friends, and therefore I charge you upon my blessing, if it please God that you outlive me and return that you never question the Lord Boyle for any thing that I have sold him, for I do lay my curse upon my wife and children if they ever question any of the purchases his lordship had made to me, for if he had not purchased any Irish land of me by my fall it would have come to the crown and then one Scot or other would have begged it from whom neither I nor mine would have had any thing for it, nor such courtesies as now I have received.

No such courtesies awaited Raleigh when he again stopped in Ireland on his way from Guiana a broken man who had lost his son. But his previous dealings there haunted him as he lodged in the Tower before his execution, and one of his final acts was to retract the evidence that he had presented against Henry Pyne in Ireland the previous year.[52] In doing so he was no doubt hoping for a more favorable judgment from his maker than he had received from his earthly monarch.

Notes

*John Neville, in presenting Nicholas Canny, said: "Several days ago a newspaper reporter asked me why we planned a paper entitled 'Raleigh's Ireland.' Rather than give you the explanation I gave the reporter, I want to introduce our speaker. Nicholas Canny is a native of Ireland, and his secondary education was at St. Flannan's College in County Clare. From the University College, Galway, he earned his bachelor's and master's degrees, then he came to the United States for his doctorate from the University of Pennsylvania. In 1974–75 he was senior Fulbright Fellow from Ireland and spent a semester each at Harvard and Yale and the summer at the Institute for Early American History and Culture at Williamsburg. For 1979–80 he was a member of the Institute for Advanced Study at Princeton. Returning to Ireland, he was dean of the Faculty of Arts from 1982–85 at University College, Galway, where he is now professor of modern history.

"Professor Canny has published on both sides of the Atlantic. His first book, *The Elizabethan Conquest of Ireland*, won the Irish Historical Research Prize in 1976. He is also author of *The Upstart Earl* (1982), and he was co-editor of *The Westward Enterprise*, a festschrift for David Beers Quinn (1978). His *From Reformation to Restoration: Ireland 1534–1660*, and an edited volume, *Colonial Identity in the Atlantic World 1500–1800*, are scheduled for publication this year. He holds membership in the Royal Irish Academy and is this year a fellow at the National Humanities Center."

[1]Nicholas Canny, *The Elizabethan Conquest of Ireland: A Pattern Established, 1565–76* (Hassocks near Brighton and New York: 1976), esp. pp. 66–92.

[2]For the details of his early career see Cecil S. Emden, "Sir Walter Ralegh 1552 or 1554–1618: His Friends at Oriel," in Cecil S. Emden, *Oriel Papers* (Oxford: 1948), pp. 9–21.

[3]For the advocacy of Ireland as a place in which younger sons might make their careers see *A Letter Sent by J.B. gentleman unto . . . Mayster R.C. esquire* (London: 1571, S.T.C. 1048); and for the presence in Ireland of younger sons see Thomas Churchyard, *Churchyarde's Choise: A generall Rehersall of Warres* (London: 1579, S.T.C., 5235).

[4]Canny, *The Elizabethan Conquest of Ireland*, pp. 93–116.

[5]For an example of how local office could thus be turned to personal advantage in Ireland see Terence O. Ranger, "Richard Boyle and the Making of an Irish Fortune," in *Irish Historical Studies*, 10 (1957): 257–297.

[6]For Grey see *D.N.B.* under Grey, Arthur, fourteenth Baron Grey de Wilton.

[7]Arthur Collins, *Letters and Memorials of State*, 2 vols., (London: 1746), vol. 1, pp. 279–83.

[8]For the careful selection by Sidney of his subordinates in Ireland, see Canny, *The Elizabethan Conquest of Ireland*, pp. 69–70 and 137–153.

[9]*Ibid.*, pp. 45–65.

[10]*A New History of Ireland, Vol. III, Early Modern Ireland, 1534–1691*, ed. T.W. Moody, F.X. Martin and F.J. Byrne (Oxford: 1976), pp. 103–111.

[11]For the causes and consequences of these revolts see Ciaran Brady, "Faction and the Origins of the Desmond Rebellion of 1579," in *Irish Historical Studies*, 22 (1981): 289–312, and Nicholas Canny, "Identity Formation in Ireland: the Emergence of the Anglo-Irish," in *Colonial Identity in the Atlantic World, 1500–1800*, ed. Nicholas Canny and Anthony Pagden (Princeton: 1987), pp. 159–213, esp. pp. 163–177.

[12]One of his letters is conveniently transcribed in Norman Lloyd Williams, *Sir Walter Raleigh* (London: 1962), pp. 33–35.

[13]Ormond to Burghley, Sept. 4, 1583, in Public Record Office (London), S.P. 63/104/60.

[14]*A New History of Ireland*, Vol. III, pp. 107–8; see also Alfred O'Rahilly, *The Massacre at Smerwick, 1580* (Cork: 1938).

[15]Lloyd Williams, *Sir Walter Raleigh*, pp. 29–31.

[16]*Ibid.*, pp. 31–35.

[17]For an account of this episode by a contemporary who was sympathetic to Lord Grey's position, see Edmund Spenser, *A View of the Present State of Ireland*, ed. W.L. Renwick (Oxford: 1970), pp. 105–7. In this account Spenser was careful to suggest that Ormond was manipulated into opposing Grey's policy.

[18]Lord Gray to Walsingham, Dec. 9, 1581, in Public Record Office, S.P. 63/87/18.

[19]*A New History of Ireland*, Vol. III, pp. 108–9.

[20]Ormond to Burghley, March 4, 1584, in Public Record Office, S.P. 63/108/5.

[21]David B. Quinn, "The Munster Plantation: Problems and Opportunities," in *Journal of the Cork Archaeological and Historical Society*, 71 (1966): 19–40; Michael MacCarthy Morrogh, *The Munster Plantation: English Migration to Southern Ireland, 1583–1641* (Oxford, 1986), pp. 38–45.

[22]Fenton to Walsingham, Sept. 29, 1587, in Public Record Office, S.P. 63/131/33.

[23]Sir Robert Naunton, *Memoirs of Elizabeth, Her Court and Favourites* (London, 1824), pp. 109–10.

[24]Norman Lloyd Williams, *Sir Walter Raleigh*, pp. 49–50; Quinn, "The Munster Plantation"; MacCarthy Morrogh, *The Munster Plantation*, pp. 19–38.

[25]Canny, *The Elizabethan Conquest of Ireland*, pp. 83–84; MacCarthy Morrogh, *The Munster Plantation*, pp. 20–21.

[26]MacCarthy Morrogh, *The Munster Plantation*, pp. 30–38; for the favourable reaction of one senior official to woad-growing in Ireland, see Wallop to Walsingham, 19 April 1585 (London, P.R.O., S.P. 63/116/18).

[27]MacCarthy Morrogh, *The Munster Plantation*, pp. 73–75.

[28]*Ibid.*, pp. 52–55.

[29]*Ibid.*, p. 52.

[30]D.B. Quinn, *Raleigh and the British Empire* (London: 1947), pp. 153–54.

[31]MacCarthy Morrogh, *The Munster Plantation*, p. 19.

[32]St. Leger to Queen Elizabeth, May 1589, in Public Record Office, S.P. 63/144/82.

[33]D.B. Quinn, *Raleigh and the British Empire*, pp. 139–52; for Raleigh's leases see Dublin, National Library of Ireland, MS 6135.

[34]"The names of Sir Walter Raleigh his tenants: my Lord Warden his book," in London, Public Record Office, S.P. 63/144/28; ff. 62–5.

[35]*Ibid.*

[36]D.B. Quinn, *Raleigh and the British Empire*, pp. 142–43; MacCarthy Morrogh, *The Munster Plantation*, pp. 114–15.

[37]The enumeration of livestock and implements as well as remarks on fallow land were provided after each group of settlers listed in S.P. 63/144/28, cited at note 34 above.

[38]Raleigh's leases, N.L.I., MS 6135; MacCarthy Morrogh, *The Munster Plantation*, pp. 228–29.

[39]D.B. Quinn, *Raleigh and the British Empire*, pp. 123–24; MacCarthy Morrogh, *The Munster Plantation*, p. 240.

[40]That it was feasible to grow the potato in Ireland is evident from J.G. Hawkes, "Masters Memorial Lecture, 1966, The History of the Potato," in *Journal of the Royal Horticultural Society*, 92 (1967): 207–24 and 288–302. That potatoes were, in fact, grown in the southern half of Ireland during the first half of the seventeenth century is evident from the depositions taken in the aftermath of the 1641 Rebellion. See for example the deposition of Richard Prudderagh of Whitchurch, County Waterford (Trinity College, Dublin, MS 820, f. 177).

[41]London, Public Record Office, LR9/86; file marked Alexander King. I am grateful to Joan Thirsk for supplying me with her notes from this file which concerns the alleged frauds associated with an attempt to grow woad, madder and oilseed on Hatton's lands in Ireland.

[42]The details of what had been achieved in the matter of urban development only came to light in 1598 when they were destroyed, on which see A.J. Sheehan, "The Overthrow of the Plantation of Munster in October, 1598," in *The Irish Sword*, 15 (1982): 11–22.

[43]This Mogeley map is housed in the National Library of Ireland and is reproduced as map no. 12, in J.H. Andrews, *Irish Maps*, Irish Heritage Series, No. 18 (Dublin: 1978).

[44]MacCarthy Morrogh, *The Munster Plantation*, pp. 150–1; Nicholas Canny, *The Upstart Earl: A Study of the Social and Mental World of Richard Boyle, first Earl of Cork, 1566–1643* (Cambridge: 1982), pp. 19–25.

[45]A.J. Sheehan, "The Overthrow of the Plantation of Munster in October, 1598."

[46]MacCarthy Morrogh, *The Munster Plantation*, pp. 121, 141. On the pessimism of Spenser, see Ciaran Brady, "Spenser's Irish Crisis: Humanism and Experience in the 1590s," in *Past & Present*, no. 111 (May 1986): 17–49, and Nicholas Canny, "Edmund Spenser as Political Theorist: A Comment on 'Spenser's Irish Crisis'," in *Past & Present*, forthcoming.

[47]MacCarthy Morrogh, *The Munster Plantation*, p. 141.

[48]Canny, *The Upstart Earl*, p. 6.

[49]*Ibid.*

[50]MacCarthy Morrogh, *The Munster Plantation*, pp. 186–87.

[51]Cork to Carew Raleigh, 16 Jan. 1632 (Chatsworth, Cork Letter Book, I, ff. 389–92).

[52]MacCarthy Morrogh, *The Munster Plantation*, p. 187.

American Colonization through Raleigh's Eyes

John W. Shirley*

It is fitting that the American celebration of the quadricentennial of the English colonization of North America should close with a memorial to Sir Walter Raleigh. Though historians are rarely totally in agreement, there is general consensus in one thing: that in spite of his failures, this proud favorite of the Virgin Queen made a greater contribution to the concept of a British Empire than did all the ministers and officials of the Tudor state.

Dr. Jones has asked me at this conference to address the subject of "American Colonization Through Raleigh's Eyes"[1] — a most interesting and important subject which I approach with some diffidence. It raises the questions: What did Raleigh think of colonization in the New World? And when did he think it? Since no man can ever know what another man thinks, you can understand my diffidence. But since you cannot prove me wrong, let me try.

Raleigh's interest in the colonization of the New World falls into three periods of his life. The first, his youthful introduction to America and its potential, extended from the 1580s through the mid-1590s and covered the Virginia period so important to this conference. The second, during his mature years from the mid-1590s to the death of Elizabeth in which he took his most personally active role, involved the search for El Dorado and a vigorous effort to establish colonies in South America. The third, short and tragic, was his frenzied South American expedition of 1617 which led to his beheading in the following year. As we shall see, Raleigh's dreams of empire changed somewhat with each of these new experiences.

The Virginia period of exploration and settlement bore the marks of the young Raleigh: imaginative, daring, impetuous. From generations on both sides of his lineage young Walter had inherited qualities which dominated his actions for the rest of his life: a pride in family and country, a love of the sea, a quick passion, and a strong sense of the dramatic.[2] Raleigh had already enjoyed the wide experiences of the young Elizabethan of good family. He had been registered at Oriel College, Oxford, at the age of fourteen and was on the rolls until 1571, but spent much of that time in France, learning the art of war aiding the Huguenots in their wars against the Catholics. By age twenty-three, Raleigh was in London, center of the Court and intellectual society of England, a member of the Inner Temple, and one of the young poets and courtiers who were hangers-on of the Court.

Here in the late 1570s, Raleigh began to focus on the New World. In the Inner Temple lived Richard Hakluyt the elder, whose major interest was navigation and geography, who was stimulating much discussion on the new lands to the west. Raleigh's blustering half-brother, Sir Humphrey Gilbert, was also in London, pushing in the Court and in the city for exploration of the far reaches of the world, both for commercial profit and to annoy the Queen's enemy, the King of Spain. Gilbert's persuasive arguments resulted in his being granted, on 11 June 1578, the first letters patent giving him and his heirs permission to seek out and discover any heathen and barbarous lands in the New World not occupied by any Christian king.

Walter Raleigh, alert to fresh opportunities and sharing Gilbert's thirst for gold and his hatred of Catholic Spain, was quickly in the midst of these activities. He not only joined many members of his family in offering financial support to Sir Humphrey for a preliminary voyage of discovery, but he volunteered his own person, inexperienced as he was, to the expedition. And, since in Elizabethan days leaders were often chosen for family status rather than experience or ability, Raleigh was named commander of the *Falcon*, which had formerly been one of the Queen's own ships.[3] Master of the *Falcon* was a Portuguese pilot, Simon Fernandes, described by the Spanish Ambassador as "a great rogue who knows that coast well," to be intimately linked with Raleigh in years to come. The *Falcon* flew a bold motto: *Nec mortem peto nec finem fugio* ("I neither seek death nor flee the end"), which Raleigh might well have taken as his own.

Sir Humphrey Gilbert was, as the Queen said, "a man noted for no good hap at sea." Though his enthusiasm ran high, his capacity for organization was limited. As a result, this first assault on the unclaimed lands for which Gilbert and Raleigh had such high hopes was a fiasco. Ships were provisioned and ready to go in early summer, but delays kept them in harbor until summer was gone and supplies were beginning to spoil. Three of the ships deserted to go privateering on their own. Starting late, the other seven ships encountered severe storms which forced them back to Dartmouth harbor. Raleigh, no doubt under the influence of Fernandes and looking for loot, took off in the *Falcon* for the West Indies, met up with some Spanish ships, engaged them, and after a fierce fight was badly beaten. Shamefacedly, he was forced to return to England with a badly damaged ship, for whose repair he was responsible. The only prizes taken by the expedition were reviewed by the Privy Council and ordered returned to their owners, and both Gilbert and Raleigh were placed under surety not to engage in piracy. Raleigh learned much from this first brush with the exploration of the New World: contingencies must be prepared for; the Spaniards were formidable foes on the water; and he personally was not a good sailor — contact with the sea made him violently seasick, as it was to do for the rest of his life.

This experience may have led Raleigh to accept a commission as a captain in the English colonial empire in Ireland. The eighteen months he spent there were most valuable in giving him experience in colonization.[4] Raleigh went to Ireland imbued with the stern and rigid principles of justice espoused earlier by his idol Humphrey Gilbert. As Gilbert had done, Raleigh, under orders, unflinchingly slaughtered soldiers, women, and children in the surrendered garrison of Smerwick. But when named as one of the commissioners governing the city of Munster, Raleigh wisely concluded that he should learn the people's problems, to stop revolts before they started. For some months he travelled widely, observing conditions and listening to the problems of the Irish.

This strategy worked: in a few months Raleigh had won the respect and confidence of the Munster English and became dissatisfied with English political policy. The mass of the peasants and many of the lesser nobles, he found, distrusted or hated the tyrannical overlords who were leading the rebellion. If given protection from these few leaders, he argued, they would rally to the support of the English government. He advocated that the English representatives assist the Irish in solving their economic problems and enlist their support and allegiance for a friendly Queen who could subdue the treasonable few who wanted to return Ireland to the Pope. This radical view enraged Lord Grey and led to Raleigh's return to Court, "bringing letters in post for her Majesty's affairs."

Raleigh wasted no time in expressing his views about England's colonial policies at Court. His presentations on Ireland to Walsingham, the Privy Council, and the Queen herself were direct and forceful. Raleigh as a young man was an impressive figure—tall, handsome, and self-assured. The gossip John Aubrey reported that Raleigh "told his tale so well, and with so good a grace and presence, that the Queen took especial notice of him and presently preferred him."[5] Under the absolute monarchy of the Tudors, such favoritism paid off very quickly. When Raleigh's commission expired in April, the Queen renewed his title and salary, but demanded he remain in England near the Court. She granted him the lease of the town house of the Bishop of Durham, which gave Raleigh a London center near the Court in public view. In May the Queen granted him leases of two estates, and shortly awarded him the right to levy charges against every English vintner licensed to sell wines. The thirty-year-old Raleigh was almost overnight one of the richest men in England.

Raleigh's new wealth whetted his interest in the development of a colonial empire for Elizabeth. Gilbert's charter for discovery and settlement of the New World was to expire in 1584, and except for a few exploratory expeditions by Simon Fernandes nothing significant had been done since the aborted venture of 1578; now in 1582 preparations for a larger voyage began in earnest. To finance it, Sir Humphrey offered grants of land to supporters and drew up elaborate plans concerning the governance, public services, churches, and economic development of lands yet to be discovered. Raleigh was enthusiastic about the potential of new colonies; he not only bought shares in the company, but used some of his new wealth to build an experimental ship of 200 tons, the *Bark Raleigh*, which he planned to command in the voyage.

Raleigh's Durham House, on the Thames embarkment, became a center of activity as experts of all sorts were enlisted in the enterprise. The famous John

Dee, England's foremost authority on geography and theoretical navigation, was a consultant. The younger Richard Hakluyt, who was giving instruction in geography and navigation at Oxford, was drafted to help, and probably brought with him his "bedfellow at Oxford," Stephen Parmenius of Buda, who asked to be a member of the expedition.[6] A case could be made that it was at this time that one of Hakluyt's Oxford students, Thomas Harriot, and another Oxford friend, Lawrence Keymis, were also brought into the planning.[7] Though Raleigh planned to be second-in-command, again Elizabeth wanted him to remain near her. For Raleigh's sake, this was fortunate, for Gilbert's second attempt was no more successful than his first.[8] In spite of the frenzy of preparation, the fleet was again poorly outfitted and victualed. Not even the route plans were firm, and at the last minute sailing routes were in confusion. Illness and inadequate food supplies forced the *Bark Raleigh* to return to port and from that point on the voyage lost focus. The vessels separated, rendezvous were missed, ill sailors refused to sail, the *Delight* ran aground and was wrecked; more than eighty men drowned, all of Gilbert's maps, charts, and logs were lost, and when the few remaining men were returning to England, the ten-ton *Squirrel* on which Gilbert chose to sail was caught in a violent storm off the Newfoundland coast and disappeared with all aboard.

The death of Sir Humphrey and the impending termination of his patent stirred his brothers into even greater activity at the Court. Adrian Gilbert joined forces with John Dee to seek a new charter to permit him to explore for a northwest passage to China. Though Raleigh originally had a large hand in this venture, he soon dropped out to seek a renewal of Sir Humphrey's patent for the colonization of the New World in his own name. In February 1594, five months after Sir Humphrey's death, Sir Adrian was granted his request and obtained rights to explore for new and shorter mercantile routes to the riches of the Orient. A month later, on 25 March, Walter Raleigh was given a new lease for the colonization of the New World.

Raleigh accepted his leadership role in American colonization with his usual enthusiasm and energy. Obviously his motives were mixed: his desire for great wealth for his Queen and country (which he seemed to view as identical) and, not incidentally, for himself, was mixed with his hatred of the vile Catholic Spaniards who were the antithesis of everything good Englishmen believed.

Activities increased at Durham House, to the extent that in many ways it resembled the navigation school of the Portuguese established by Prince Henry the Navigator. The two magi, John Dee and Thomas Harriot, collected maps and rutters of the coastlines of the emerging continent collating new information as it was obtained. Detailed information on ship design was brought to the Durham library, analyzed, revised, and passed on to shipbuilders to improve their products. Harriot attacked the monumental problem of determining the correction factor which needed to be applied to compass readings in diagonal sailing in different latitudes, solving the complex problem of the rhumbs in tables one decimal point more accurate than those used by the British Royal Navy today.[9] To insure that these innovations were not left in the Durham library, Harriot taught scientific navigation to Raleigh's masters and pilots, for which he wrote a text, called *Antarcticon*, which has unfortunately disappeared.

Within a month of the receipt of the charter, Raleigh sent off an exploratory expedition under two of his young servants. Philip Amadas commanded the *Bark Raleigh* with Simon Fernandes as master, and Arthur Barlow followed in one of Raleigh's pinnaces. Raleigh again was not permitted to go; his new duties as junior knight for Devonshire in the House of Commons may have kept him at home. Almost certainly John White, later so closely tied to his colonizing ventures, was aboard, and quite likely Thomas Harriot, on whom Raleigh relied more than any other for advice. From late April to mid-September 1594 Raleigh's first commitment to the "remote heathen and barbarous landes" of Virginia — which this quadricentennial celebration is all about — was under way.

Professor Quinn has made available the many extant documents about the Virginia colonies which exist to give some insight into Raleigh's hopes and ambitions.[10] Harriot's *Briefe and True Report* gives an amazingly modern overview of the economic wealth the colonies might provide and a fascinating first-hand account of the natives and their beliefs. White's superb drawings of Virginia and its people as seen by the colonists is of inestimable value to the historian. And an unpublished propaganda pamphlet is also very revealing of Raleigh's dream of empire.

Shortly after the departure of Amadas and Barlowe on his first exploratory probe, probably in July, Raleigh conspired with Walsingham to bring back to London the Reverend Richard Hakluyt, who had been serving as chaplain to the English embassy in Paris, to help prepare a paper which might induce the Queen to support this new program. Remarkably, this tract has survived, though not published until this century. Hakluyt again joined Raleigh's entourage in Durham House and used Raleigh's books and maps and his own vast knowledge of voyages and explorations to produce a detailed pamphlet. Shortly after the return of Amadas and Barlow in mid-September, the treatise, bearing the formidable title,[11]

> *A particular discourse concerninge the greate necessitie and manifolde commodyties that are like to growe to this Realme of Englande by the Western discoveries lately attempted, Written in the yere 1584. by Richarde Hackluyt of Oxforde at the requeste and direction of the righte worshipfull Mr. Walter Raghly nowe Knight, before the comynge home of his Twoo Barkes:*

was completed and on October 5th, Hakluyt waited on the Queen in person to present his "Discourse."

Hakluyt's *Discourse* stresses the benefits Raleigh felt could ensue from this expansion of Elizabeth's empire. It is interesting to note that in the presentation to the Queen, the first and most cogent argument for settling the New World was the need to win the heathen natives away from the false gospel of the Spanish Catholics to the true religion of England. Hakluyt spelled this out clearly:[12]

> Nowe the Kinges and Queenes of England have the name of Defendors
> of the Faithe: by which title I thinke they are not onely chardged to
> mayneteyne and patronize the faithe of Christe, but also to inlarge and
> advaunce the same: Neither oughte this to be their last worke, but rather
> the principall and chefe of allothers, according to the comaundemente
> of our Saviour Christe.

Unquestionably this was Hakluyt the preacher rather than Raleigh speaking. Though Raleigh might approve the argument to win over the Queen, there is no evidence that any preacher or religious leader was included among the colonists sent to Virginia, and the only colonist who appeared interested in the religious beliefs of the natives was Thomas Harriot, who, like Raleigh, was accused of too liberal interpretation of the scriptures.

Quickly, however, to appeal to the more worldly character of the Queen, the argument turned economic: bases in the New World would open new natural resources to English merchants and give shorter trade routes to the remote countries of the western world. English strongholds in the New World would furnish deep-water ports for the English fishing and merchant vessels during the inclement part of the year, and furnish safe harborage for English shipping currently endangered by their Spanish enemies. Holding such territory would "be a great bridle to the Indies of the kinge of Spaine"[13] making difficult the return voyages of his plate fleet. Spain, Hakluyt argued, must be restrained, for the great wealth being extracted from the New World was being used for evil purposes — endangering all Protestant countries, stealing properties properly the Queen's, and even supporting uprisings in Ireland and Scotland and threatening English peaceable enterprise.

Into this picture of economic growth and development Hakluyt introduced — again probably at Raleigh's instigation — the sociological theme which Raleigh had exploited in his advice on Ireland. This was the theme that an oppressed people would join and support a benevolent ruler. In his tirade against the Spanish cruelties in treating the natives of the West Indies and New Spain, Hakluyt produced testimony that during the last forty years the Spaniards had "don to deathe unjustly and tyranously more than xij millions of soules men women and children."[14] Such oppressed people would quickly revolt and "shake off from their shoulders the moste intollerable and insupportable yoke of Spaine, which in many places they have already begonne to doo of themselves withoute the helpe of any christian Prynce."[15]

It was with such high hopes that Raleigh launched his second colonial effort under the leadership of Grenville and Lane in 1585. The expedition was more thoroughly planned, better manned and provisioned than any which had gone before.[16] Six ships and barks, carrying approximately six hundred men, were mustered. Richard Grenville and Ralph Lane, both experienced military men, were in command, charged with the responsibility of protecting the expedition from both the natives and the Spaniards, and of locating and seizing a suitable deep-water harbor for English shipping. Thomas Harriot, loaded down with the latest scientific instruments and a fair command of Algonquian, was Raleigh's special emissary, charged with surveying Virginia both for its geography and its economic resources and for a sociological study of the native inhabitants. His firsthand study was to be the base for later colonizing efforts and, if favorable, for gaining support to augment the settlement program. For this latter purpose (and for general interest), John White was to work with Harriot in drawing maps of the newfound land and in depicting representatives of the native population and their way of life. Soldiers enough to protect the expedition were equipped, and fresh and ample supplies for the whole colony for a full first year were to accompany them. Nothing that Sir Walter, now a wealthy man, could contribute, solicit, or borrow to insure the success of the colony was omitted.

As we all know, Raleigh's first colony did not live up to the high dreams of Raleigh, Hakluyt, Harriot, and White. The chosen leaders, Grenville and Lane, were too close to their violent battles with the Irish and too intense in their hatred of the Spaniards and Portuguese to approach the natives with the sympathy and understanding which would rally them to the cause of the Virgin Queen. The colonists, recruited with rosy promises of easy living, with gold and pearls to be had for the asking, were ill prepared for a hard pioneer life devoted to husbanding of the resources which actually were all around them. Bad feelings developed, and discipline and organization deteriorated instead of improving with experience. The frantic return of the colony with Drake a fortnight before Raleigh's supply ships arrived at Roanoke was a most disastrous blow to the steady growth and development of a colonial empire as envisioned by Sir Walter.

Raleigh learned many lessons from the disappointing first settlement in Virginia. The reports of Harriot and White encouraged the economic potential of a permanent colony if relations with the natives could be improved. Roanoke Island had proved to be an unsatisfactory site for a major settlement, neither healthful for the colonists nor adequate as a harbor for major ships, merchantman or privateer. But explorations had found an alternative site on the shores of Chesapeake Bay. Experiences of the first winter had shown that to stabilize the colony and give a feeling of permanence to the settlement, family units would be vastly superior to an all-male group of citizens. Leadership should be civil rather than military.

It was with these modifications that the second colonial effort was planned.[17] John White, experienced and moderate, was to be governor. Families were to be recruited (including White's own pregnant daughter and her husband). And after a preliminary recovery of everything left in the Roanoke village, a new city was to be established on the Chesapeake. This group, the fourth American voyage sponsored by Sir Walter, "departed the sixth and twentieth of April [1587] from Portsmouth" to become the famous and mysterious Lost Colony, whose story need not be retold here. Only the caprices of fate kept Raleigh's youthful dreams of establishing an English settlement in Virginia from the rich success it deserved.

The next few years when colonization efforts were most badly needed were hectic ones for England and for Raleigh. Though the fate of the colonists and Raleigh's hopes for England's overseas empire were not forgotten, they were forced by circumstances into a secondary role in his thinking. The imminence of Spain's assault on the English mainland was of prime importance, marked by reprisals, counterassaults, and open naval warfare in which Raleigh had a significant hand. His position on Elizabeth's war council took much of his time in the late 1580s, and the early 1590s found him as "Fortune's tennis ball,"[18] preoccupied almost completely with his personal problems. His secret marriage to one of her attendants, Elizabeth Throckmorton, infuriated Queen Elizabeth and put Raleigh in the Tower in disgrace. He had enough to do preserving his own head and any vestige of his fortune without worrying about the expansion of the Queen's empire. It was not until the middle of the 1590s, when Raleigh had begun to work himself back into favor, that he could again devote his thoughts to the New World.

In Raleigh's eyes the situation had changed, both in America and in England. Only a bold and dramatic gesture could arouse the tired and jaded Elizabeth. He no longer had the resources to send English colonies to an undeveloped wilderness. What was needed was quick wealth or the acquisition of territories already developed. Prospects of limitless riches turned his thoughts again to Spain. The huge caches of precious metals and jewels stolen by Cortez and Pizzaro had been emptied. But had all the treasure cities west of the Andes been located? And had all the Inca warriors been destroyed? Both rumor and tradition suggested they had not. Gossip had it that some of the Inca and Aztec rulers had escaped, carrying with them vast stores of golden idols and treasures. Others spoke of undiscovered civilizations buried in the reaches of South America, not yet visited by Europeans. Tales of a lost Inca empire, El Dorado, city of gold, continued to circulate. This was a bait that a man like Raleigh could not resist.

Raleigh's second dream of empire was clear. He would discover this lost city and lay its treasures before the Queen.[19] And, as his dreams grew, he expanded on the idea of establishing new colonies for Elizabeth in the South American region he named Guiana—not colonies of imported settlers living in a hostile environment, but of native Indians who could be converted to English religion, English social customs, and citizenship. These new citizens would live under the beneficent hand of Gloriana and would serve as local defenders of Englishmen and English trade against their Spanish enemies. These new colonies would meet all his dreams of empire: they would enrich England by pouring the gold of the Incas into her treasury; they would cripple Spain by removing her chief assets; and they would make England the preeminent world power by increasing her armies with powerful Indian hosts. The rich colony of Guiana would be Raleigh's gift to the world's preeminent monarch and the jewel of a precious new colonial empire.

Though less well known than his efforts in Virginia, these South American ventures reveal much about Raleigh's ideas of colonization and give us our best view of the New World through his eyes. Not only did he personally take part in the venture, but he has himself furnished us with a detailed account of the whole expedition. Stimulated by the malicious gossip which accompanied this bold venture, Raleigh rose to his own defense and explained his motives. His account, titled *The Discoverie of the Large, Rich, and Bewtiful Empyre of Guiana*, published in 1596,[20] reveals what he saw, did, and felt from February to August 1595 while he was attempting to found a new empire for Elizabeth in the New World.

Raleigh's charter for this voyage was much like those of the past, but since he was entering enemy waters, it authorized him to "offend and enfeeble the King of Spain" as well—a license for privateering, thievery, and hostile acts that must have thrilled his soldier's heart. Captain Whiddon, as usual, made a preliminary voyage in 1594 to explore the Orinoco delta (thought to lead to the site of El Dorado) and to sound out the Spanish defenses. Meanwhile Raleigh strained his resources for his major assault. Lord High Admiral Charles Howard offered one ship, and Raleigh mustered two of his own, the *Bark Raleigh* or the *Roebuck*, which he commanded himself, and an unnamed galley commanded by his close associate Lawrence Keymis.

Arriving at Trinidad on 22 March, Raleigh began to gather information. That evening a small canoe came alongside, bearing two Indians, one of whom was a local *casique* or lord known by Whiddon. Raleigh used his charm to win them over, and from his questioning reports "wee vnderstood what strength the Spaniardes had, how farre it was to their Citie, and of *Don Anthonio de Berreo*, the gouernour, who was said to be slaine in his second attempt of *Guiana*, but was not."[21] Raleigh also charmed the native Spaniards who came to trade:[22]

> ... all which I entertained kindly and feasted after our manner: by means whereof I learned of one and another as much of the estate of *Guiana* as I could, or as they knew, for those poore souldiers hauing beene many yeares without wine, a fewe draughtes made them merry, in which moode they vaunted of *Guiana* and of the riches thereof, and all what they knew of the waies and passages, my selfe seeming to purpose nothing lesse then the enterance or discouerie thereof, but bred in them an opinion that I was bound onely for the reliefe of those english, which I had planted in *Virginia*, whereof the brute was come among them....

Raleigh lingered at Port of Spain: he continued to gather information from both Indians and Spaniards as he waited the chance to avenge the treasonable actions of the Spanish captain, Antonio de Berreo, who had ambushed and killed a number of Captain Whiddon's men the year before. At last convinced that Berreo was completely untrustworthy and that the search for Manoa required him to travel the Orinoco River in small boats, Raleigh concluded that "to enter *Guiana* by small boats, to depart 400 or 500 miles from my ships, and to leaue a garrison in my backe . . . I should haue sauoured very much of the Asse. . . ."[23] Raleigh was not an ass, and he took the action he felt doubly needed:[24]

> . . . taking a time of most aduauntage, I set vpon the *Corp du guard* in the euening, and hauing put them to the sword, sente Captaine *Calfeild* onwards with 60 soldiers, and my self followed with 40 more and so toke their new city which they called *S. Ioseph*, by breake of day: they abode not any fight after a few shot, and al being dismissed but onely *Berreo* and his companion, I brought them with me abord, and at the instance of the Indians I set their new city of *S. Iosephs* on fire.

In complete control after this quick victory, Raleigh spent some days questioning Berreo, getting from him all he knew about the country, the native tribes, the names and dispositions of their *casiques*, and especially the location of the mines reported to be the source of Indian gold and silver. The gallega was cut down for more shallow draft, and in this, with one of the small ship's boats, Raleigh with 100 of his men started up the Orinoco.

The hardships of the journey were very trying to a courtier accustomed to life at court. A hundred men were to spend a month[25]

> in the raine and wether, in the open aire, in the burning sunne, & vpon the hard boards . . . that what with victuals being most fish . . . and the heate of the sunne, I will vndertake there was neuer any prison in England, that could be founde more vnsauory and lothsome, especially to my selfe, who had for many yeares before beene dieted and cared for in a sort farre differing.

But like most Europeans seeing America for the first time, Raleigh forgot his discomfort in the glories of the countryside and the nobility of the natives. The first Indians they met were most impressive. "These Tiuitiuas are a very goodlie people and verie valiant, and haue the most manlie speech and most deliberate that euer I heard of what nation soeuer." Again, at the farthest point of their advance on the Caroni river, near the entrance to the fabled mine, where the men were led by a series of six waterfalls each as high as a church steeple, the fact that he admitted he was "a very ill footeman"[26] did not diminish Raleigh's poetic appreciation:[27]

> I neuer saw a more beawtifull countrey, nor more liuely prospectes, hils
> so raised heere and there ouer the vallies, the riuer winding into diuers
> braunches, the plaines adioyning without bush or stubble, all faire greene
> grasse, the ground of hard sand easy to march on, eyther for horse or
> foote, the deare crossing in euery path, the birds towardes the euening
> singing on euery tree with a thousand seueral tunes, cranes & herons
> of white, crimson, and carnation pearching on the riuers side, the ayre
> fresh with a gentle easterlie wind, and euery stone that we stopped to
> take vp, promised eyther golde or siluer by his complexion.

Surely this was a land fit for a Queen like Elizabeth!

But Raleigh's main effort was to convince the native chiefs to ally with the English as enemies of the Spaniards and to embrace Elizabeth as their sovereign. From his first meeting with the native *casiques*[28]

> by my Indian interpreter . . . I made them vnderstand that I was the
> seruant of a Queene, who was the great *Casique* of the north, and a
> virgin, and had more *Casiqui* vnder her then there were trees in their
> Iland: that she was an enemy to the *Castellans* in respect of their tyrannie
> and oppression, and that she . . . had sent me to free them also. . . . I
> shewed them her maiesties picture which they so admired and honored,
> as it had been easie to haue brought them Idolatrous thereof.

This message, Raleigh wrote, he "made to the rest of the nations both in passing to *Guiana*, & to those of the borders, so as in that part of the world her maiesty is very famous and admirable."[29]

The high emotional points of Raleigh's Orinoco voyage were undoubtedly his two visits with his "old friend" Topiawari, the hundred-year-old chief of the mighty province of Arromaia, which might be the key to the entrance to El Dorado. Topiawari had succeeded to the throne when his nephew, Morequito, had been slain by Berreo for his gold. In spite of his great age, Topiawari was "a man of great vnderstanding and pollicie . . . and yet of a very able bodie."[30] On their voyage up the Orinoco Raleigh made a special point of stopping at the port of Morequito, sending an emissary to the old king. "The next day following, before noone he came to vs on foote from his house, which was 14 English miles (himself being 110 years old) and returned on foote the same daie."[31] A host of warriers, women, and children accompanied him bearing gifts: bread and wine, parakeets, even an armadillo the powder of whose horn, Raleigh the chemist wrote, cured deafness.

After the old king had rested in Raleigh's tent from his long walk in the burning sun, Sir Walter began his campaign:[32]

> . . . ere I went anie farther I made him know the cause of my coming
> thither, whose seruant I was, and that the Queenes pleasure was, I should
> vndertake the voiage for their defence, and to deliuer them from the
> tyrannie of the Spaniards, dilating at large (as I had done before to those

of *Trinedado*) her Maiesties greatnes, her iustice, her charitie to all oppressed nations, with as manie of the rest of her beauties and vertues, as either I coulde expresse, or they conceiue, all which being with great admiration attentiuely heard, and maruellously admired. . . .

After questioning Topiawari about the lands surrounding Guiana, their riches, and the willingness of the old king to ally himself with Raleigh's colonial venture, the two parted as close friends. Raleigh was to proceed with his explorations, and Topiawari would confer with the neighboring provinces and have an answer for Raleigh on his return.

The coming of the rainy season and the consequent swelling of the Orinoco and its tributaries cut short the explorations which Raleigh hoped to accomplish. The fabled mine on which the hopes of the expedition rested was always reported in the lands beyond. From Morequito to the river Caroni they heard tales of gold in the villages ahead, but none was found. Yet in spite of the urgency of their return to their base in Trinidad, the cortege stopped off a second time at the port of Morequito.[33]

> As soon as I came to ancor I sent away one for old Topiawari, with whom I much desired to haue farther conference, & also to deal with him for some one of his countrey, to bring with vs into England, as well to learne the language, as to conferre withall by the way.

Within three hours of receiving Raleigh's message, Topiawari was at his side, "and with him such a rabble of all sortes of people, and euery one loden with somewhat, as if it had beene a great market or faire in England."[34] Raleigh, Topiawari, and a translator retired to Raleigh's tent to discuss strategy.

Raleigh was reluctant to leave Guiana without the Inca gold which Topiawari assured him was not too distant. But Topiawari urged caution: the season was late and travel difficult; Raleigh's forces were too small to wage war and at the same time protect the natives; time did not permit mustering all the Indian nations to fight the Spaniards. Though Topiawari himself would probably not live for another year, discretion urged deferring the all-out assault until the better season of the next year, when Raleigh could furnish a stronger force and Topiawari would have united the natives to augment his numbers. Raleigh then gave Topiawari, and his chiefs some "of the new money of 20. shillings with her Maiesties picture to wear."[35] In return, Topiawari gave his solemn pledge that "the principallest of those prouinces [would] become seruauntes to her Maiestie, and to resist the Spanyardes, if they made any attempt in our absence." Agreement reached on this strategy,[36]

> he freely gaue me his onelie sonne to take with me into England, and hoped, that though he himselfe had but a short tyme to liue, yet by that meanes his sonne shoulde be established after his death: and I left with him one *Frauncis Sparrow*, a seruant of captaine *Gifford*, (who was

desirous to tarry, and could describe a cuntrey with his pen) and a boy
of mine called *Hugh Goodwin*, to learne the language.

On every stop on the journey down the swollen river, Raleigh found welcome
from the native chiefs. Word of the great Queen and her rich emissary and
of their approval by Topiawari had spread throughout the land. More and more
Raleigh had become convinced that Elizabeth's empire could well embrace the
lands of the south of America and the wealth which had hitherto gone to her
Spanish enemy.

Raleigh was pleased with his future prospects, but unhappy about his failure
to find gold. Leaving Trinidad he planned to visit the site of his Virginia colonies,
but on the way decided to exercise the authority of his charter by raiding some
of the Spanish towns to return some profit for his investors and himself. Raleigh
claimed success, but reliable Spanish sources indicate that he was driven off with
heavy losses. Raleigh himself conceded that he buried Captain Whiddon on
Trinidad, and that he failed to collect the ransom he demanded for his captives,
Alvaro Jorge and Antonio de Berreo. Even the fond hope of setting foot on
Roanoke and seeing the Chesapeake was denied Raleigh, as he complained, "the
extremity of weather forced me from the coast."[37] His small fleet was forced
to turn back to England, where it arrived in August, six months after departure.

Raleigh's empty-handed return to England aroused the anger of the few
supporters he had. Many even doubted that he had been to America at all, accusing
him of hiding out in Devon or lolling on the Barbary coast and purchasing
samples of ore while his vessels sailed without him. Even the Queen seemed
unmoved by his accounts of her American popularity. Indignant, and sincere
in his firm belief of an American Elizabethan colony, Raleigh wrote his account
of *The Discoverie* which, partly because of fancied accounts of the Amazons and
Anthropophagi (in which Raleigh truly believed), became an immediate success,
going through a second edition before 1596 was out.

Raleigh took seriously his pledge to Topiawari and the other *casiques* to return
with military and naval support for the building of the new Elizabethan empire.
But first, he realized, he must locate a channel through the shallow deltas of
the Orinoco and Amazon to accommodate ships of greater draft. Though few
backers would support his venture, he continued to muster his own resources.
Less than seven months after his return, in January 1596, Lawrence Keymis,
in the *Darling of London*, followed by the pinnace *Discovery*, set sail on this new
mission, hoping to take advantage of more propitious weather in the lands of
the equator. The story of this mission was also published by Keymis under the
title *A Relation of the second Voyage to Guiana. Perfourmed and written in the yeare
1596. By Lawrence Keymis, Gent.*[38]

On this third voyage, again, the ocean crossing was made in foul weather;
it was mid-March before the *Darling* reached the coast of Guiana and the pinnace
did not arrive at all. For twenty-three days Keymis and his crew cruised the

delta, charting the coast and entrances and seeking a deep-channel entrance. On April 6 they discovered a channel and sailed their ship directly into the Orinoco mainstream, which Keymis renamed Raleana for his patron. All along the way, Keymis reported, the natives rushed to greet them, thinking they brought the reinforcements promised by Raleigh to defeat their Spanish oppressors.

From two *casiques*—Anawra and Aparwa—Keymis learned of developments during the past year. Topiawari had died and his only son (now christened Gualtero after Sir Walter) would be king on his return from England. In his absence, the tribes had gone into hiding to escape Spanish persecution. Meanwhile, the Spanish reinforcements under Berreo's son had overrun the entire area surrounding the Caroni River, bringing not only soldiers to strengthen their positions, but more than 600 colonists to establish permanent communities along the river, and sixty Negro slaves to work the mines.

In his larger vessels, it took Keymis just eight days to reach the juncture with the Caroni where the mine was supposed to be. But here again his plans were foiled. During the year, Berreo's son had built a fort and garrison there, effectively blocking entrance to what Berreo (as well as Raleigh and Keymis) believed to be the source of Inca gold. Unable to reach the mine, the disappointed Keymis had sailed back to the open sea. There he found the *Discovery* had arrived in such foul shape that he had to burn it to keep it from the Spaniards. On his return voyage, though he hoped to seize some Spanish prizes or at least to purchase some tobacco to recoup their investment, he failed to find either, and reached England empty handed.

Keymis' report to Raleigh of his failure to return gold, ore, or even the location of the gold mine, sounded the death knell for Raleigh's hopes to establish a Guiana empire under the aegis of his queen. The Queen was more concerned about the massing of Spanish warships in the harbor of Cadiz than the tribulations of a few primitive Indians on the Orinoco. Sir Robert Cecil wanted more from his investments than political promises and a few doubtful rocks. And the London merchants found it more profitable to raid Spanish shipping—to steal the gold the Spaniards had stolen from the Indians—than to extract wealth by hard labor. England was not ready for Sir Walter's dreams of empire. Although the day of empire was close at hand, it was not to dawn under the aegis of the Virgin Queen.

Raleigh had little real pleasure for the rest of his life. England was still sparring with Spain for control of the seas, and Raleigh was much preoccupied in naval activities. When a great fleet was raised to assault the port of Cadiz in June 1596, Raleigh, in command of his new two-decked warship *Warspite*, proved himself to be the hero of the occasion. It was the Earl of Essex, however, who took the fancy of the people. The Queen disappointed Raleigh by seizing the rewards for her own purse; badly wounded in battle, he complained, "What the Generals have gotten, I know least; they protest it is little. For my part

I have gotten a lame leg and a deformed. . . . I have possession of naught but poverty and pain."[39]

The next year, however, as payment for his loyalty, the Queen restored Sir Walter to his position of Captain of the Queen's Guards. By now, however, he was no longer a romantic favorite (that position was held by Essex), but an old and trusted friend and counselor of the court who was only able to send occasional vessels to seek for his lost colonists. The execution of Essex following his attempt to take over the throne, however, brought Raleigh into great disfavor with the masses. As Captain of the Queen's Guard he had been forced to attend the execution of his friend, and the people were inclined to blame him for the downfall of their favorite and booed him when he appeared.

The accession of James VI of Scotland as James I of England brought Raleigh's final degradation. Before the first year of James's reign was out, Raleigh had been stripped of all offices and sources of income, had lost his estates, and, on trumped-up charges had been convicted of treason and thrown in the Tower, his very life subject to the "pleasure" of the King. Two rooms in "The Bloody Tower" were his home for the rest of his life.

V. T. Harlow, the most assiduous scholar of his Guiana ventures, concluded that "the idea that dominated Raleigh's mind for the last thirty years of his life was the complete destruction of Spanish power in South America and the establishment of an English empire in its place."[40] He filled his Tower hours in writing his monumental *History of the World*, the most widely read book of the seventeenth century, but his major concern was for his own release and the establishment of an estate for his wife and son Walter. The Spanish gold which had earlier eluded him might still accomplish this. Raleigh deluged James with plans to wrest the riches of Guiana away from the Spaniards, and James (though he did still not trust Raleigh) was intrigued with the thought of quick and easy riches. On 16 March 1616, after holding him imprisoned for more than a dozen years, James, over the objections of the Spanish Ambassador, granted Raleigh a release from prison to prepare for another expedition to Guiana. This commission was issued under the privy seal instead of the royal seal, however, changed "trusty and well-beloved" into "under peril of the law," and included injunctions against harming any Spaniard who might be encountered.[41] The King was to receive all taxes and duties on everything Raleigh brought back, including one fifth of all gold, silver, and ores. And, hard to believe, to counter the objections of the Spanish Ambassador, Gondomar, James secretly agreed to reveal to him complete information about Raleigh's plans, ships, men, armaments, and schedules. In short, James was giving the expedition the kiss of death in advance.

Raleigh's second voyage to Guiana is almost too tragic to recount. Even after thirteen years of disfavor and imprisonment, Raleigh was able to raise nearly 30,000 pounds for the venture. A 500-ton warship, appropriately named the

Destiny, was built and outfitted as flagship to a fleet listed as six warships and one pinnace totalling 1,215 tons and carrying 431 men and 121 pieces of ordnance. But nothing went right. Adverse winds forced the fleet back to port on its first attempt to sail. The same thing happened the second time. On the third a gale drove them past the Scilly islands and sank their pinnace. Winds, high seas, and spoiled foods caused much illness. Sir Walter was seasick before he lost the sight of land. In the Canaries they were mistaken for Barbary pirates and fired upon with some loss of life. And on the way to Guiana the men were struck by raging fevers and put completely out of action. Raleigh wrote his wife that he "suffered the most violent [tropical fever] for fifteen days that ever man did and lived."[42] His ship lost forty-two men, including his military commander, chief lieutenant, master surgeon, master refiner, provost marshal, the governor of the Bermudas, and two personal servants. Their bodies were cast overboard without ceremony.

By the time they reached Trinidad it had become obvious that neither Sir Walter nor his kinsman, Sir Warham St. Leger, was well enough to lead the expedition. A reorganization was made: Lawrence Keymis was to lead the party; George Raleigh, a nephew, was to be sergeant-major, and Walter Raleigh, his son and heir, one of his captains. Using force only for self-defense, they were to proceed to the Caroni River to locate the mine, to bring back as much of the richest ore as they could carry, most of which would go to James as ransom. Raleigh was to wait near the Orinoco delta for the return of his mission.

Just what went wrong is not clear. For some inexplicable reason, Keymis, instead of stealing past the Spanish fort of St. Thome in darkness to reach the entrance to the Caroni as had been planned, landed his forces on the south bank a few miles before reaching the town and anchored opposite the fort, remaining just out of range of the Spaniards. His soldiers, uncertain what to do, were settling for the night when they were attacked. Rallying his troops, young Walter ("Wat") Raleigh, rushed into the fray. A single shot rang out, and Raleigh's heir fell dead, because (as an eye witness wrote) of "his unadvised daringness."

The fiasco continued. Keymis made a half-hearted attempt to ascend the Caroni, but snipers from the shore continued to kill his men. Finally, after twenty-nine days, they returned to St. Thome, carrying white flags, but were fired upon. With only 150 men of his original 400 remaining, Keymis burned the city and turned downstream to face Sir Walter with the news of the death of his son and the end of his hopes for freedom.

Raleigh had more sorrows than he could bear. The death of young Wat meant the end of his dreams of family, fame, and fortune. In his bitterness he upbraided Keymis, who, having told his tragic tale, retired to his cabin and shot himself. The ill Raleigh was half mad with pain and grief as he wrote a final letter from Trinidad:[43]

What shall become of me now, I know not: I am unpardoned in England, and my poor estate consumed; and whether any other Prince or State will give me bread, I know not.

Seven months later, after long negotiations with Spain as to which nation should punish the grievous sinner Raleigh, King James withdrew his "pleasure" and the original punishment of 1603 was to be meted to the old knight. But again the soft heart of James mitigated the punishment. Raleigh was not be hanged, drawn, and quartered: he was to have a nobler punishment—beheading. So on 28 October 1618 Raleigh went to the scaffold where he played out his last act: Raleigh the man was dead; Raleigh the legend was born.[44]

Following his execution, a foolscap sheet was found in Raleigh's Bible, apparently written on the night before his death.[45] The first six lines were a slightly revised portion of a love poem he had written in his happier youth, while he was favored by his Queen:

> Even such is Time who takes in trust
> Our youth, our joys, and all we have,
> And pays us but with earth and dust:
> Who in the dark and silent grave,
> When we have wandered all our ways,
> Shuts up the stories of our days.

To these Sir Walter had added a final couplet:

> But from that earth, that grave, that dust,
> The Lord shall raise me up, I trust.

Notes

*Harry L. Watson, associate professor of history at the University of North Carolina at Chapel Hill, introduced John W. Shirley as follows: "Like our principal subject, Walter Raleigh himself, John W. Shirley has distinguished himself as a renaissance man. His undergraduate training lay in the widely separated fields of literature and physics and he has continued to excell in the scientific and humanistic fields ever since, with a disdain for narrow specialization which has been most unfashionable in the twentieth century. He first taught English for five years at Michigan State University. With the outbreak of World War II, he deftly shifted to a stint in the Physics Department. After further experience teaching the history of science at Cal Tech and English once more, he joined the administration of North Carolina State University. From 1962 to 1974, he served as H. Fletcher Brown professor in the history of science at the University of Delaware, as well as provost and vice president for academic affairs there, and acting president of the university in 1967 and 1968.

"Retiring from those positions in 1974, John Shirley's real career—for our purposes—took off. In the thirteen years of his retirement, he has published five books on Renaissance men of science, including *Thomas Harriot, A Biography* and *Sir Walter Ralegh and the New World*. He has been honored with a Guggenheim fellowship, a medal from the University of Delaware, and two honorary degrees. His topic today is 'American Colonization Through Raleigh's Eyes.'"

[1]Much of this paper is based on the pamphlet written by the author for America's Four Hundredth Anniversary Committee, *Sir Walter Ralegh and the New World* (Raleigh: North Carolina Department of Cultural Resources, 1985). The most valuable work on this subject is still David B. Quinn's *Raleigh and the British Empire* (London: 1947, 1962, 1973). Also interesting is the Penguin Book edition of Andrew Sinclair's *Sir Walter Raleigh and the Age of Discovery* (Harmondsworth: 1984).

[2]See A.L. Rowse, *Sir Walter Ralegh, His Family and Private Life* (New York: Harper and Brothers, 1962).

[3]William Gilbert Gosling, *The Life of Sir Humphrey Gilbert: England's First Empire Builder* (Originally published, 1911: reprint Westport, Conn.: Greenwood Press, 1970). pp. 148–50. According to Quinn, this ship was in very bad condition and had been sold.

[4]See the old but still standard work by Edward Edwards, *The Life of Sir Walter Raleigh, Based on Contemporary Documents*, (London: Macmillan, 2 vols., 1868). For Raleigh's Irish service, see vol. II, chapter 3, pp. 35–47.

[5]John Aubrey, *Brief Lives Chiefly of Contemporaries, Set Down by John Aubrey, Between the Years 1669 and 1696*, edited by Andrew Clark (Oxford: University Press, 2 vols., 1898. This from II, p. 180.

[6]David B. Quinn, "Stephen Parmenius of Buda, The First Hungarian in North America," *New Hungarian Quarterly*, 14 (1974): 152–57.

[7]John W. Shirley, *Thomas Harriot: a Biography* (Oxford: Clarendon Press, 1983), pp. 105–7.

[8]The first-hand account of this voyage by Captain Edward Haies is given in Gosling's *Life of Sir Humphrey Gilbert*, pp. 223–71.

[9]Jon V. Pepper, "Harriot's Earlier Work on Mathematical Navigation: Theory and Practice," in John W. Shirley (ed.), *Thomas Harriot, Renaissance Scientist* (Oxford, Clarendon Press, 1974), pp. 54–90.

[10]A full bibliography of the publications of David B. Quinn up to mid-1976 is included in *The Westward Enterprise: English Activities in Ireland, the Atlantic, and America 1480–1650*, edited by K.R. Andrews, N.P. Canny, and P.E.H. Hair (Detroit: Wayne State University Press, 1979), pp. 303–9. Most important for this study are *The Roanoke Voyages, 1584–90* (London: The Hakluyt Society, 2 vols. 1955); *Virginia Voyages from Hakluyt* (with Alison M. Quinn) (London: Oxford University Press, 1973); *North America from Earliest Discovery to First Settlements, The Norse Voyages to 1612* (New York: Harper & Row, 1975); and *Set Fair for Roanoke, Voyages and Colonies, 1584–1606* (Chapel Hill: University of North Carolina Press, 1985).

[11]This was originally published in 1935 by E.G.R. Taylor in *The Original Writings and Correspondence of the Two Richard Hakluyts* (London: The Hakluyt Society, 1938), Document 46, vol. 2, pp. 211–326.

[12]*Ibid.*, p. 215.

[13]*Ibid.*, p. 239.

[14]*Ibid.*, p. 259.

[15]*Ibid.*, pp. 257–58.

[16]What is known and reasonably surmised about all the Roanoke colonies may be found in detail in Quinn, *Set Fair for Roanoke*.

[17]Quinn, *Set Fair for Roanoke*, pp. 295–97.

[18]Sir Robert Naunton, *Fragmenta Regalia, or, Observations on Queen Elizabeth, her Times & Favorites*, John S. Cerovski (ed.), (Washington: The Folger Shakespeare Library, 1985), p. 71.

[19]Raleigh's two voyages to South Ameria and the Spanish documents relating to them are fully covered in two volumes by V.T. Harlow: *The Discoverie of the large and bewtifull Empire of Guiana by Sir Walter Raleigh* (London: The Argonaut Press, 1928); and *Ralegh's Last Voyage, Being an account drawn out of contemporary letters and relations, both Spanish and English, of which the most part are now for the first time made public, concerning the voyage of Sir Walter Ralegh, knight, to Guiana in the year 1617 and the fatal consequences of the same* (London: The Argonaut Press, 1932).

[20]Quotations from this work are from the facsimile edition published by Theatrvm Orbis Terrarvm (Amsterdam and New York: 1968). The facsimile retains the original pagination.

[21]*Ibid.*, p. 4.

[22]*Ibid.*, pp. 4–5.

[23]*Ibid.*, p. 6.

[24]*Ibid.*, pp. 6–7.

[25]*Ibid.*, pp. 8–9.

[26]*Ibid.*, p. 67.

[27]*Ibid.*, pp. 67–68.

[28]*Ibid.*, p. 7.

[29]*Ibid.*, p. 7.

[30]*Ibid.*, p. 33.

[31]*Ibid.*, p. 61.

[32]*Ibid.*, p. 62.

[33]*Ibid.*, p. 74.

[34]*Idem.*

[35]*Ibid.*, p. 81.

[36]*Ibid.*, p. 80.

[37]*Ibid.*, p. 5.

[38]This work has also been published in facsimile as number 65 of "The English Experience" by Theatrvm Orbis Terrarvm (Amsterdam: 1968).

[39]Edwards, *Life of Ralegh*, vol. II, letter LXIX, 156.

[40]*Ralegh's Last Voyage*, 1.

[41]Robert Lacey, *Sir Walter Ralegh* (New York: Atheneum, 1974), p. 344.

[42]Edwards, *Letters*, Letter CLIII, II, 147.

[43]Edwards, *Letters*, Letter CLIV, II, 356.

[44]Thomas Harriot was present at Raleigh's execution; see John W. Shirley, *Thomas Harriot, a Biography*, pp. 443–49.

[45]Aubrey, *Brief Lives*, II, p. 190.

Harry L. Watson (top), associate professsor at UNC-CH, introduced John W. Shirley (bottom right) and Karen Ordahl Kupperman. They spoke respectively on "American Colonization through Raleigh's Eyes" and "Raleigh's Dream of Empire."

Raleigh's Dream of Empire
and Its Seventeenth-Century Career

*Karen Ordahl Kupperman**

Sir Walter Raleigh's plans for a great British empire in America actually encompassed all the elements that would make future colonies succeed. His plans also included all the seeds of failure. Colonial strategists were engaged, for almost three-quarters of a century following Raleigh's pioneering ventures at Roanoke, in attempting to part the strands, to separate the ingredients of success from those of failure. Their inability easily to distinguish the two led to many trials and much suffering; but Raleigh's vision also gave promoters and colonists such hope for future accomplishments that the early feeble plantations were sustained over their rocky beginnings.

Raleigh himself came to be a great symbol to later proponents of empire, but, because his legacy was so ambiguous, he was taken to stand for different goals by each group that honored him. Before the Elizabethan inheritance could be put in proper perspective, promoters had to decide what the British empire should accomplish. Goals and means to goals had to be clearly delineated.

When England first turned its colonial sights from nearby Ireland to America in the 1580s, goals for a British empire were well-known but vague. First and foremost, England, as the leader of the Protestant nations, sought to defy the Spanish superpower, to cut off the Indian gold that fed Spain's campaign to force the return of European Protestants to Roman Catholicism. The second set of goals followed naturally from the first: ventures in America would build the English nation's wealth and honor, would raise England from a backward little country on the fringe of Europe to great nation status.

Finally, promoters looked for personal enrichment and aggrandizement from overseas adventures. Great hopes of fabled wealth were translated into the assumption that rightly conducted expeditions would return groaning under a load of gold and rich commodities. Such expectations were crucial because Queen Elizabeth, while keeping control of foreign policy in her own hands, conducted it through the ventures of private men. When relations with Spain ruptured into open war in the middle of the 1580s, the Queen opened the door to privateering, privately financed attacks on the Spanish treasure fleet as it made its slow, clumsy way from Havana to Seville. English with money to spare invested it in small fleets sent out in hopes that they might detach one of the great treasure ships from its escort and return vast profits to the investors. Even capture of much smaller independent ships loaded with cargos of cochineal or hides could make a venture worthwhile.

Those who invested did so out of a desire to enhance England's status while striking at Spain, but the chance for gain was crucial: no investments would have taken place without that incentive. Elizabeth knew this; it was the key to her strategy. The government encouraged such ventures but did not formally fund them. However, through the grant of monopolies to royal favorites such as Raleigh, Queen Elizabeth in effect redistributed the nation's resources. By allowing men she trusted to control and derive income from key import and manufacturing sectors, the Queen made possible the concentration of resources in the hands of those who would use them for great projects. She chose wisely in Raleigh.

Raleigh was prepared to reinvest the wealth produced by the vast estates and monopolies of everything from the importation of sweet wines to the mining and processing of tin in Cornwall showered on him by the Queen in the country's and his own interest. He argued that an American base to which privateers could come for repairs and victualling would prolong the season for preying on Spain's far-flung and ill-protected empire, weakening the enemy and enhancing England's power at the same time. Thus the idea for a settlement at Roanoke was born.

When models were sought for such a colony, it was natural to reach for the idea of a military outpost, able to defend itself against both Spanish and Indian enemies and knowledgeable about the needs of the privateers. Military expeditions had been sent to Ireland and to the continent, and that familiar model seemed appropriate. Such a force could also reasonably be expected to conduct reconnoitering expeditions into the interior in search of precious minerals and even the hoped-for passage through the continent to the Pacific. If sources of wealth within English-American territory were discovered and added to that to be derived from attacking the Spanish, then a great British Empire might quickly become a reality.

There was only one problem with this model: it could not succeed. Later experience proved conclusively that military outposts always failed, and the reasons now seem obvious. Colonists could not be completely dependent on a lifeline to Europe. It was just too risky; as the events of the Armada year and the desertion of the last Roanoke colony showed, events at home or the financial reverses of investors, not to mention the difficulties of Atlantic travel, all could leave colonists stranded. Plantations must be self-sustaining if they were to survive, and this meant that settlers must come expecting to devote themselves to providing food, shelter, and supplies for the colony.

So, investors must not expect colonists to return valuable commodities to England for some time; they must even expect to put in money over many years without such a return because no colony could become completely self-sufficient. In the event, promoters found that the privateering war of the 1590s went very well without a base such as had been planned at Roanoke. English ships were able to spend long periods in the West Indies and did not need access to an English station for relief.[1] As long as the main goals of English American expeditions remained hit and run attacks on Spanish territory and the wealth they brought in, colonies were an expensive irrelevance.

Most of the Elizabethans were content to restrict English activities to such patriotic piracy, but Raleigh's vision was much more complex and farseeing. In the final attempt to found a colony at Roanoke under his monopoly patent, he and his associates completely restructured the venture. Though this set of colonists was abandoned and therefore "lost," the 1587 Roanoke plantation had all the design elements of a successful settlement. Seventeenth-century promoters finally returned to this model after prolonged and repeated failures. Though Jamestown was founded just twenty years after the final Roanoke colony, a decade of failure would intervene before the new Virginia colony gave up the fatally flawed military outpost model and moved to introduce private ownership of land and the family life that made such property rights meaningful. Plymouth Colony in New England, founded near the time of this transition, followed the correct plan from the beginning, as did all mainland English colonies from this time forward.

What were the ingredients of a successful colony that can be seen in plans for the 1587 City of Raleigh? In the first place, it was sponsored by a small corporation, the institution which, in future colonies, would provide the consistency of support impossible for a single individual. Settlers were recruited as families, and the lure of freehold estates in land, as much as 500 acres, was held out to them. No colony made up exclusively of young men ever sustained itself; the military outpost form implied rotation back to the home country. Only the presence of women and children led to that permanent commitment without which success was always elusive, and only private property in land would attract the kind of substantial and hard-working families who could endure the isolation and uncertainty and build a replica of English society in America.

Most important of all, the plans for the City of Raleigh meant a wholly new concept of what colonies were to accomplish for England. Though Raleigh's interest in the privateering war continued, he demonstrated his understanding that the real future of English America lay in a long-term commitment, and the painstaking construction of a new polity on American shores. Implicitly the City of Raleigh plans acknowledged that the search for gold, and swashbuckling adventures such as Raleigh was still to seek in Guiana, were only one model and much less solid for the long run. El Dorado might exist, and he devoutly hoped so, but the City of Raleigh was to exist in fact.

This element had always been present in Raleigh's thinking, as can be seen in his sending John White and Thomas Hariot to Roanoke to document the economic possibilities of the area. Hariot's *Briefe and True Report of the New Found Land of Virginia* (1588) emphasized that America was a land filled with economic resources, but he spotlighted humble commodities for development rather than rich prizes to be picked up and carried home by soldiers. His report made clear that only through a long process of settlement and experimentation could a colony reach an acceptable stage of productivity. Once that stage was reached, the products would be items of importance to the English economy, dyes and fibers for the textile industry or wood for the timber-poor country, but not glamorous or intrinsically valuable commodities. Mundane goods produced by ordinary people would be the wave of the future.[2]

Raleigh's vision thus held two lines of thought about the future of English America. On the one hand he believed to his last day that there was gold for England in the New World and that bold strokes and daring adventures would uncover it. In these exploits the English David would confront the Spanish Goliath, "the sword of that Antichrist of Rome,"[3] and, by crippling the flow of gold to Hapsburg coffers, protect beleaguered Protestants everywhere. Personal aggrandizement, patriotism, and religious nationalism all worked together in the grand scheme. This was not a game for the faint of heart; only the daring would win.

But at the same time Raleigh looked to development of true colonies, settlements of English men and women working toward self-sufficiency, who would contribute to the growth of a very different British Empire, one founded on world trade in basic commodities. Whereas the first line of thought involved enormous waste both of lives and money, expenditure that would be repaid only when and if the big strike occurred, the second required investment of labor, skills and lives on a very different level. These two traditions were compatible in Raleigh's mind. Even though he had moved to the second model with the 1587 colony, there is evidence that he still hoped to found a privateering base on the coast. And his first voyage to Guiana in search of gold and in defiance of Spain was to occur in the next decade.

The plain fact is that the two approaches to an American empire were never compatible. In the seventeenth century promoters and colonists would unravel the two strands that Raleigh had twisted together and would eventually understand that each blocked the realization of the other goal. This should have been apparent even in the sixteenth century; the expectations built by Roanoke's origins in the privateering war led to actions that destroyed the chances of the 1587 plantation.[4] The writings of John White, governor of that "lost" colony, are filled with his anguish as he related how the ships carrying the settlers, and later vessels that went to find them, diverted from course time and again for privateering opportunities. And of course, the settlement would not have been abandoned had it not been for the threat of the Spanish Armada, itself an attempt to cut off English privateering at its source.[5]

Clarity about goals and means would not be won so easily. Anyone could see that Roanoke had failed twice with two different models; it would have taken unusual insight to see that one model was always doomed to failure and the other would ultimately be the key to success. The Virginia Companies, founding their colonies just two decades after the last Roanoke colonists were left in America, did not possess extraordinary insight. It must have been galling to Raleigh as he watched from his prison in the Tower of London the suffering and defeats of the new Virginia colonies.

Raleigh's exclusive right to control colonization in Virginia, as all of North America's east coast was then known, lapsed with his arrest. New, more limited, patents were issued to two Virginia companies in 1606. The western merchants' company, headquartered in Bristol, was to sponsor colonization in the "North Part" of Virginia, sometimes called Norembega and later New England, and the London company was to found a settlement in Chesapeake Bay, the ideal location discovered by an exploring venture from Roanoke.

Both these colonies repeated the mistakes of Roanoke. Each was planned as a military outpost and neither, therefore, benefited from clear notions of how the colony would serve England. Jamestown's planners had learned one significant lesson: this venture was backed by a joint-stock company of massive proportions. Shares were sold throughout the country and patriots invested, thus guaranteeing a level and continuity of support Raleigh could never have supplied. But they returned to the military outpost model with its assumption that all colonists worked for the company and would be rotated home eventually. Raleigh himself, with his taint of treason, was not consulted by the new colony's designers. Thomas Hariot, the greatest English expert on America and its resources, appeared before a meeting of the Council for Virginia in London to answer questions, and his book was read avidly, but apparently there was no attempt to include him systematically in the planning process.[6]

The outpouring of support for the Jamestown colony reflected patriotic frustration over the pacifist policies of the new king, James I, first of the Stuart line. At his accession James, determined to avoid that most expensive of early modern projects, war, brought privateering to a screeching halt. Saddled with a king who seemed determined to conciliate rather than confront Spain, English patriots sought to defy the national enemy in the one way that remained open: the settlement of a colony that would forever preclude Spanish expansion northward from the Florida peninsula.

But Virginia Company planners, ignoring the lessons of Roanoke, commanded their emissaries to find gold, and quickly. As they sought sources of gold up the mighty rivers that flowed into Chesapeake Bay, the explorers were also to find the passage through the American continent to the riches of the East. No one doubted that such a passage existed, and no one had any idea of the extent of the continent. The Virginia settlers spent the crucial first weeks on such searches rather than preparing for independent life over the winter. John Smith's scorn still resounds as he wrote of the "gilded refiners with their golden promises,

[who] made all men their slaves in hope of recompence; there was no talke, no hope, no worke, but dig gold, wash gold, refine gold, load gold. . . ." As a result, Smith and the few other experienced men saw "all necessarie businesse neglected, to fraught such a drunken ship with so much gilded durt."[7] And in that first winter, unusually severe even for the Little Ice Age of the sixteenth and seventeenth centuries, the little colony saw the deaths of two thirds of its members.

Nothing so clearly shows the muddle-headedness of the outpost's leaders as their neglect of the third charge in their commission: to search for "them there left by Sir Walter Raleigh." The settlers must have realized that these immigrants of twenty years' experience could have provided invaluable aid to the new venture. Though they heard various rumors of people clothed like Europeans whose skills made them valuable to the villages in which they lived, small and belated efforts were made to find the Roanoke remnant, and the idea that they were all dead was readily accepted. All the colonists' energies went into the search for immediate profits; as they had little left to construct a viable town, they also spared few for such a vague and possibly fruitless search.[8]

Meanwhile the equally small Bristol merchants' settlement at Sagadahoc in Maine experienced that severe winter in discouragement so great that the colonists returned to England in less than a year. The reasons for that failure are complex, but at heart the problem lay in the western merchants' inability to provide the level and continuity of support such a venture required. Dashed hopes for commodities, built by summer-only ventures whose reports on the New England environment had been very favorable, made the task of attracting investors all but impossible. Sagadahoc was too far from the Caribbean to provide a base from which Spanish ships could be attacked if a new twist in foreign policy should make that possible. Nor did its cold climate and rocky shores hold out much hope for rich commodities. New England settlements would never be attractive until the goals for British America were clarified. Once again, the problem centered on deciding what colonies were to be for.[9]

Sagadahoc was allowed to die, but Jamestown, though its career had been as wretched, was the object of a renewed effort to attract investors and continued royal support. Preachers made an English presence in America a Protestant crusade and hopes were rekindled. Softness in government and lack of a critical mass were diagnosed as the causes of failure. The fresh charter of 1609 made possible a new government and a large fleet filled with colonists. One positive benefit was lost in the new plans: the presence of John Smith, who was pushed out of the presidency and the colony by his antagonists, now reinforced from London.

John Smith's career in America was essentially over; one brief reconnaissance in New England in 1614 was his only contact here after he left Virginia. What the colonies lost in leadership, the empire gained in his new role as theorist and publicist. As he wrote he developed his notions, implicit in his earliest writings, of what the British Empire should be into a mature plan for England's future. Though he and Raleigh could not have been more different in their origins and style, in many ways Smith became the Raleigh of the early Stuart period. He fought for his vision of a great English nation just as Raleigh had done, and he combined writing and action to create a powerful case and a degree of authority few could approach.

At first glance Raleigh and Smith could not seem more dissimilar. We think of Sir Walter as the witty favorite at the glittering Elizabethan court, his great pearl earring his trademark, while plain John Smith was the son of a yeoman farmer whose aspirations for his son reached only to the status of a provincial merchant. Raleigh was educated at Oxford and the Inns of Court; Smith was lucky to receive a grammar school education.

But in some ways the differences are apparent only. Both men went off to the European wars of religion, the university of war as Smith called it, at about fourteen or fifteen; it was a brutal transition to adult life. Though Raleigh returned to attend the universities, both men were largely self-taught through their reading, and, though at different stages of life, through their membership in literary circles in the capital. Raleigh had a distinguished family name, but neither man inherited wealth; each had to make his own way to fame. And, for both the path to renown was self-advertisement and advocacy of a vigorous imperial policy.

When we think of John Smith, his denunciations of the effete gentlemen who fell apart in the hardships of Jamestown, where "a plaine Souldier that can use a Pick-axe and spade, is better than five Knights," always come to mind. But would he not have included Raleigh in his argument that "discovering things unknowne" and adding a new kingdom to "our Native mother-countrie" was a role for "men that have great spirits, and smal meanes"? His scorn was reserved for those "descended nobly" who consumed their substance idly, not returning service for the honors and wealth they inherited.[10]

The real difference between the two imperialists from our point of view lies in the single-mindedness of Smith. Whereas Raleigh at the height of his power presided over manifold schemes, including competing colonies in Ireland, and the division of his attention contributed to the abandonment of the Roanoke colony, Smith devoted himself exclusively and tirelessly to the promotion of a British empire in America. Smith called Virginia and New England his children, "for they have bin my wife, my hawks, my hounds, my cards, my dice, and in totall my best content."[11]

Other men claimed the mantle of the great Elizabethans. These were, like Raleigh, great gentlemen and aristocrats, grandees for whom direction of national policy was a natural role. Men such as Robert Rich, Earl of Warwick, and his cousin and man of business Sir Nathaniel Rich; William Fiennes, first

Viscount Saye and Sele; Robert Greville, Lord Brooke; Edward Montague, Lord Mandeville and the Civil War Earl of Manchester; Sir Thomas Barington; Sir Benjamin Rudyerd; and John Pym would have expected in normal times to be close advisors of the government. In the increasingly polarized English political situation of the 1620s and 1630s, however, these Puritan lords and gentlemen found themselves frozen out. They saw England, the Elect Nation, turning its back on the cause of true religion as the Hapsburg war machine fought to re-establish Roman Catholicism in reformed states. When Charles I and Buckingham were pushed to aid the Protestant cause in Europe, the expeditions were so poorly planned and mounted that they accomplished little except humiliation; accumulations of troops in England led to suspicion that the government's goal was to harry the English into an unwelcome Arminian religious settlement leading ultimately to restoration of Roman Catholicism.

Religious and political causes were seen as intertwined; popery and tyranny were two sides of the same coin. These grandees, as Puritans, were viewed with suspicion by a monarch and his advisors who saw them as a potentially hostile force and who denied them the leadership role they saw as theirs by right. In the civil war of the 1640s these Puritan lords and gentlemen would take up that position; in the 1620s and 1630s they put their energies into encouraging colonization and, where possible, into Elizabethan-style privateering attacks on Spanish ships.[12]

Raleigh, executed to conciliate the king of Spain in 1618, was claimed as a symbol by these men. John Pym, the acknowledged leader of the Parliament during the early years of civil war, recorded his impressions of Raleigh's execution in his manuscript of *Memorable Accidents:* "A.D. 1618. Sir Walter Raleigh 'had the favour to be beheaded at Westminister, where he died with great applause of the beholders, most constantly, most Christianly, most religiously.'" Pym's speeches, like those of most in his circle, show the powerful influence of Raleigh's writings.[13] They kept alive his aggressive anti-Spanish policies and his dream of a glorious British empire in America. Some of them were involved in the Virginia Company and oversaw the splitting off of the Somers Islands or Bermuda Company as a separate entity which they largely controlled. In 1630 they founded their own colony, sponsored by a company whose membership was forever to be restricted to a handful of great men, on Providence Island off the coast of Nicaragua. This plantation was expected to develop commodities of value, but privateering was clearly a primary goal from the very beginning. They were to be the Raleighs of the mid-seventeenth century.

How can both John Smith and the Puritan grandees be the heirs of the Elizabethan tradition? The answer is that the contradictory strands of Raleigh's policies were untwisted in the seventeenth century; Smith took up one aspect of Raleigh's thinking, and the lords and gentlemen made the other their own. The Puritan grandees seem the obvious inheritors of the Elizabethan tradition.

Though they lacked the patronage of the court, they had the necessary style. Their social and political positions gave them the self-confidence, their educations the vision, of a Raleigh. They willingly took up his brief in the 1620s and 1630; in their minds as in the previous generation's, national greatness and defiance of Spain were irresistably bound together with American empire. As long as the monarchy turned its back on these historic aims England was doomed to a secondary status among the nations of Europe. If the light of true religion were allowed to go out on the continent, then God might withdraw his election of England. They wanted nothing less than that the nation live up to its responsibilities.

Their goal was a government that would, as in the days of Elizabeth, take up the leadership role natural to a country preeminent among Protestant nations. When faced with Stuart intransigence, they determined to do what they could and to bide their time until the government came to its senses. Though their attention ultimately was on Europe, they, like Raleigh, saw the New World as crucial to their campaign. American gold fueled the vast Hapsburg bureaucracy and armies; to the extent that privateers could choke off that supply, the effectiveness of the Roman Catholic forces in Europe would be diminished.

Cutting Spain off from American treasure was only half the battle. True greatness would come to England with the development of its own sources of Indian riches. In this quest the Puritan grandees, like Raleigh, looked to the south. Scientific lore of the day connected treasure with hot regions. Gold and precious minerals were said to be nurtured in the earth by the warmth of the sun's rays and drawn to the surface by its magnetic power. Moreover, England, with its northern location and cool maritime climate, lacked ability to produce the rich commodities that thrive only in frost-free regions. Britain would never be great till it established free access to the centers from which such products came.

This was not an effete search for spices and silks; it was a hard-headed response to England's problems. The county seats of these lords and gentlemen lay in England's cloth-producing areas, regions hit hard by the massive depression of the 1620s. Bad harvests, resulting from Little Ice Age conditions, sharpened suffering, and the grandees determined to help. One problem was that the English textile industry, leader of the nation's economy, was being outclassed by new continental techniques. The fibers, dyes, oils, and fixatives necessary to a revival of the cloth industry came largely from warmer areas. Thus England was captive to the whim of countries who were at least potential enemies. Only a secure source of such commodities, owned and run by Englishmen, would free the country of such lurking danger.

Charles I, who succeeded to the crown in 1625, quickly made it clear that he would not choose his advisors from among these Puritan lords and gentlemen; as he seemed to move closer to Arminianism in religion and defiance of Parliament in his politics, they determined to act. Shortly after Charles's dissolution of Parliament and his determination to call it no more in 1629, they met to organize the Providence Island Company. The colony they founded, planted in 1630 and falling to Spanish attack on the eve of the English Civil War in 1641, was intended to develop the products England needed. Every year settlers there received directions to develop dozens of commodities, most of which they ignored. In fact the economy of the island quickly focused on tobacco, which was never of good quality, and some cotton; the demands that they develop dozens of exotic crops were largely ignored.

Providence Island failed in part because the grandees perpetuated those elements in Raleigh's thinking that could not succeed. The small size of the company, reminiscent of the small City of Raleigh corporation, meant that the investors, rich as they were, would find the venture a continual drain on their resources. Colonists also found the experience draining; though the company encouraged families to emigrate, all settlers were tenants working for the company as much as for themselves. The many suggestions for new commodities were interpreted by the planters as intolerable pressure, which was met by obstinate refusal to shift from the tobacco that, poor as it was, still represented a sort of security to the beleaguered colonists.

Most important, the company's demand for gain and for exotic products for England when combined with their desire to continue Elizabethan defiance of Spain required that the colony be planted deep in the Spanish empire. It was important to the company's program that the island be an outpost of godly English people, but its location and mixture of goals meant that its government must always be in the hands of military men. As in the first Roanoke colony, the captains and their lieutenants often saw matters very differently than did those whose goal was to develop agricultural commodities. Tension was inevitable and often threatened to tear the little colony apart.

From the beginning the Providence Island Company hoped to use the island, as Raleigh had planned for Roanoke, as a base for privateering attacks on Spanish ships. When that became possible halfway through the settlement's decade of life, the tensions were intolerable. The adventurers confronted the lesson that Raleigh had faced in the sixteenth century: planting a replica of English society was incompatible with the goal of providing a military base for buccaneering activities. Though the two goals were inextricably linked in backers' minds because both were meant to enhance English power, in fact they must be separated if either were to be realized.[14]

The Puritan grandees were still unclear about the nature of the lesson. They extrapolated from the wreckage of their colony the notion that failure had been due, not to ill-conceived goals, but to paucity of support: success would come only when the Stuarts put the full power of the government behind a national foreign policy that aimed to cripple the Roman Catholic forces led by Spain and to found a great British Empire. Like Raleigh, they believed that if England were to participate in this high-stakes game, the focus must be on the Caribbean, source of wealth and crossroads of world trade.

When the civil war brought Oliver Cromwell to power, the dream was at last within reach. Cromwell was grounded in the great Protestant imperial tradition; as Lord Protector he put his full moral and political authority behind the Western Design, a scheme to oust the Spanish and build a mighty British presence in the Caribbean. Many of his advisors argued that, so corrupt and weak had the Iberians become, it would be possible from island beachheads to seize the mainland of Central America and possibly even to spread English influence throughout the southern regions.

Bitter lessons had to be learned again. Cromwell, like Elizabeth, tried to substitute enthusiasm for support. The combined naval and military operation was poorly planned and undersupplied; men died in large numbers, and, as in Jamestown, disorientation and despair led to apathetic behavior that doomed many. The Western Design that aimed at Hispaniola but succeeded in taking only Jamaica was truly the heir of almost a century of propaganda. So thoroughly had Cromwell and his closest advisors absorbed the notion that God intended the English, as bearers of true religion, to control the New World that they substituted faith in divine providence for hard-headed assessment of the problems and prospects of their plans.[15]

The apparent judgement of God, reflected in failure of the great campaign, was so stunning that Cromwell repeatedly sought its meaning in national days of prayer and fasting. Blair Worden argues that it was his dejection over failure of the Western Design that led Cromwell to make what Worden calls his most devastating mistake: the refusal of the crown.[16]

With the failure of the Western Design the weakness of one strand of the Raleigh legacy was clearly demonstrated. As Cromwell and his advisors contemplated their failure, the English island colonies that would make their contribution in commodity production and trade were building for a very different future. The Caribbean would be important to the English empire, but in a way unlike that envisaged in the great Elizabethan tradition. Sugar, not gold, was to bring prosperity; and prosperity was to be built on a system as exploitative of unwilling human labor as any that the Spanish had instituted. True religion had very little to do with it.

The other strand in Raleigh's legacy was also being woven into a pattern in the first half of the seventeenth century, and this fabric quietly and unexpectedly proved its durability. The City of Raleigh model proved to be the key to success in North America. No colony flourished unless it adopted this form. Successful colonies were sponsored by corporations that guaranteed continuity of support. More important, they were composed of families that came to America with the intention of supporting themselves and of committing themselves to life here. In order to attract such families, promoters had to offer private property in land. This proved to be the single most important element: substantial and hardworking English people would emigrate to secure the stake that land ownership represented. Other promises were simply much less important than this one; all manner of other inducements would not suffice if this was lacking and little else was needed if land was guaranteed.

The successful model involved production of commodities; all who emigrated must expect to get their hands dirty. Glorious military exploits that led to acquisition of gold were not part of this program; nor were the great gentlemen who expected to perform such feats. Solid, middling English subjects would build true colonies through their own labor.

John Smith was one of the first to realize that only commodity-producing plantations would flourish. As he reflected on the experience of Virginia and his own impressions of New England, as well as his thorough knowledge of the Roanoke documents, he began to develop an increasingly sophisticated theory of empire and of England's future. It was to be a future in which the merchants, not grandees, would make and carry out plans. Great gentlemen would lend their names, their connections at court and, perhaps, money, as Raleigh did in the final Roanoke colony but, as in that venture, control would stay with the merchants. Much of Smith's theory could have been generated by anyone who studied the empires of the early seventeenth century. It was Smith who put all the pieces together in a coherent program.

Rather than focus on the south as the Puritan grandees did, Smith sought to attract attention for New England which he said had been "esteemed as a cold, barren, mountainous, rocky Desart" after the Sagadahoc plantation's failure.[17] Smith was disturbed by Virginia's commitment to planting tobacco, not a commodity to make England great, and pictured the settlers "rooting in the ground about Tobacco like Swine."[18]

Smith's basic argument was that, in seeking to emulate Spain, England was backing the wrong model entirely. Spain was merely a conduit through which Indian gold flowed to European banks that held the bankrupt monarchy's notes. Gold, any easily won wealth, could never lead to proper growth of a true society that must be based on commitment and hard work. While Smith admired the great early Spanish explorers and colonizers, he argued that the empire they established had become soft and parasitic because no proper foundation had been laid.[19] He believed it was the height of folly for the English, seduced by dreams of wealth and blinded by propaganda, to become in their turn parasitic on that already corrupt empire.

The correct model was Holland. While the lords and gentlemen had been hypnotized by the lure of southern gold, the Dutch had become "mighty, strong, and rich" by dealing in the "contemptible trade of fish." Smith devoted himself to laying out the opportunities that the north offered, and he underscored his point by christening the region New England, emphasizing its affinity with his native land. He wrote page after page about the kinds of fish there taken, the small outlay necessary to set up in fishing which opened the trade to humble men, and the probable rewards, and he returned repeatedly to his lesson: "let not the meannesse of the word fish distaste you, for it will afford as good gold as the Mines of Guiana or Potassie, with lesse hazard and charge, and more certainty and facility.[20]

Smith pictured America as a land of independent smallholders, each of whom worked hard because he worked for his own posterity. In trade as on the land, the small venturer was increasingly important; merchants with one or two ships built the nation's wealth as they increased their own. Perhaps nothing sets Smith off from the grandees and their interpretation of the Raleigh legacy so much as his attitude toward privateering; where they pictured patriotic ravaging of the treasure ships of Antichrist's sword, Smith saw instead activities that harmed those very small merchants who were doing the real work. He wrote that "It is strange to see what great adventures the hopes of setting forth men of war to rob the industrious innocent, would procure."[21] In fact, Smith was correct; though we always hear of capture of a few great Spanish carracks loaded with treasure, most privateers made their money in taking small ships loaded with commodities; ventures indeed were sent out "to rob some poore Merchant or honest fisher men."[22]

Smith's program—widespread ownership of family farms and small entrepreneurship on the seas combined in a commitment to build a secure new English society in America—places the captain in company that at first sight looks impossible. His model was first tried in its entirety by the Puritan settlers of Massachusetts Bay. They did not, of course, set out to emulate Smith's plan; it was he who pointed out to them that they were in fact following his program. His last and most philosophical book, *Advertisements for the Unexperienced Planters of New England, or Any Where*, written as the Bay Colony was established, gloried in the fact that at last a true British Empire existed in America. If Massachusetts Bay succeeded as he thought it would, it would be "a great glory and exceeding good to the Kingdome, to make good at last what all our former conclusions have disgraced." He acknowledged that the Puritan settlers might be "more precise [in religion] than needs," but argued that they, unlike the Separatists struggling to hold on at Plymouth, were good and loyal subjects as well as substantial planters.[23]

It is ironic that the two strands of the Raleigh legacy were both taken up by Puritan activists in the 1630s and beyond. One, the line that argued for defiance of Spain and settlement as an aid to privateering, failed as it had failed before. The other, the thread that at first looked so slender, the erection of plantations of nearly self-sufficient smallholders, ultimately proved successful. The Puritanism of Massachusetts Bay's founders has often been pointed to as the special ingredient that led to success, but when that colony's experience is set against that of the grandees the argument falls apart, for the grandees were equally Puritan.

John Smith, as usual, had the answer to the puzzle. Though throughout his life he was protected and sponsored by high-born benefactors, Smith addressed his appeal to the broad middling group and the merchants. His conception of empire offered the independence they valued. He portrayed an America where neither the landlord nor the lawyer troubled planters, and the lure was powerful. Once Virginia instituted the headright system, servants signed on in the thousands at least in part because of the promise of fifty acres when their indenture was up. The thousands who emigrated to New England went primarily for religious reasons, but the land offered by Massachusetts communities was also a powerful magnet.

English men and women did not want to go to America to work for others, even if such work held out the promise of great wealth. They sought the liberty that came only with ownership of a homestead, even if that land produced a rude sufficiency. Raleigh realized this when he endorsed the plan for the City of Raleigh with its grandiose offer of 500 acres. Only after much suffering and waste of resources and human life would colonizers return to this realization. John Smith and the substantial men who organized the Bay Colony were the first who saw this lesson with clarity.

Raleigh's dream of empire thus lived on in the seventeenth century; it carried with it both success and failure. Even after the successful model had been established in Massachusetts and accepted in the Chesapeake, Puritan gentlemen in England hoped for realization of the first, the militant Protestant and anti-Spanish, strand. Not until the failure of the Western Design in the 1650s did they come to accept that the promise held out by that line of thought, the establishment of a British Empire in the south based on privateering, was illusory and perhaps unworthy. It was a dream that died hard; the reality, trade in "contemptible" commodities, was difficult to accept, involving as it did a wholly different view of England's future and of the aristocrat's place in that future. Few were as keen as Smith on a world where merchants dominated.

Notes

*Introducing Karen Kupperman, Harry L. Watson said: "Like our first speaker, Karen Ordahl Kupperman is an outstanding historian of early America who has made special contributions to our understanding of that field through applications of the history of science—in her case, through knowledge of ethnohistory, the historical effect of climate, and the history of medicine. She received her graduate training at Harvard University and Cambridge University. She has taught at the University of Connecticut since 1978 and now holds the rank of full professor. She has received distinguished fellowships from the American Philosophical Society, the Mellon Foundation, the American Council of Learned Societies, and most recently, the National Humanities Center at Research Triangle Park.

"Dr. Kupperman is the author of twelve scholarly essays on early colonial history, one of which, 'Apathy and Death in Early Jamestown,' won her the Binkley-Stephenson Award in 1984 for the best article published in the *Journal of American History*. We in North Carolina know her best, perhaps, as the author of *Roanoke: The Abandoned Colony*, an excellent short book on Sir Walter Raleigh's most famous experiment. She is also the author of *Settling with the Indians: The Meeting of English and Indian Cultures in America, 1580–1640* and the editor of two forthcoming collections of important documents, a one-volume edition of the works of Captain John Smith and a microfilm edition of the papers relating to the settlement of Providence Island in the Caribbean. She will speak to us today on 'Raleigh's Dream of Empire and Its Seventeenth Century Career.'"

[1]On the privateering war of the 1590s, see Kenneth R. Andrews, *Elizabethan Privateering: English Privateering During the Spanish War, 1585–1603* (Cambridge: 1964).

[2]Thomas Hariot's *Briefe and True Report* is available in several forms. A fully annotated version, along with all other documents pertaining to the Roanoke colonies, can be found in David Beers Quinn (ed.), *The Roanoke Voyages, 1584–1590*, (London: 2 vols. 1955). A facsimile of the 1590 edition, with the woodcuts made by Theodor DeBry of the John White paintings, has been published by Dover Books (New York: 1972). A selection of Roanoke documents, including the *Briefe and True Report*, is available from the North Carolina Department of Cultural Resources, Division of Archives and History: David and Alison Quinn (eds.), *The First Colonists: Documents on the Planting of the First English Settlements in North America, 1584–1590* (Raleigh: 1982).

[3]This phrase occurs in a letter sent by Ralph Lane, governor of the 1585 Roanoke colony, to Sir Francis Walsingham, August 12, 1585. Quinn (ed.), *The Roanoke Voyages*, I, 203.

[4]Kenneth Andrews argues that the emphasis on privateering and on "petty enterprise" of the 1590s diverted Elizabethan foreign policy from more important goals and therefore was destructive of more than Roanoke. "Elizabethan Privateering," The Harte Lecture, 1985, in Joyce Youings (ed.), *Raleigh in Exeter 1985: Privateering and Colonisation in the Reign of Elizabeth I* (Exeter: 1986), 1–20, esp. 12–20.

[5]For the full story of the Roanoke colony, see David Beers Quinn, *Set Fair for Roanoke: Voyages and Colonies, 1584–1606* (Chapel Hill: 1985), and Karen Ordahl Kupperman, *Roanoke: The Abandoned Colony* (Totowa, N.J.: 1984).

[6]See the note by Richard Hakluyt, 1609, in Quinn (ed.), *Roanoke Voyages*, I, 388.

[7]Smith, *The Proceedings of the English Colony in Virginia*, 1612, known as *The Map of Virginia, Part II*, in Philip L. Barbour (ed.), *The Complete Works of Captain John Smith* (Chapel Hill: 3 vols. 1986), I, 218–219.

[8]John Smith reported hints of the Roanoke colonists and expeditions to seek them in his *True Relation of Such Occurrences and Accidents of Noate as Hath Hapned in Virginia* (1608), in Barbour (ed.), *Complete Works of Captain John Smith*, I, 49, 55, 63; in his *Map of Virginia, Parts I and II, ibid.*, 150, 265–266; and in his *Generall Historie of Virginia, New-England, and the Summer Isles* (1624), *ibid.*, II, 226, 291. William Strachey reported evidence that the Roanoke colonists had lived with the Chesapeake Indians and that all had been exterminated by Powhatan's forces; *The Historie of Travell into Virginia Britania*, Louis B. Wright and Virginia Freund (eds.), (London: 1953), 15, 91, 104–108, 150. Samuel Purchas wrote that Smith had evidence of this deed: "Virginia's Verger" in *Hakluytus Posthumus or Purchas His Pilgrimes* (1625; rpt. Glasgow, 1906), 19, 228; and note, *ibid.*, 18, 527.

[9]On Sagadahoc, see David B. and Alison M. Quinn (eds.), *The English New England Voyages, 1602–1608* (London: 1983), especially 74–90 and 331–468. See also Richard A. Preston, *Gorges of Plymouth Fort* (Toronto: 1953), 141–150, and Douglas R. McManis, *European Impressions of the New England Coast, 1497–1620*, University of Chicago Department of Geography Research Paper no. 139 (Chicago: 1972), 106–108, 137.

[10]Smith, *Generall Historie,* in Barbour (ed.), *Complete Works of John Smith,* II, 263–264; and *A Description of New England,* 1616, *ibid.,* I, 343–345.

[11]Smith, *New Englands Trials,* 1622, *ibid.,* I, 434.

[12]On English domestic and foreign policy in this period, see Derek Hirst, *Authority and Conflict: England, 1603–1658* (Cambridge, Mass.: 1986), chapter 5.

[13]Historical Manuscripts Commission, Appendix to Tenth *Report* (1887), Part VI, 85; Christopher Hill, *Intellectual Origins of the English Revolution* (Oxford: 1965), 208–211.

[14]The basic sources for the history of the Providence Island Company and colony are the company's records in the Public Record Office at Kew (CO 1/124, 1 and 2). These are two large folio volumes, one of which contains records of company meetings, and the other copies of letters and instructions sent to the colony. These and related primary documents are available in the Microform Academic Publishers series *British Records Relating to America in Microform,* ed. W.E. Minchinton, *The Providence Island Venture, 1630–1641,* ed. Karen Ordahl Kupperman. The Providence Island Company is the subject of A.P. Newton's *The Colonising Activities of the English Puritans* (New Haven: 1914). For a brief modern treatment, see Karen Ordahl Kupperman, "A Puritan Colony in the Tropics: Providence Island, 1630–1641," in Ralph Bennett (ed.), *Settlements in the Americas* (University of Delaware Press, forthcoming).

[15]This point is developed at length in Karen Ordahl Kupperman, "Errand to the Indies: Puritan Colonization from Providence Island to the Western Design," *William and Mary Quarterly* (forthcoming). See also Roger Crabtree, "The Idea of a Protestant Foreign Policy," in Ivan Roots (ed.), *Cromwell: A Profile* (London: 1973), 160–189, and John F. Battick, "A New Interpretation of Cromwell's Western Design," *Journal of the Barbados Museum and Historical Society,* 34 (1972): 76–84.

[16]Blair Worden, "Oliver Cromwell and the Sin of Achan," in Derek Beales and Geoffrey Best (eds.), *History, Society and the Churches: Essays in Honour of Owen Chadwick* (Cambridge: 1985), 127, 135–141.

[17]Smith, *Generall Historie,* in Barbour (ed.), *Complete Works of Captain John Smith,* II, 399.

[18]*Ibid.,* 285. See also *The True Travels, Adventures, and Observations of Captaine John Smith,* 1630, *ibid,* III, 237.

[19]Smith, *Description of New England, ibid.,* I, 327, 350; and *Advertisements for the Unexperienced Planters of New England, or Any Where,* 1631, *ibid.,* III, 277, 299.

[20]Smith, *Description of New England, ibid.,* I, 312, 330–332, 360; *New England's Trials, ibid.,* 424–425, 437–438, 441; and *Generall Historie, ibid.,* 43, 462, 474.

[21]Smith, *Description of New England, ibid.,* I, 330, 350. See also his *True Travels, ibid.,* 223, 238–241.

[22]Smith, *Advertisements, ibid.,* III, 284–286.

[23]*Advertisements, ibid.,* III, 269–270.

"Fortune's Tennis Ball," or Bouncing About with the Bibliography of Sir Walter

Christopher M. Armitage*

While enjoying this luncheon, we acknowledge the fine way that H. G. Jones has organized the whole conference. But I am going to make a startling revelation about him: I recently discovered that he is a closet alchemist. By "closet" I do not refer to the fact that in order to find him in his office one must thread a labyrinth of tables and bookstacks until in the furthest, darkest recess one beards him in his cell, where, like Prospero, he sits amid his books, "all dedicated to the bettering of his mind." No: by "closet alchemist" I mean that he had hidden, at least from me, his belief that dull lead can be transmuted into bright gold. This belief came out when he told me that I was to be the speaker at this luncheon and that I was to make the subject of bibliography "entertaining and amusing." This command is akin to ordering a miner at the coalface not to get dirty, or a swimmer to stay dry.

My conclusion, after toiling at the Sisyphean task of compiling a bibliography of so Protean a character as Sir Walter Ralegh, is that a bibliographer is also described by Dr. Johnson's definition of a lexicographer as "a harmless drudge." Moreover, since Ralegh was involved in such diverse matters as navigation, politics, poetry, colonization, writing a *History of the World,* concocting medicines, attacking Spaniards, attending law school, intriguing at court (the list could continue), any attempt to account for all that has been written about him is bound to contain omissions and errors. Here his bibliographer may again have recourse to Dr. Johnson, who, when asked by a lady why he had incorrectly defined "pastern" as the knee of a horse, replied "Ignorance, madam, pure ignorance."

The phrase "Fortune's Tennis Ball" in my title has nothing to do with the meteoric rises and falls of Bjorn Borg or John McEnroe. "Fortune's tennis ball" was a verdict on Ralegh rendered by Sir Robert Naunton in the seventeenth century, when tennis meant real or royal tennis played on an indoor court with terms and rules very different from those of tennis today.[1] But on numerous occasions this bibliographer has felt slammed around the chases and hazards of the royal tennis court. Let me identify two instances.

For many years I sauntered carefree into—or past—the North Carolina Collection, never dreaming that I would have greatness thrust upon me in the form of a project which required constant use of its splendid resources. But when that moment came, alas, the Wilson Library was closed for refurbishing and the Ralegh material locked away in a massive steel cage. Dr. Jones permitted me access to the material, provided that I was locked in with it. His staff were

Christopher M. Armitage, associate professor at UNC-CH, discussed his forthcoming bibliography of Raleigh in a paper titled "Fortune's Tennis Ball."

most helpful in letting me in and out: on those rare occasions when they forgot to release me for lunch, they did rescue me at 5:00 P.M.!

The second instance arose last summer. I knew that some of the gaps could be filled in through the Bodleian Library at Oxford. I did not anticipate that last summer would be the very period chosen for the most unEnglish activity of installing air-conditioning in the Bodleian. As a result, most of the items I needed to see were inaccessible.

Though not particularly paranoiac, after these two frustrating blocks I began to murmur "The time is out of joint, o cursed spite, / That ever I was born to set it right." But then my Prufrockian alter ego reminded me that "I am not Prince Hamlet, nor was meant to be; / Am an attendant lord, one that will do / To swell a" conference.

Ralegh, however, has been compared to Prince Hamlet—and Bottom, and Othello, and Iago, and Prospero, and to Shakespeare himself. As a prominent Elizabethan and acknowledged writer Ralegh was bound to attract the attention of the anti-Stratfordian zealots, particularly since he had a dozen years of enforced leisure in the Tower of London, during which he wrote Shakespeare's plays while pretending to be occupied with *The History of the World.* Such stuff the exasperated bibliographer must wade through. In quest of Raleghana he also learns more than he may have wished to know about potatoes, the crompster or hog (a coastal ship), obsolete medicinal formulae, customs and excise practices on the isle of Jersey, whether or not the Lost Colonists were absorbed into the Lumbee Indians of Robeson County in North Carolina, and so on. He also grapples with such problems as whether to spell Hariot and Harington with one "r" or two; whether the captured treasure-ship was the "Madre de Dios" (Spanish) or "Deus" (Portuguese); which spelling of Sir Walter's patronymic to adopt (as late as the mid-nineteenth century Isaac D'Israeli, father of Britain's future Prime Minister, used Rawleigh); under which letter of the alphabet to place William Least Heat Moon, the American Indian author of *Blue Highways*; and many other knotty issues.

On rare occasions the bibliographer may have some fun. I found, for instance, that what went to the word-processor as "he espoused a maid of honor" came out as "he exposed a maid of honor." Had the machine automatically recalled John Aubrey's scandalous anecdote about Ralegh's compelling seduction of the lady who as a result bore them a son? This is the son whose portrait, standing in front of his father, was shown yesterday on one of Helen Wallis's slides. Apparently he was a chip off the old block, to judge from another of Aubrey's anecdotes:

> Sir Walter Raleigh, being invited to dinner with some great person, where his son was to go with him, said to his son, Thou art such a quarrelsome, affronting creature that I am ashamed to have such a bear in my company. Mr Walt humbled himself to his father, and promised he would behave himself mightily mannerly. So away they went. He sat next to his father and was very demure at least half dinner time. Then said he, I this morning, not having the fear of God before my eyes, but by the instigation of the devil, went to a whore. I was very eager of her, kissed and embraced her and went to enjoy her, but she thrust me from her and vowed I should not, For your Father lay with me but an hour ago. Sir Walt, being so strangely surprized and put out of his countenance at so great a table, gives his son a damned blow over the face; his son, as rude as he was, would not strike his father, but strikes over the face of the gentleman that sat next to him, and said, Box about, 'twill come to my Father anon. 'Tis now a common used proverb.[2]

Young Walt was sent to France in 1613 under the governorship of Ben Jonson, whom he got dead drunk and caused to be carried around Paris in a cart, Walt telling the spectators that Jonson was a more lively image of the Crucifix than any they had. Unabashedly telling this story to William Drummond of Hawthornden, Jonson added that Walt's mother was delighted about the escapade, saying "that his father, young, was so inclined, though the father abhorred it." Four years later, however, escapades turned deadly: Walt was killed during Keymis's ill-judged attack on San Tômé, as recounted in Professor Shirley's paper. This tragedy was a further disaster in the debacle of Ralegh's last voyage to Guiana.

Ralegh's courage and grace at his execution, which was vindictively demanded by King James I soon after Ralegh's return from that voyage, made a deep impression. One source of information about his behavior at his beheading is a letter written by Robert Tounson. The letter is reproduced in a book entitled *Walteri Hemingford, Historia de Rebus Gestis Edvardi I, II, et III.* In this case, knowledge of English history could be downright disadvantageous, because a seventeenth-century letter is hardly to be expected amid a history about monarchs of several centuries earlier. The compiler of the volume was Thomas Hearne of St. Edmund Hall in Oxford University, another harmless drudge, who gave rise to the couplet:

> "Pox on't!" said Time to Thomas Hearne,
> "Whatever I forget, you learn."

When his Stuart sympathies led to his being locked out of his job in the Bodleian Library after he refused to swear allegiance to the Hanoverian regime, he retired to St. Edmund Hall and filled many volumes with comments on his contemporaries, such as calling George Frederick Handel and his musicians "a lousy crew of foreign fiddlers."

In conclusion, I would like to share with you two pieces about Ralegh that may be unfamiliar. (When a speaker announces a wish to share something, the announcement often is a prologue to bad news. Such is not, I hope, the case here.) The pieces are by two poets, one Anglo-Irish and one American, who both died in 1963. They touch, in a complementary way, on many of the diverse aspects of Ralegh. The first is by Louis MacNeice, classical scholar and writer for the British Broadcasting Corporation, whose "Suite for Recorders" treats Elizabethan poets as recorders living in a dangerous era of political intrigue and treachery. The poem begins with an epigraph from Shakespeare which is thought to allude to Christopher Marlowe's death in a brawl over a tavern bill, and the first quatrains introduce a series of allusions to the pastoral conventions in "The Passionate Shepherd to his Love" by Marlowe and "The Nymph's Reply" by Ralegh.

SUITE FOR RECORDERS

... it strikes a man more dead than a great reckoning in a little room.

As You Like It

I

If shepherd to nymph were the whole story
Dying in holocausts of blossom,
No midwife and no middleman
Would contravene the upright sun.

If Raleigh to Marlowe on the other
Hand were an uncontested audit,
Then Thames need only flow to mock
A death in tavern or on block;

Nor swimming Hellespont nor climbing
Starwards could answer the inquiring
Blade that would spill each threaded bead,
Each grace-note of a broken reed;

While far sou'wested Eldorado,
Old pipe-dream in the Tower of London,
Would be no more than history claims —
A long axe handle spliced for James.

. . . .

II

In a little room, a little plot, a little lifetime
Hark, the shrill recorders after meat, the Elizabethan
Mayflies in a silver web which dangled over chaos,
    Twirling round and round,
Waited for the silent headsman, countering his silence
    With arabesques of sound.

Courtier with the knife behind the smile, ecclesiastic
With faggots in his eyes, tight-lipped scholar with
    forbidden
Fruit in his back garden, all were conscious in their bowels
    Of the web and whose it was
And beneath it of the void where not old faith nor yet new
    learning
Dare breathe the word Because.

. . . .

Golden age? Age of discovery? Age of madrigals and liars,
Age when men died young. We envy what we think an
    innocent ardour,
What in fact was staged revolt upon a tightrope, a creative
    Despair, a blithe despair of youth,
Which in that swivelling dubious web essayed its white lies
    in defiance
Of the black void of truth.

Violent men with salt in their nostrils, blood on their
    hands, whose gentler moments

Conjured up, for lack of sleep, a land which ancient
    literati,
Careless of the starved and sweaty facts, had filled with
    mimic
Shepherds fluting to their sheep
For Spenser, Sidney, Kit and Will to loll and count and then
    recounting
Their antics fall asleep.

Life as a game? An art? An orgy? Something of each; a
    mortification
Also. Prematurely dead—or dumb—they left behind them
What for us? A bed of flowers? A second best? A starting
    point? Or
Blind end, blind spring, spring of a trap?
Yet still they pipe and still from No Man's Pastures trip
    their white, their ringstraked,
Their black sheep through the gap.

III

. . . .

The windblown web in which we live
Presumes a yawning negative,
A nothing which cries out to see
A something flout its vacancy.

To singe the beard of the King of Spain
Was but a token; Tamburlaine
Found no more in his earthly crown
Than was allowed to Corydon;

And both demanded something more
Than their set piece of love or war,
Than what faint echoes drift to us
Of muffled drums or calamus.

Yet read between those lines and peer
Down through the mesh of gossamer
And you will sense the darkness which
Made either guttering candle rich;

And you, a would-be player too,
Will give those angry ghosts their due
Who threw their voices far as doom
Greatly in a little room.[3]

The second piece is by William Carlos Williams, the New Jersey pediatrician. His essay "Sir Walter Raleigh" includes a rhapsodic account of the Virginia which Ralegh sought to colonize. The last of these paragraphs could serve as a comment upon the impulse behind this conference and the studies which Sir Walter continues to inspire.

O Muse, in that still pasture where you dwell amid the hardly noticed sounds of water falling and the little cries of crickets and small birds, sing of Virginia floating off: the broken chips of Raleigh: the Queen is dead.

O Virginia! who will gather you again as Raleigh had you gathered? science, wisdom, love, despair. O America, the deathplace of his son! It is Raleigh. anti-tropical. It is the cold north, flaring up in ice again.

What might he have known, what seen, O Muse? — Shoal water where we smelt so sweet and so strong a smell, as if we had been in the midst of some delicate garden; and keeping good watch and keeping but slack sail — we arrived upon the coast; a land so full of grapes as the very beating and surge of the sea overflow them, such plenty, as well there as in all places else, on the sand and on the green soil on the hills, as well as every little shrub, as also climbing towards the tops of high cedars, that in all the world I think a like abundance is not to be found. And from below the hill such a flock of cranes, mostly white, arose with such a cry as if an army of men had shouted all together. — He might have seen the brother of the king, Granganimo, with copper cap, whose wife, comely and bashful, might have come aboard the ship, her brows bound with white coral; or running out to meet them very cheerfully, at Roanoak, plucked off his socks and washed his feet in warm water. A people gentle, loving, faithful, void of all guile and treason. Earthen pots, large, white and sweet and wooden platters of sweet timber.

Sing, O Muse and say, there is a spirit that is seeking through America for Raleigh: in the earth, the air, the waters, up and down, for Raleigh, that lost man: seer who failed, planter who never planted, poet whose works are questioned, leader without command, favorite deposed — but one who yet gave title for his Queen, his England, to a coast he never saw but grazed alone with genius.[4]

Notes

[*]H.G. Jones presented the speaker as follows: "Christopher M. Armitage, holder of a Bowman and Gordon Gray chair of undergraduate teaching in English at the University of North Carolina at Chapel Hill, earned his master's degrees from both Oxford University and the University of Western Ontario and a doctorate from Duke University. He has taught at Huron College, Université Laval, University of Guelph, and currently he is also a visiting associate professor of Canadian literature at Duke. His books include *Manual of Service Writing for the Royal Canadian*

Air Force (1958) and *A Bibliography of the Works of Louis MacNeice* (1973). Professor Armitage's teaching effectiveness has been recognized by the Standard Oil Foundation Award and the Nicholas Salgo Distinguished Teacher Award. In addition to his classroom duties, he serves as acting director of the Office of International Programs and director of the UNC Study-Travel Program in Oxford.

"At the request of America's Four Hundredth Anniversary Committee, Chris Armitage took on the formidable task of completing a comprehensive annotated bibliography of Sir Walter Raleigh. His courage flagged only momentarily when he was told that all previously commissioned compilers had died on the job; and, judging from his robust health, *An Annotated Bibliography of Sir Walter Raleigh* will be published in the fall by the University of North Carolina Press. Today he proves to us that bibliographical work is not always deadly to either the mind or the body."

[1] Sir Robert Naunton, "Rawleigh," *Fragmenta Regalia, or Observations on the late Queen Elizabeth, Her Times and Favorits [sic]* (London: 1641), p. 30.

[2] *Aubrey's Brief Lives*, edited by Oliver Lawson Dick (London: Secker and Warburg, 1949; Ann Arbor: University of Michigan Press, 1957), p. 256.

[3] Louis MacNeice, "Suite for Recorders," *Ten Burnt Offerings* (London: Faber, 1952), pp. 13–18. Reprinted in *The Collected Poems of Louis MacNeice*, edited by E.R. Dodds (London: Faber, 1966; New York: Oxford University Press, 1967), pp. 283–87.

[4] William Carlos Williams, "Sir Walter Raleigh," *In the American Grain* (Norfolk, Conn.: New Directions, 1925), pp. 59–62. Reprinted in *The William Carlos Williams Reader*, edited by M.L. Rosenthal (Norfolk, Conn.: New Directions; London: MacGibbon & Kee, 1966), pp. 336–39.

Ralegh and Drake

Norman J. W. Thrower*

The roster of Elizabethan overseas adventures includes a number of well-known names such as Cavendish, Chancellor, Davis, Drake, Frobisher, Gilbert, Grenville, Hawkins, Ralegh, and Willoughby.[1] Among these it could be demonstrated, statistically if need be, that none have such enduring reputations as Ralegh and Drake. There are many similarities in the lives and work of these two men — both were born in the West Country of England, both were soldiers in Ireland, both received favors from the Queen, both were members of Parliament, both promoted and engaged in voyages of discovery, both died under tragic circumstances, and memories of both live on through popular stories as folk heroes. However, there are important differences between these men, and it might be illuminating to compare the careers of two of the greatest of the Elizabethans.

Although we properly honor Ralegh as the founder of England's first settlement on the Atlantic coast of what is now the United States, he was never able to visit the colony he promoted in North America, but, surprisingly, Drake did. I don't intend to focus on the Roanoke Colony, of which much has been said in this conference.[2] Rather, as well as comparing Ralegh and Drake, I will attempt to put their lives in the context of the signal events that were taking place when England was still in the process of breaking away from the Church of Rome and, for most of the period, saw Spain as the implacable enemy.

Before the discovery of America in 1492, England and Spain had been political and commercial allies. This changed dramatically after Pope Alexander VI issued a bull dividing the unknown world between Spain and Portugal in 1493. The next year the bull was ratified by the Treaty of Tordesillas. Only three years after this, in 1497, King Henry VII of England sponsored a voyage out of Bristol commanded by the Venetian, John Cabot, during which Newfoundland was discovered. This was quickly followed by other English and French voyages to North America, which was claimed but not occupied by Spain and Portugal. By the 1540s, Plymouth, the English port with which Drake and Ralegh are both associated, came to rival Bristol as a point of departure for Atlantic voyages. The English Navy was built up at this time by Henry VIII, who had succeeded his father Henry VII in 1509, but the King's ships were heavily involved in wars with France, and English overseas voyages in the sixteenth century were largely private affairs.[3]

Within this setting, the county of Devon, two boys were born who were to greatly affect their age; much that has been written about the early years of Drake and Ralegh is probably apocryphal. Francis Drake was born on a farm at Crowndale near Tavistock, about ten miles north of Plymouth, the family

Court artist Nicholas Hillliard in the 1580s painted miniatures of Sir Walter Raleigh (left) and Sir Francis Drake (right). *By permission of the National Portrait Gallery, London (Raleigh) and the Victoria and Albert Museum (Drake).*

believes in 1543.[4] This was during the last years of the reign of Henry VIII, and some fifty years after the New World had been discovered by Columbus. Drake's father, Edmund Drake, had most probably been a seaman before marrying and settling down. Though not well off, the Drake family had excellent connections. Francis, later Earl of Bedford, is said to have been godfather to Francis Drake and that the baby was his namesake. Edmund Drake's mother, and therefore Francis Drake's grandmother, was a Hawkins—a prominent family in Plymouth. In the 1530s and 40s the Hawkins family made profitable trading voyages to Guinea and Brazil. This family relationship was later to be of great significance in the career of Francis Drake.

As the result of a Catholic uprising in the West Country in 1549 the Drake family, which was fiercely Protestant, was forced to leave Devon. Francis Drake, now six years of age, was taken by his parents to the London area where they lived on a hulk at the mouth of the Medway, a small river on the coast of Kent. Edmund Drake was employed as a Bible reader in the Navy, and the young Francis grew up knowing about ships and seamen. He was the oldest of twelve brothers, at least three others of whom (John, Joseph, and Thomas) went to sea. During his childhood, religious troubles continued in England as Henry VIII was succeeded by his son Edward VI (the boy king) in 1547 who, in turn, was succeeded by Queen Mary I (Bloody Mary) in 1553. In this year matters were further complicated when Mary married Philip, son of King Charles V of Spain. Wars continued on the Continent in the course of which England lost Calais, its last possession on mainland France, in 1557. During this period Francis Drake, now in his teens, was apprenticed to a merchant captain engaged in coastal trade. It was in the difficult waters of the Thames estuary that young Drake developed his navigational skills. When the master died, he bequeathed his ship to Drake, who soon sold it and left the London area to seek his fortune with his relatives in Devon.

In 1548 Sebastian Cabot, the son of John, had accepted an invitation to come to England from Spain, where he held the position of pilot major. This proved to be a turning point in the training of English navigators who, in the next half century, became "great sea dogs."[5] In 1553 Richard Chancellor was appointed pilot of an expedition to discover the northeast passage to the Far East under the command of Sir Hugh Willoughby. Willoughby was lost, but Chancellor eventually made his way overland to Moscow to the court of Ivan IV (the Terrible) as a result of which the Muscovy Company was founded. In 1558 Elizabeth I became Queen of England; Edmund Drake was made Vicar of Upchurch, Kent as a reward for his fidelity to the Protestant cause.

Prior to this, in the early 1550s, at Hayes Barton near East Budleigh, some ten miles from Exeter in South Devon, a son, Walter, was born to Walter Ralegh of Fardell and his third wife, Katherine.[6] Thus Francis Drake was about nine years of age when Walter Ralegh was born. The birthplaces of Drake and Ralegh are about forty miles apart as the crow flies. There is a family connection between Drake and Ralegh, for the senior Walter Ralegh's first wife was Joan Drake, daughter of John Drake of Exmouth, cousin of Francis's family. There was a second wife, but it was by his third wife that the senior Walter Ralegh had two sons, first Carew and then Walter junior. Walter's mother was the widow of Otho Gilbert, by whom she had three sons—John, Humphrey, and Adrian Gilbert. Like the Drakes, the Raleghs and Gilberts were Protestants and were affected adversely by the troubles associated with the Catholic uprisings in the West Country, but it was not necessary for them to leave Devon involuntarily. However, when he was in his teens, in 1568, young Walter Ralegh joined a group of West Countrymen who went to France to support the Huguenot cause. He spent four years campaigning in religious wars on the Continent which culminated, much later, in the revocation of the Edict of Nantes (1598) through which Huguenots were dispersed throughout northern Europe.

By the time Ralegh returned to England in 1572 a number of events had taken place which were to affect the course of history and, with this, the lives of Ralegh and Drake. In 1568, Mary, Queen of Scots, took refuge in England, and in the same year the Netherlands rebelled against Spain. Meanwhile, Drake had made three voyages to Middle America, and was embarked on a fourth.[7] Drake's first transoceanic voyage was in a ship owned by his relatives, William and John Hawkins, and commanded by Captain John Lovell, in 1566-67. This was followed by an expedition by John Hawkins in 1567-8 in which Drake was given command of the *Judith*, one of six ships in the flotilla. This venture proved to be a disaster since the English were caught and attacked by a superior Spanish fleet at San Juan de Ulua (Vera Cruz) off the coast of Mexico. Only the flagship with Hawkins aboard and the *Judith*, under Drake, escaped. Drake thought they had been deceived by a promise of protection and felt that, because of this, all his subsequent depredations against the Spanish were justified. On the return to England Drake was sent to deliver a letter from William Hawkins to Queen Elizabeth's Principal Secretary of State Sir William Cecil (later Lord Burghley) reporting the disaster. This was probably Drake's first contact with the Court.

Hawkins was not happy with Drake's conduct at the Battle of San Juan and wrote, "The *Judith* . . . forsook us in our great misery."[8] Soon after his return to England Drake, now thoroughly experienced in piratical seamanship, married Mary Newman, the daughter of a West Country seaman, in 1569. Two years later he was again in the Caribbean—this time on his own account. The next year, 1572, he embarked on his daring raid on Panama. As Balboa had done nearly sixty years earlier, Drake crossed the Isthmus; he vowed he would be the first Englishman to sail on the Pacific. It was on his return to the Caribbean coast that Drake captured a mule train carrying Spanish treasure and returned to Plymouth a rich man in 1573. He now joined the expedition of the Earl of Essex in Ireland to attempt to colonize Antrim. This failed, but it was in Ireland that Drake met Thomas Doughty, a young aristocrat with close connections at Court who, in 1577, was to embark with Drake with fatal consequences for Doughty.

Five years earlier in 1572, the young Walter Ralegh had enrolled in Oriel College Oxford but, like many undergraduates of that time, he seems not to have taken a degree although possessed of considerable book learning. He was registered in the Middle Temple (one of the Inns of Court) in 1575 and was well enough off to have servants, for two of whom he had to post bail for rowdiness. Ralegh was himself imprisoned for dueling but, in retrospect, everything he did seemed to lead to the Court of Queen Elizabeth, where his half brother Humphrey Gilbert had preceded him. It was Gilbert who introduced Ralegh to George Gascoigne, a poet, publisher, and soldier. Gascoigne had published Gilbert's *Discourse to Prove a Passage by the North West to Cathay* and now published one of Ralegh's early poems.

Gilbert had been planning an expedition to the Orient by way of the north of North America for a decade and received letters patent from the Queen for this purpose in 1578. The northwest passage seemed a more promising way to reach the Far East than the northeast passage. Although Chancellor's venture in the latter direction and the subsequent establishment of the Muscovy Company had led to the remarkable overland journey from Russia to Persia by the Englishman Anthony Jenkinson in 1561–64, this had not initiated direct trade with eastern Asia, the ultimate objective of Gilbert's voyages. Ralegh now associated himself with Gilbert's plan for overseas exploration, and a squadron of ten ships left Dartmouth harbor in September 1578 with Ralegh in command of the *Falcon*. A storm dispersed the fleet which put but back into Dartmouth. Through this unsuccessful action Ralegh seems to have become known at the Court of Elizabeth which included, in addition to Lord Burghley, the Earl of Oxford, the Earl of Leicester, Sir Christopher Hatton, and Sir Francis Walsingham.

Just prior to Ralegh's return to England in the *Falcon*, Walsingham, Leicester, Hatton, and John Hawkins, now treasurer of the Queen's shipyards, were promoters of what was to become Drake's most ambitious project. Queen Elizabeth was probably a supporter of this venture of 1577, which was not approved by Burghley. The same promoters of Drake's venture had also been supporters of the attempt of Martin Frobisher to find the northwest passage in the previous year, and now they were backers of his second attempt. We are not certain of the motives behind Drake's voyage—whether to look for possible English settlements in South America south of the sphere of Spanish influence, whether to explore the approaches to the northwest passage from the Pacific, or others. In any case, Drake left Plymouth on 13 December 1577 and sailed south with a squadron of five vessels including his flagship, the *Pelican*. On the way Doughty challenged Drake's authority and at St. Julian, in Patagonia, Drake had Doughty executed. Drake now navigated the strait (found by Magellan sixty years earlier) in sixteen days, a record for the century. Once in the Pacific a great storm drove him southward into what is known today as Drake Passage, between Tierra del Fuego and Antarctica. When the storm abated Drake found he had only one ship left, the *Pelican*, which he renamed *Golden Hind* after a device on the crest of his patron, Hatton.

The *Golden Hind* now sailed northward along the Pacific coast of South America, attacking towns and shipping along the way. From one Spanish ship, called by the English "Cacafuego," Drake took a vast treasure, which he loaded on the *Golden Hind*. Drake dared not now return the way he had come, so he sailed north beyond any Spanish settlements to what is now the latitude of Washington state. He may have been looking for the Pacific entrance to the northwest passage, but the weather deteriorated, and he turned southward to California where the *Golden Hind* was careened and replenished for the projected voyage across the Pacific. Drake's six-week stay in California, 16 June–23 July 1579, on what the Tudors called the back side of America, was the earliest English presence in any part of what was to become the United States. He took possession of the land from the Miwok Indians as *Nova Albion* — the first New England — for Queen Elizabeth before leaving the coast of California.[9]

Drake now sailed across the Pacific to Mindanao and on to the Moluccas, where the *Golden Hind* anchored at the Island of Ternate. Here Drake made a treaty with the local Sultan that some have seen as the beginning of the British Empire in Asia, formalized later, in the establishment of the East India Company. Drake sailed on to a remote island to careen his ship. Shortly after this, the *Golden Hind* struck a rock in the Celebes and Drake had to jettison part of his cargo of spices. The ship was extricated from this danger and continued to thread its way through the islands of southeast Asia to Java. Following a well-travelled course via the Indian Ocean, the Cape of Good Hope and the Atlantic, Drake and his crew arrived in Plymouth on 26 September 1580, nearly three years after the voyage had begun. They had made the second global circumnavigation, after Magellan's, and the first from which the commander returned home. It was properly called the "Famous Voyage."[10]

When Queen Elizabeth heard of his return, after some hesitation, she summoned Drake to London and, in a long private audience, learned the details of the voyage. The treasure was stored in the Tower of London except for the generous prize given to Drake and the crew. Drake was knighted aboard the *Golden Hind*, and he returned to Plymouth, where he became Mayor in 1581. He bought a great country house, Buckland Abbey, from Sir Richard Grenville. Drake's first wife died about this time, and in February 1585, he married Elizabeth Sydenham, daughter of a Somerset knight, a friend of the Drake family. In the previous year he had become a member of Parliament for Bossiney, North Cornwall, and, through this, was able to benefit Plymouth and the West Country generally.

During the period of Drake's circumnavigation and its immediate aftermath Ralegh had not been idle. In 1580 he followed his half brother Sir Humphrey Gilbert as a soldier in southwestern Ireland, a very different area from the northeast where Drake had served. There is no special value in detailing both the grisly and the romantic episodes of Ralegh's service in Ireland, which has been sufficiently covered in this conference, except to say that he eventually obtained large grants of land there and advanced his position at the Court of Elizabeth by his exploits. Within a few months of his return from Ireland in 1582 he became a favorite of the Queen, to whom he would send his poems during his rare absences. The absence of the Earl of Leicester and the Earl of Essex, who were fighting for the Protestant cause in the Netherlands, 1585–87, left the field at home freer for Ralegh. Naturally his advance at the Court did not please those being reduced or displaced in the favor of the Queen. She rewarded Ralegh with appointments and monopolies, which were the basis of his power. In 1584 Ralegh became member of Parliament for Devon and was knighted by the Queen.

Such was the background for Ralegh's enterprises in the New World, the sketchiest account of which only need be passed in review in this essay. Ralegh had helped finance Humphrey Gilbert in another ill-starred overseas venture in 1583 during which his half brother was lost at sea. Ralegh now became the major protagonist for transatlantic English settlements in support of which he employed the propagandist, Richard Hakluyt, and the navigator-scholar, Thomas Harriot. Backed by letters patent from Queen Elizabeth, Ralegh sent out a reconnaissance expedition to the New World in 1584. This was followed by the colonization of 1585 led by Sir Richard Grenville, since the Queen would not let Ralegh go overseas. The party that reached what is now North Carolina included, besides Grenville, Harriot and the future (third) circumnavigator, Thomas Cavendish. After the Roanoke colonists were landed, Grenville, Cavendish, and others left for England with the understanding that the over one hundred settlers remaining under Governor Ralph Lane and Harriot would be visited and replenished the next year. Meanwhile Ralegh had been increasing his power at home with more monopolies and further appointments, including Lord Lieutenant of Cornwall. At one time he had as many as five hundred servants.

In the meantime Francis Drake had organized a large expedition (in which the Queen and Ralegh, among others, had an investment) to attack Spanish possessions in the Caribbean. Meanwhile, through many vicissitudes Governor Lane, Harriot, and most of the colonists had survived a winter in Roanoke, and now it was summer again and no ship had arrived from England. Imagine their surprise when, on 11 June 1586, instead of a relief squadron, the colonists saw Drake's large fleet off the coast, as it transpired, returning from the Caribbean. Although not his original intention, Drake heeded the pleas of the colonists and took them back to England.[11] Grenville, who had been dispatched by Ralegh to provide succour to the colony, arrived a short time after Drake's departure to find Roanoke deserted. Grenville left a small holding party on the island and returned to England, where Lane's hasty departure was being explained to the unhappy Ralegh. In late 1586 Ralegh was disillusioned about his overseas venture in North America and offered to sell out to any bidders; it was Grenville who wished to carry on with the idea of forming a military base against Spain in America. Ralegh now further consolidated his position in England by the acquisition of large estates which were formerly the property of Anthony Babington, who had plotted the assassination of Queen Elizabeth and the release of Mary, Queen of Scots. The plot was discovered, and Mary was executed by order of Queen Elizabeth in 1587. In the same year, on Hatton's promotion to Lord Chancellor, Ralegh became Captain of the Queen's Guard and reached the peak of his influence. This was also the year when Ralegh approved another expedition to "plant" a colony in North America in which he had a modest investment. Upon their arrival the colonists found that none of the small party left earlier by Grenville had survived. The same fate later awaited them except for the few, including the governor, John White, who returned home in August 1587.

In Europe events were now leading inexorably toward the climactic event of Elizabeth's reign—the defeat of the Spanish Armada. In April 1587 Drake with a large force had attacked shipping in Cadiz and "singed the King of Spain's beard."[12] This action had the effect of delaying the sailing of the Armada for a year, which gave Hawkins (building ships for the Queen), Ralegh, and others time to supervise preparations against a possible invasion on land, and Drake to muster the fleet. The commander of the English Navy was Charles, Lord Howard of Effingham, Lord High Admiral, with Drake being appointed Vice Admiral. When the Armada came in the summer of 1588, Drake was in Plymouth; he waited until the Spanish had sailed beyond the town and attacked them from the rear. The Armada was driven up the English Channel and the North Sea, where the winds completed the destruction of the Spanish fleet. For his role in the defeat of the Armada John Hawkins was knighted, thus, in this distinction, joining Drake and Ralegh, who had received the honor earlier.

However, King Philip tried again to build a fleet to invade England, and Drake, with a large force, attacked Lisbon (a port available to the Spanish fleet since the forcible union of Spain and Portugal in 1580). This venture proved disastrous to the English, and the Queen was greatly displeased. So Drake returned to Plymouth and immersed himself in his duties as Mayor and member of Parliament for the next five years. One enduring result of this was the building of a leat or conduit to bring fresh water from Dartmoor to Plymouth. In the meantime Thomas Cavendish had made the second English global circumnavigation, 1586–88. He attempted another circumnavigation in 1591, in company with John Davis, an experienced Arctic explorer and chartmaker, but the voyage was unsuccessful and Cavendish died without reaching the Pacific a second time.[13]

In these eventful years Ralegh had been so occupied that the promised relief expedition he had induced London merchants to finance to provide succour for the Roanoke colonists had been delayed until 1590. When White and his little fleet arrived at the site of the settlement in August of that year, they found no sign of life in what has come to be known as the Lost Colony. Meanwhile the English continued their predations against Spanish shipping and, in 1591, Lord Thomas Howard was appointed to lead an expedition to intercept the returning treasure fleet in the Atlantic. Ralegh was named Vice Admiral but the Queen would not let him sail, so Grenville was assigned to the position. The Spanish fleet had recovered from the defeat of the Armada and, with the main English force immobilized, Grenville in the *Revenge* fought a losing battle against fifty-three enemy ships. This heroic-tragic action, in which Grenville died in late August 1591, was celebrated by Ralegh in his *Report of the Truth of the Fight about the Isles of Acores this last Summer*. Already an accomplished poet, Ralegh by this piece established himself as a writer of prose. Early in 1592 Ralegh was installed in Sherborne Castle in Dorset by the Queen, who was soon to punish him for indiscretion at her court.

Ralegh had met and fallen in love with one of Elizabeth's maids-of-honour, Elizabeth (Bess) Throckmorton, daughter of Sir Nicholas Throckmorton, the Queen's first Ambassador to Paris. The couple married secretly sometime in 1591 and the affair was kept from the Queen until Bess became obviously pregnant. She gave birth to a boy on 29 March 1592 who was named Damerei, and it seemed for a time that life could go on as usual for the new parents. However, the jealous Queen imprisoned Bess and Ralegh in the Tower of London in August 1592 only to have him released the next month. The reason for the premature release was to enable Ralegh to control the looting by English sailors of a Spanish treasure ship *Madre de Dios* which had been taken in a raid, as successful as the *Revenge* affair of the previous year had been unsuccessful. Ralegh was one of the principal organizers and investors in this enterprise, but he did not receive as large a share as others and claimed to have lost money in the venture. When the assignment was completed Ralegh returned to his imprisonment in the Tower, to be released again, with Bess, at the end of the year. Like Drake after he had displeased the Queen some three years earlier, Ralegh now went back to his home in the West Country. Also, like Drake, he continued to represent that part of the country in Parliament and to work on various local projects. Ralegh enjoyed the pleasant life of Squire of Sherborne where, in 1593, Bess gave birth to a second son, Walter (known as Wat). But both Ralegh and Drake wanted nothing more than to be fully restored to the Queen's favor.

For Drake the opportunity came in 1594 when he and Sir John Hawkins were appointed as joint commanders of an expedition to attack Spanish overseas settlements. A large fleet sailed from Plymouth in the late summer of 1595. Las Palmas in the Canary Islands was unsuccessfully attacked before the now depleted force sailed across the Atlantic to the Virgin Islands and on to Puerto Rico. Here the Spanish defenders had been warned and the English sustained big losses, Hawkins dying on shipboard on 12 November. Drake and the remainder of the fleet sailed on to sack Panama, but they were again defeated, and Drake contracted fever and dysentery. He died aboard his ship 28 January 1596 and was buried at sea off Portobelo, a few miles from the eastern end of what is now the Panama Canal.[14] This sad ending makes it obviously impossible to continue a parallel discussion of Drake and Ralegh in relation to contemporary events. Accordingly, the remainder of Ralegh's life will be sketched only in the broadest outlines and a comparison will be made between the careers of these two great adventurers.

As early as 1593 Ralegh had become obsessed with the idea of finding El Dorado. The legend had grown up during the early years of European expansion into South America, and the possibility of finding great wealth had impelled others, before Ralegh, to explore the interior of the continent. The focus of

Ralegh's expeditions would be the Orinoco—the first of the great rivers of South America to be experienced by Europeans and the last to be thoroughly explored.[15] In 1594 Ralegh sent a reconnaissance ship to Guiana, followed by a full-scale expedition the next year. Although not yet fully rehabilitated by the Queen, Ralegh was authorized to take any land not already possessed by Europeans and to engage in privateering. He was now leader of the expedition and crossed the Atlantic for the first time. The ships were left at the coast and, with the help of Indian guides, Ralegh and his exploring party made their way by barge through the delta to the main course of the Orinoco. At length they came to the confluence of the Orinoco and Caroni rivers, and Ralegh elected to ascend this large tributary of the main stream. The party had travelled over two hundred miles upstream and seen much beautiful country but had not found the elusive El Dorado. They returned to the coast and eventually to England, which was reached in September 1595, nine months after setting out. The investors in the project were understandably disappointed that no great quantity of valuable metals had been brought back, but Ralegh wrote a glowing account of the Empire of Guiana, which was an immediate success and provided useful propaganda for further expeditions.

But it was through a naval action, rather than through his writings and explorations, that Ralegh finally became reconciled to his Queen. He was given command of one of the five squadrons in the fleet of over one hundred ships that was sent out to attack Cadiz in the summer of 1596. The leaders of the expedition were Lord Charles Howard and the Earl of Essex; Ralegh thought of it as an opportunity to avenge the death of Grenville. The Spanish were quite unprepared, and the sacking of Cadiz by the English was as successful as Drake's expedition had been to the same place nearly a decade earlier. In the action in which he distinguished himself greatly, Ralegh was wounded in the leg as a result of which he limped for the remainder of his life. Upon his return he was reinstated as Captain of the Queen's Guard, a position he would retain until the death of Elizabeth. But he was now frequently absent from Court as, in 1597, when he was Vice Admiral and commander of a squadron in an expedition led by Essex which attempted, without success, to intercept the Spanish treasure fleet in the Azores. As the result of this action relations between the Earl and Ralegh deteriorated. Essex now plotted against the Queen, was arrested for treason and condemned to death. Ralegh as Captain of the Guard was present at the execution of his rival on Ash Wednesday, 1601.

The Virgin Queen who had been on the throne for over four decades was now growing old and the problem of succession loomed large in the minds of her councillors. The strongest claimant was King James VI of Scotland, the son of Mary, Queen of Scots. Some years before his fall Essex had prejudiced the King against Ralegh who, in turn, had spurned James's representative, the Earl of Lennox. Influential ministers and prominent courtiers now turned against

Ralegh so that when James became King of England in March 1603 on the death of Elizabeth, peace was made with Spain and Ralegh was sacrificed. He was deprived of many offices and within four months was once more thrown into the Tower of London. The charge was treason, but the evidence was vague and insubstantial. In the end, the sentence of death was commuted to further imprisonment in the Tower. The incarceration was humane; he had separate quarters and was allowed servants and visitors. During his imprisonment Ralegh and Bess, who visited him frequently, had another son, Carew, born in 1605.

After this date among Ralegh's fellow prisoners was his friend Henry Percy, Earl of Northumberland (the Wizard Earl), who was supposedly implicated in the Gunpowder Plot. The Earl and Ralegh, who were both scientifically inclined, conducted experiments at the Tower. In spite of the precaution of having Sherborne Castle made over to their son Wat, the Raleghs were forced by the King to relinquish this property for reasonable compensation. A number of prominent people came to the Tower to consult with Ralegh, among them the eldest son of King James, Prince Henry, who, however, died in 1612. Ralegh thus lost his greatest potential ally and patron. During his four-year friendship with the Prince, Ralegh threw himself into his greatest literary work, *The History of the World* (published 1614). Harriot, who had returned from Roanoke to England with Drake's fleet in 1586, was permitted frequent access to the Tower and assisted Ralegh with *The History* and with various experiments. The book was denounced by the King because of its implied unfavorable comparison between his reign and the previous one, but no effective ban was achieved. But because of this, and its assumed opposition to the doctrine of the Divine Right of Kings, it became influential among the rising Parliamentary faction.

Since Ralegh's expedition to Guiana in 1594, a number of English adventurers, some of them his servants, had been in the area. On the promise of locating a gold mine in Guiana if allowed to go once again himself, Ralegh secured his release from the Tower in 1616. Now over sixty years of age and not in good health, Ralegh, with the help of his wife, raised enough money to outfit a fleet of a dozen ships. The flagship *Destiny* was commanded by his son Wat, now in his twenties. In the summer of 1617 the ships left England on a voyage which, because of a royal restriction placed on it that there should be no conflict with the Spanairds, was doomed before it began. On arrival in the Caribbean Ralegh stayed off Trinidad while an expeditionary force, including Wat Ralegh, landed in Guiana and advanced up the Orinoco. Here the inevitable confrontation between the Spanish and the English took place, and Wat and others were killed. They had also failed to find the promised gold mine.

Ralegh returned to England in the *Destiny* in June 1618 and in August was again incarcerated in the Tower. After a trial on charges that were not really proved but mostly to placate Spain, his condemnation of 1603 was reviewed, and he was sentenced to die. A late attempt to escape failed, and with great dignity and bravery Sir Walter Ralegh faced his execution on 28 October 1618. He was buried not as his wife Bess had requested at Beddington Church but in St. Margaret's Westminister. "This was the end," as John Aubrey says, "of the great Sir Walter Raleigh, great sometimes in the favor of Queen Elizabeth and (next to Sir Francis Drake) the great scourge and hate of the Spaniard."[16]

Much was written about Drake and Ralegh during their lives and much more has been written since. Some of this may be apocryphal, but from the abundant literature it is possible to gain an idea of the character of these men. The best-known story concerning each, whether true or not, well summarizes the nature of Drake and Ralegh, respectively. When the message came at 3:00 P.M. on Friday, 13 July 1588, that the Armada had been sighted in the Channel, Drake was reputedly playing bowls on Plymouth Hoe. "There's time to finish the game and beat the Spaniards too"[17] was Drake's cool reaction to the news. He knew that the English fleet was prepared and that nothing could be done until the next ebb tide six hours later. There was, therefore, no need to panic. Similarly, the episode concerning Ralegh freshly back from Ireland at the English court spreading his "plush cloak" on the ground so that Queen Elizabeth could tread dryshod over a *"plashy place"* or puddle, is entirely in keeping with Ralegh's character.[18] This story was written down after Ralegh's death but, like the Drake incident, it may be more than merely a fable.

As far as their ancestery is concerned both Drake and Ralegh came from solid West Country stock but were related, in each case, to more prominent families. Drake had little formal education but, no doubt, learned reading and writing from his father who, as Bible reader and later Vicar, would have been at least reasonably literate. By contrast Ralegh attended Oxford University, knew several foreign languages and also received training as a lawyer. However, he was more interested in life at Court than in academic pursuits. When necessary Drake could express himself well as, for example, the speech he delivered to his crew on the coast of South America and also could speak Spanish freely. However, he preferred action to words, and his reputation may have temporarily suffered because he failed to publish an account of his voyages himself and left this to others.[19] On the other hand Ralegh was a man of letters, skilled in both poetry and prose. His prose work, notably *The History of the World* (even if only a first part of a longer work), is still consulted and his poetry is to be found in anthologies to this day.[20] Ralegh also associated with some of the most gifted poets of his age, including Sir Philip Sidney and Edmund Spenser, and wrote a clever satire on Christopher Marlowe's "The Passionate Shepherd to his Love."

In personal appearance Drake and Ralegh presented an interesting contrast. A number of contemporary portraits of each survive; both Ralegh and Drake were painted by the miniaturist, Nicholas Hilliard, when at the height of their manhood. Drake was described as "low of stature, of strong limbs, broad Breasted, round-headed, brown hayre[d], full Bearded, his eyes rounde, Large and Cleare, well favoured, fayre and of a cheerfull countenance."[21] Ralegh "was a tall, handsome and bold man.... His beard turned up naturally.... He spake broad Devonshire to his dyeing day. He had a most remarkeable aspect, an exceeding[ly] high forehead."[22] He was of a swarthy complexion with dark hair and beard. As far as his character is concerned, an anonymous contemporary wrote to Lord Burghley of Ralegh "... no man is more hated than him, none cursed more daily by the poor.... His pride is intolerable...." But his friend, the Earl of Northumberland, writing to King James, said of Ralegh, "... although I know him [to be] insolent, [and] extremely heated ... yet must I needs confess what I know, that there is excellent good parts of nature in him...."[23] Of Drake, after he was knighted, Stow tells us that "... his name and fame, became admirable in all places, the People swarming Dayly in the Streetes, to behold him vowing hatred to all that durst mislike him.... In his imperfections he was Ambitious for honor. Unconstant in amity. Greatly affected to popularity."[24] His prisoner, Francisco de Zarate, said that Drake treated his men with affection and they treated him with respect, and that he had no favorites. Both Ralegh and Drake loved luxury. Ralegh became famous for his clothes, which were described as being "a considerable part of his estate"[25] while, even at sea, Drake had his food "served on silver dishes with gold borders and gilded garlands."[26] Both had great success in their relations with women and both were happily married. Drake had no children by either of his wives; and only Carew, of the three sons Ralegh had with Bess, survived him.

At the height of their powers both Ralegh and Drake were bold leaders but, in the end, this charismatic quality deserted them. Only when he was past his prime was Ralegh himself permitted the opportunity to travel to newly discovered lands overseas. By contrast Drake, early in his life gained fame from such ventures and contributed significantly to geographical discovery himself. His circumnavigation was his greatest achievement and best illustrates his belief in the freedom of the seas. Gaspar de Vargas, his enemy, said of Drake that "there was no one in the world that understood the art [of navigation] better than he."[27] It was through the capture of Spanish treasure, directly in the case of Drake and more indirectly through Ralegh, that the English economy was immediately improved. As a result of Drake's enterprise in Asia and Ralegh's in North America, others were to establish colonial possessions in those areas which contributed remarkably to the expansion of British influence worldwide in the eighteenth and nineteenth centuries, particularly. In the long run the most important effect of this colonization has been the spread of the English language.

Although not appointed to the Privy Council, as members of Parliament Drake and Ralegh had considerable political influence but neither was a "politician" nor an important policy maker. In the matter of religion, through association with others rather than through his own words and actions, Ralegh was accused of being an atheist. Ralegh was a philosophical theologian while Drake was a thoroughly evangelical Protestant. Ralegh's interest in chemical experiments, which he carried out while in the Tower, where he prepared medications, made him suspect of witchcraft in some quarters. These interests were shared by his fellow prisoner, Northumberland, and also by Harriot, who was a skeptic, though not an atheist. Although it is too much to claim that Ralegh introduced tobacco into England (it was known long before the 1580s), he most certainly popularized its use. Aromatic plants were collected on Drake's circumnavigation, and the first scientific account of the voyage was a botanical work by Charles de l'Ecluse.[28] Both Ralegh and Drake did much to promote navigation, scientific illustration, and cartography. The contributions of Harriot to navigation, though unpublished, were considerable;[29] and White's delineations of coastal Carolina, its inhabitants, flora, and fauna were the best of the area for many years.[30] Ralegh mapped the coast of the island of Trinidad himself during his visit in 1595. Similarly, Drake had a great concern with drawing and cartography, as well as navigation, as indicated by Nuno da Silva, his Portuguese prisoner who reported: "Francis Drake kept a book in which he entered his navigation and in which he delineated birds, trees and sealions. He is adept at painting and has with him a boy [his young cousin John Drake] who is a great painter."[31] Zarate commented that Drake's coastal views were so natural that "no one who guides himself according to these paintings can possibly go astray."[32] Unfortunately all these original Drake materials are lost, unlike the splendid maps and drawings by John White and Thomas Harriot of coastal Carolina, which we can still enjoy today.[33]

In the flamboyant Sir Walter Ralegh and the more pragmatic Sir Francis Drake we see two figures whose lives exaggerate certain characteristics of the Elizabethan age. Drake was fortunate enough not to live into the new reign while Ralegh, whose loyalty to the Queen was absolute, could not come to terms with the Jacobean age.

Notes

*Stephen B. Baxter, Kenan professor of history at the University of North Carolina at Chapel Hill, introduced Norman Thrower as follows: "Norman Thrower was born in England in 1919 and came to this country in 1947 after seven years' service in the British Army. He is probably too modest to want you to know that he was awarded the Burma Star. He took his B.A. at Charlottesville and his advanced degrees at Madison, joining the geography faculty at UCLA in 1957. For the past thirty years he has been exceptionally successful there as a teacher, as a scholar, as an administrator, and indeed as a grantsman. Since 1981 he has combined his professorship in geography with the post of director of the William Andrews Clark Memorial Library at UCLA. In these years he has not only administered the library but raised a good deal of money for its endowment.

"Norman's early publications were in the field of cartography, both of Burma and of southern California. This led on naturally enough to an interest in the work of Edmond Halley, who made major contributions in the field of cartography at the turn of the eighteenth century before going on to the astronomical observations for which he is best known. In 1981 the Hakluyt Society published his two-volume work, *The Three Voyages of Edmond Halley in the Paramore 1698–1701*. As the research for this work went on, Norman became interested in the South Atlantic voyages of an earlier Englishman, Francis Drake.

"None of us who have felt only the leg or the trunk of the elephant can appreciate the full extent of our debt to Norman, and to Dr. Helen Wallis and Professor Quinn, for their great work in the celebrations of the past ten years. The labours of the Sir Francis Drake Commission actually began in 1973, and here fourteen years later we are still celebrating with this International Sir Walter Raleigh Conference. The parties have been important in focusing public attention on the discoveries of the first Elizabethans. The papers and books which have been written for the occasion have deepened our knowledge of those discoveries and of the English world of four hundred years ago which made those discoveries possible. We are now a plural society, and happy with it, but it would be shameful for us to forget our English heritage.

"Norman served on the Sir Francis Drake Commission, and became its President. He also edited the book published to celebrate Drake's landing in 1579, *Sir Francis Drake and the Famous Voyage, 1577–1580*. I was rather suspicious of all this interest in naval affairs on the part of an Army man until I discovered that Norman's grandfather had been one Captain Bailey, a naval officer. So he comes by the sea naturally enough, as do most Englishmen. It is a real pleasure to have Professor Thrower with us today. He will speak to us on 'Raleigh and Drake.'"

[1]In the *Dictionary of National Biography* (Oxford: Oxford University Press, 1917 and later) which has articles on all of these men, some nineteen pages are devoted to Ralegh and sixteen to Drake. Of the others Sir John Hawkins has the largest biography in this source, slightly over seven pages.

[2]For recent authoritative accounts of these voyages see especially the writings of David B. Quinn, including *Set Fair For Roanoke: Voyages and Colonies, 1584–1606* (Chapel Hill and London: University of North Carolina Press, 1985). This was published for America's Four Hundreth Anniversary Committee.

[3]For an up-to-date description of a major Tudor ship, see Margaret Rule, *The Mary Rose: The Excavation and Raising of Henry VIII's Flagship* (Leicester: Windward Press, 1982).

[4]There is considerable literature on Drake recently augmented by, and referred to in, Norman J.W. Thrower (editor), *Sir Francis Drake and the Famous Voyage: Essays Commemorating the Quadricentennial of Drake's Circumnavigation of the Earth* (Berkeley, Los Angeles and London: University of California Press, 1984). This work, which contains ten specialized essays and an extensive bibliography, was published for the Sir Francis Drake Commission, State of California.

[5]David W. Waters, *The Art of Navigation in Elizabethan and Early Stuart Times* (London: Hollis and Carter, 1958) is the authoritative work on this topic.

[6]Robert Lacey, *Sir Walter Ralegh* (London: Weidenfield and Nicolson, 1973), and Norman Lloyd Williams, *Sir Walter Ralegh* (London: Eyre and Spottiswoode, 1962) are the fairly recent and standard works on the life of Ralegh. The latter contains long quotations from the original writings of Ralegh and others.

[7]John Hampden (editor), *Francis Drake, Privateer: Contemporary Narratives and Documents* (University, Alabama: University of Alabama Press, 1972) reprints important accounts of Drake's earlier voyages with annotations. Later voyages are the subject of two Hakluyt Society Publications, Mary Frear Keeler (editor), *Sir Francis Drake's West Indian Voyages, 1585–86* (London: Hakluyt Society, Second Series, 148, 1981) and Kenneth R. Andrews (editor), *The Last Voyage of Drake and Hawkins* (Cambridge: Hakluyt Society, Second Series, 142, 1972).

[8]Hampden, *op. cit.,* p. 45.

[9]Warren L. Hanna, *Lost Harbor: The Controversy over Drake's California Anchorage* (Berkeley, Los Angeles and London: University of California Press, 1979).

[10]The term is Richard Hakluyt's, from his account of Drake's circumnavigation in *The principall navigations, voiages and discoveries of the English nation* (London: 1589).

[11]Quinn, *Set Fair for Roanoke, op. cit.,* especially pp. 131–139, and Keeler, *op. cit.,* pp. 40 and 270–274.

[12]The report in the town records of Plymouth states that Drake "did greatly annoy the King of Spain's flete." Quoted in Crispin Gill, "Drake and Plymouth" in Thrower (editor), *op. cit.,* p. 86.

[13]David B. Quinn (editor), *The Last Voyage of Thomas Cavendish, 1591–1592* (Chicago: Society for the History of Discoveries and the Newberry Library, University of Chicago Press, 1975).

[14]Gill in Thrower, (editor), *op. cit.,* p. 89.

[15]Christopher Columbus on his third voyage to the New World in 1598 passed along the southern shore of the Island of Trinidad and, by the great amount of fresh water being emptied into the sea, believed he was off the coast of a continent (Asia). Angel Falls, the highest waterfall in the world, on a tributary of the Caroni River, was discovered by air by James (Jimmy) Angel in 1935.

[16]John Aubrey, *Brief Lives,* 6 fol. 78, edited by A. Clark (Oxford: Clarendon Press, 1898), p. 189.

[17]Richard Boulind, Crispin Gill, Martin Wright, and G. Chowdary-Best, "That Game of Bowls," *Mariner's Mirror,* (November 1971): 447–450. A series of letters on the subject.

[18]Thomas Fuller, *The History of the Worthies of England* (London: 1662), p. 262.

[19]This matter is discussed at length in "Early Accounts of the Famous Voyage" by David B. Quinn in Thrower (editor), *op. cit.,* pp. 33–49.

[20]Sir Arthur Quiller-Couch (editor), *The Oxford Book of English Verse,* (London: Oxford University Press, 1940). Three pages are devoted to four of Ralegh's poems in this authoritative anthology. In *The New Oxford Book of English Verse 1250–1950,* chosen and edited by Helen Gardner (Oxford: Oxford University Press, 1972) there are also four poems by Ralegh covering over six pages. Ralegh is similarly represented in other major anthologies of English verse.

[21]John Stow, *The Annals or Generall Chronicle of England* (London: 1615), p. 808.

[22]John Aubrey, *Brief Lives, op. cit.,* 6 fol. 75, 75v.

[23]Quoted in Williams, *op. cit.,* pp. 69–70, 164.

[24]Stow, *op. cit.,* p. 807–8.

[25]Fuller, *op. cit.,* p. 262.

[26]Hampden, *op. cit.,* p. 214, quoting Don Francisco de Zarate.

[27]Hampden, *op. cit.,* p. 216.

[28]Charles de l'Ecluse, *Caroli Clvsii Atreb aliqvot notae in Garciae Aromatum Historiam. Eisudem descriptiones nonnullarum Stirpium, & aliarum exoticarum rerum, que a Generoso vir Francisco Drake* (Antewerp: 1582).

[29]David W. Waters, "Elizabethan Navigation" in Thrower (editor), *op. cit.,* p. 31.

[30]Paul Hulton and David Quinn (editors), *The American Drawings of John White* (London and Chapel Hill: University of North Carolina Press, 2 volumes, 1964).

[31]Helen Wallis, "The Cartography of Drake's Voyage" in Thrower (editor), *op. cit.,* p. 123.

[32]*Op. cit.,* p. 123. Several maps with elements derived from Drake's delineations which can be dated some years after "The Famous Voyage" are extant; see Helen Wallis, "The Cartography of Drake's Voyage" in Thrower, *op. cit.* These include the Drake-Mellon map with insets showing incidents on the voyage in Asia and flags of St. George: at Drake's two most important discoveries in the Americas, Drake Passage (1578) and Nova Albion (1579); at Baffin Island (Frobisher's claim of 1576); and at Ralegh's Roanoke Colony, dated on the map, 1585.

[33]Hulton and Quinn (editors), *op. cit.*

Stephen B. Baxter (top), Kenan professor of history at UNC-CH, introduced Norman J. W. Thrower (bottom right) and Jerry W. Mills. They spoke respectively on "Raleigh and Drake" and "Raleigh as a Man of Letters."

Sir Walter Raleigh as a Man of Letters

Jerry Leath Mills*

My title is one I arrived at, as some might say, in the spirit of colonialism itself: I expropriated it from its previous owner. That owner was Professor Frank Hersey, who used it for a paper he prepared for a conference very similar to our present meeting, scheduled in North Carolina in 1918 but cancelled because of the influenza epidemic. Its intended proceedings were published by the State Literary and Historical Association the same year. Hersey's purpose was the same as my own—a general overview of Raleigh's literary activity—and our shared title is thus appropriately general, if not vague.

Our emphases, however, are somewhat different, and they reflect the critical climates of the respective times. For Hersey, Raleigh's poetry—his earliest literary mode—was interesting as a repository of catchy phrases and for selected examples of Raleigh's tough-mindedness; but Raleigh, for him, was essentially a master of prose, and specifically the prose of a man of action: "He did not carve his sentences in alabaster," Hersey writes, "he cut them out with his sword." And he adds: "Sometimes hacked them, too."[1]

This is a view—Raleigh's literary achievement as synonymous with his achievement in prose—that remained more or less constant from Raleigh's death to well into our century. Henry David Thoreau, for one, regretted that Raleigh wrote any poetry at all. But in recent decades the poems have earned revaluation and a new appreciation. One factor in this has been the researches of Professor Lefranc[2] and others toward establishing a reliable canon of his writings. Another is a growing interest among literary scholars in Raleigh's influence, as a poet, on his great poetic contemporary, Edmund Spenser.[3]

These, at any rate, are major factors in *my* interest in Raleigh the poet, because nothing in my background as a North Carolinian prepared me to see him in that light, even though, in this state, we all grow up with Sir Walter the man. If you grew up here, as I did, you probably don't remember ever *not* knowing about him. As a youth you may have tended, as I did, to confuse him with Prince Albert, since both have achieved a kind of aromatic immortality on tobacco packages, and if you saw him in *The Lost Colony* in the 1950s you may remember that he talked a lot like the Sheriff of Mayberry, since Andrew Griffith played the role. You knew him as an adventurer, a founder and loser of colonies, a man who flung ships across the ocean and his cloak in the mud before the Queen. You may have heard that he established the vogue of tobacco-smoking in England and that he introduced the potato to Ireland, thus inventing the Irish potato. You may even have been aware that he wrote a million words on *The History of the World* before giving up at 131 B.C. But you probably didn't think of him as a poet, and certainly not the author of anything like this:

Hir face, Hir tong, Hir wit

Hir face,	Hir tong,	Hir wit,
So faire,	So sweete,	So sharpe,
First bent,	Then drew,	Then hit,
Mine eie,	Mine eare,	My hart.
Mine eie,	Mine eare	My hart,
To like,	To learne,	To loue,
Hir face,	Hir tong	Hir wit,
Doth lead,	doth teach,	Doth moue.
Oh face,	Oh tong,	Oh wit,
With frownes,	With checke,	With smart,
Wrong not,	Vexe not,	Wound not,
Mine eie,	Mine eare,	My hart.
Mine eie,	Mine eare,	My hart,
To learne,	To knowe,	To feare
Hir face,	Hir tong,	Hir wit,
Doth lead,	Doth teach,	Doth sweare.[4]

We aren't absolutely sure that Raleigh wrote this poem (I'll mention some of the authorship problems later on), and perhaps we should hope that he didn't. It is, of course, as much a riddle as a poem, capable of being read at least three ways: vertically, stanza by stanza and column by column; horizontally, stanza by stanza; and horizontally, line by line ("Hir face, Hir tong, Hir wit,/So faire, so sweete, So sharpe," etc.). The evidence for Raleigh's authorship is rather strong, whether we like it or not, and this poem, like several others that probably date from the late 1580s, is so different from what we usually think of as his public personality that it provides a focal point for the question, why did Sir Walter Raleigh write poetry?

One answer is readily available and often repeated: writing poetry was one of the expected accomplishments of a courtier in Raleigh's time, like dancing, horsemanship, facility in French and Italian, and the ability to lie with a straight face. This is true; but the essential reasons go deeper than that. They repose, first of all, in the major emphases of education in the sixteenth century, and, second, in the initially political uses Raleigh was to perceive for the prevailing literary fashions of the day.

We don't know a great deal about Raleigh's individual educational experience, but unless it was markedly different from that of other young men of his class it was based on several assumptions we now think of as typical of a Renaissance world view. It was aimed, at least in theory, at producing the Whole Man, the integrated personality—the "Renaissance Man," as we now say—for whom contemplation and study were not goals to be pursued for themselves, but rather as a basis for informed and purposeful action in the real world. Although based solidly on the Greek and Roman classics, with a heavy admixture of theology, it was not an Ivory Tower education. It was, in its central interest, preparation for public service.

Public service in Elizabethan England meant the clergy, the military, and the government, with its center at the royal court. At the higher levels of all these pursuits the requisite abilities were the arts of expression, communication, and, especially, persuasion: the power, through language, to move men's minds. Destinies both personal and national were assumed to be shaped not only with the sword but with the pen and tongue. Consequently, education at almost all stages stressed literary style as well as the mastery of a body of knowledge, on the reasonable assumption that, since we think chiefly in words, a clear and elegant style provides a medium or matrix for the clear and elegant formulation of thought. Students studied logic and rhetoric both in theory and in practical situations—the great Roman historians, for example, were read not simply for historical information and political theory but also in order to analyze the orations they attribute to the statesmen and military leaders of the Ancient World. Students staged plays to improve their forensic skills, and recitation sessions were conducted largely through debate, often on paradoxes, unsolved problems, and unresolvable questions, such as "Which is better, day or night?" (One testimony to the popularity of that topic is Milton's pair of poems, "L'Allegro" and "Il Penseroso," which elevate that issue to a high metaphysical plane.) Since these problems had few possibilities of resolution, the premium was on wit, ingenuity, and rhetorical organization—the same qualities evident in the poem "Hir face, Hir tong, Hir wit"—and the exercise of these was excellent preparation for life in the labyrinth of patronage, clientage, and competitiveness that constituted the Court.

In keeping with this stress on style and verbal elegance, sixteenth-century schooling placed a special value on the study and composition of poetry. Poetry, then as now, offered a special challenge, with its strict requirements for appropriate diction, inventiveness, and the decorous conjunction of content and form. Students were made to memorize large segments of Latin verse, analyze its rhetorical strategies, and then rewrite it in English, varying and adapting it to purposes conceived by themselves. "Modern" poetry was not formally studied, but young scholars read it on their own, especially the recent continental works, and it was a dull pupil who could not quote lavishly from the Italian of Petrarch and the French of Ronsard and Du Bellay.

This taste for continental poetry, and for imitations of it in English, continued into the adult lives of many men, especially those who sought to make their way in the atmosphere of Elizabeth's Court. The Queen herself wrote poetry.

She loved symbolism, stylization, and formal elegance, and she seems to have shared the appetite, current all over Europe in the 1580s, for love poetry in the vein of the great Italian Francesco Petrarca—or, as he was known in England, Francis Petrarch.

Petrarch had lived and written two centuries before Raleigh; but most Elizabethans thought of him as a contemporary in spirit. His enduring, indeed continually growing, popularity throughout Europe lay in the formula for love poetry he developed in the 317 sonnets he wrote to his idealized lady, Laura. Petrarch in effect taught succeeding generations how to write love poetry that combined sex with spirituality and thus satisfied both the emotional and philosophical instincts of the Renaissance man. In its paradigmatic, popularized form, the Petrarchan progress goes something like this: The poet is smitten with love at the first sight of his lady, overwhelmed first by her physical beauty and, later, equally appreciative of her personality and mind—he admires not only her face, as Raleigh puts it, but also her tongue (expressive of her refined ideas) and wit.

However, in keeping with the chastity that is, for the poet, a part of her attractiveness, she remains aloof and inattentive to his pleas. He idealizes her—places her on a pedestal, as we now say—addresses her as a goddess and the sovereign mistress of his heart. He reacts violently to his passion and becomes subject to chills and fever. He burns like fire, he freezes like ice. Her every whim carries, for him, the power of life and death, and in the agony of his unrequited love he calls her cruel, unfeeling, a tyrant and murderess. He threatens to die, or move to the country.

What this pose is supposed to demonstrate, of course, is the lover's sensitivity, his capacity for refined feeling and deep appreciation of beauty. And it leads, ultimately, to a religious experience. As he suffers and loves, the lover comes to understand that the lady's beauty is simply an earthly manifestation of the greater beauty of God, who created both the lady's beauty and the poet's ability to love. Thus the adoration of Laura leads to the worship of God, and earthly love finds its justification as one rung on a ladder leading to heaven.

It was probably Raleigh's knowledge of Irish affairs that brought him to the Queen's attention around 1582. Once he had that attention he found means to keep it through a behaviorial mode based on the Petrarchism of the time. In the poems he addressed to her he created a kind of "political Petrarchism"[5] that appealed, not simply to Elizabeth's vanity, but to her love of ceremony, gamesmanship, and extravagant behavior. The story of Raleigh's spreading his cloak before the Queen is most likely untrue in a factual sense, but it is directly in keeping with the attitude he expresses in the poems he wrote to her.[6]

What Raleigh exploits in this type of poem is, as Leonard Tennenhouse has discussed in an excellent essay,[7] the *literal* applicability of a vocabulary that is only metaphorical in Petrarch's poems. Elizabeth *was* a sovereign ruler. She *did* wield power over life and death. She *was* unattainable (the Virgin Queen). And she *was* more or less literally on a pedestal — at least a throne. That she could be a tyrant was abundantly demonstrated in her treatment of her courtiers and was to be shown most forcefully in 1592 when she clapped Raleigh in the Tower. The gifts at Elizabeth's disposal — power, prestige, and riches — made the amatory favors of the ordinary love object seem paltry. The Petrarchan mode allowed Raleigh to translate these political realities into a refined and graceful idiom of praise, cajolement, and solicitation.

The following example of that kind of poem, "Praised be Diana's fair and harmless light," is typical of Raleigh's poetic idealization of the Queen and typical also in possessing an elaborate and self-serving subtext established by allusion.

> Praisd be Dianas faire and harmles light,
> Praisd be the dewes, wherwith she moists the ground;
> Praisd be hir beames, the glorie of the night,
> Praisd be hir powre, by which all powres abound.
>
> Praisd be hir Nimphs, with whom she decks the woods,
> Praisd be hir knights, in whom true honor liues,
> Praisd be that force, by which she moues the floods,
> Let that Diana shine, which all these giues.
>
> In heauen Queene she is among the spheares,
> In ay she Mistres like makes all things pure,
> Eternite in hir oft chaunge she beares,
> She beautie is, by hir the faire endure.
>
> Time weares hir not, she doth his chariot guide,
> Mortalitie below hir orbe is plaste,
> By hir the vertue of the starrs downe slide,
> In hir is vertues perfect image cast.
>
>> A knowledge pure it is hir worth to kno,
>> With Circes let them dwell that thinke not so.

Raleigh here, as frequently, addresses the Virgin Queen under the name of one of the various goddesses associated with chastity: Diana, Cynthia, Belphoebe. These figures, in myth, are all associated with the moon. The planet customarily used as a symbol for kingship, from biblical times forward, was not the moon but the sun, partially because of its primacy in the heavens and also because of its related symbolism of the virtue of Justice. Sunlight is relentless in its searching out of evil, and while it makes life possible on earth, it can also scorch, burn, and punish. The sun, in gendered languages, is inevitably a masculine noun.

But the moon, equally dominant in its own sphere of time, is soft and feminine. In contrast with the justice of the sun, the moon represents mercy, consolation, and love. By its gentle light—"harmless light," as Raleigh says—flaws are overlooked and beauty is brought to the lives of others. Thus a somewhat cynical but essentially accurate paraphrase of the first line, "Praised be Diana's fair and harmless light," might be: "Please make me warden of the tin mines. Please give me the monopoly on imported wines. Please invest a few thousand in a trip to the Outer Banks."

When Raleigh wished to appear hurt by the Queen's real or fancied inattention to him, he assumed a further extension of the Petrarchan pose, that of the lover in despair, casting himself into isolation and woe. This is the pose of "Like to a hermit poor," which contains an image of sartorial self-denial that must have seemed especially ludicrous to contemporaries familiar at first hand with Raleigh's propensity for extravagant dress and self-adornment:

> Like to a Hermite poore in place obscure,
> I meane to spend my daies of endles doubt,
> To waile such woes as time cannot recure,
> Where none but Loue shall euer finde me out.
>
> My foode shall be of care and sorow made,
> My drink nought else but teares falne from mine eies,
> And for my light in such obscured shade,
> The flames shall serue, which from my hart arise.
>
> A gowne of graie, my bodie shall attire,
> My staffe of broken hope wheron Ile staie,
> Of late repentance linckt with long desire,
> The couch is fram'de whereon my limbs Ile lay,
>
> And at my gate dispaire shall linger still,
> To let in death when Loue and Fortune will.

To the modern ear these poems sound overwrought, even fulsome. In the nineteenth century, Thoreau, as I have mentioned, didn't like them at all. He remarked that in them Raleigh's "genius seems warped by the frivolous society of the Court."[8] Such a comment overlooks the degree to which Raleigh's idealization was, apart from its function as flattery, homage to the concept of monarchy for which Elizabeth stood. Nonetheless, if these poems were all of Raleigh's verse that we possessed, his reputation as a poet would be a very minor one indeed. Fortunately he moved on from this vein, or alternated with this vein, another, more private kind of poetry in which the personality we think we know seems more accurately expressed. In these poems Raleigh's vision penetrates beyond the surface glitter of the court to the grimmer and more authentic truths of disappointment, impermanence, and the constant possibility of betrayal and loss. His best poems are preoccupied, as is *The History of the World*, with the fragile nature of human achievement in the constant process of time and inevitable change.

An excellent example of this tone, and of Raleigh's subtlety in expressing it, is the sonnet he wrote to accompany the first installment of Edmund Spenser's great epic, *The Faerie Queene*, in which, topically, Raleigh appears as a major character, thinly disguised under the name of Timias, Prince Arthur's squire. This sonnet is one of the few poems by Raleigh that we can date firmly: he wrote it in 1589, when *The Faerie Queene* was being readied for publication the next year. The ostensible purpose is to praise Spenser by declaring that his poem will eclipse all previous achievements in verse, including those of Petrarch, whose Laura will be forgotten in favor of Spenser's Gloriana. The ghosts of Homer and other Ancient poets will howl in the underworld to see their works displaced by Spenser.

> Methought I saw the graue, where *Laura* lay,
> Within that Temple, where the vestall flame
> Was wont to burne, and passing by that way,
> To see that buried dust of liuing fame,
> Whose tumbe faire loue, and fairer vertue kept,
> All suddeinly I saw the Faery Queene:
> At whose approch the soule of *Petrarke* wept,
> And from thenceforth those graces were not seene.
> For they this Queene attended, in whose steed
> Obliuion laid him downe on *Lauras* herse:
> Hereat the hardest stones were seene to bleed,
> And grones of buried ghostes the heuens did perse.
>   Where *Homers* spright did tremble all for griefe,
>   And curst th' accesse of that celestiall thiefe.

This is successful enough as witty praise; but Peter Ure has called attention to the fact that only four of the fourteen lines are on Spenser's poem, while the rest concentrate on the theme of displacement, on the abandonment and despair of those whom oblivion will now cover. And Raleigh's emotional identification, as Ure observes, is clearly with these.[9]

There is, most likely, a personal dimension to all this. In 1589 Raleigh was in fact threatened with displacement, in the Queen's hierarchy of favorites, by the young Earl of Essex. But is isn't *just* personal. Raleigh is here, in effect, finding his subject, formulating an early statement of the theme of his longest and most complex poem about Elizabeth, *The Ocean to Cynthia*, and eventually of *The History of the World*: that all good things lack permanence, and man is condemned forever to watch his finest achievements fade.

We can see Raleigh's clearest expression of this theme—and one of the most poignant expressions of it that the Renaissance produced—in the poem beginning "Nature, that washed her hands in milk." This is a poem that begins with the poet idealizing his lady, moves to the Petrarchan image of the proud and tyrannizing beauty, the "cruel fair," and then exposes the self-deluding nature of both attitudes in the presence of devouring time:

Nature that washt her hands in milke
   And had forgott to dry them,
In stead of earth tooke snow and silke
   At Loues request to trye them,
If she a mistresse could compose
To please Loues fancy out of those.

Her eyes he would should be of light,
   A Violett breath, and Lipps of Jelly,
Her hair not blacke, nor ouer bright,
   And of the softest downe her Belly,
As for her inside hee'ld haue it
Only of wantonnesse and witt.

At Loues entreaty, such a one
   Nature made, but with her beauty
She had framed a heart of stone,
   So as loue by ill destinie
Must dye for her whom nature gaue him
Because her darling would not saue him.

But Time which nature doth despise,
   And rudely giues her loue the lye,
Makes hope a foole, and sorrow wise,
   His hands doth neither wash, nor dry,
But being made of steele and rust,
Turnes snow, and silke, and milke to dust.

The Light, the Belly, lipps and breath,
   He dimms, discolours, and destroys,
With those he feedes, but fills not death,
   Which sometimes were the foode of Joyes;
Yea Time doth dull each liuely witt,
And dryes all wantonnes with it.

Oh cruell Time which takes in trust
   Our youth, our Joyes and all we haue,
And payes us but with age and dust,
   Who in the darke and silent graue
When we haue wandred all our wayes
Shutts up the story of our dayes.

A strange and haunting evocation of this transience of earthly things is the poem, "As You Came From the Holy Land." There Raleigh takes an old ballad, dating back to medieval times, when Walsingham was a popular shrine for religious pilgrims, and adapts it to a rejection of all the false promises of the world, promises symbolized by the lady of the poem, who has chosen variety and new experience over loyalty to the adoring lover in his advancing age. The pilgrim's final attitude, a rejection of earthly for philosophical and spiritual love, is the medieval attitude of *contemptus mundi*, a substitution of contemplation and retreat for more worldly involvements:

> Of women kynde suche indeed is the loue
>   Or the word Loue abused
> Vnder which many chyldysh desyres
>   And conceytes are excusde.

> Butt true Loue is a durable fyre
>   In the mynde euer burnynge;
> Neuer sycke, neuer olde, neuer dead,
>   From itt selfe neuer turnynge.

Never turning from itself, that is, to the distractions of the active life. Perhaps fortunately for the course of empire, this was a program Raleigh himself was able to follow only when he was behind bars.

We can observe Raleigh's awareness of the human propensity for self-delusion about matters of permanence and change in a witty and sardonic vein in his famous reply to Christopher Marlowe's pastoral invitation, "Come live with me and be my love." In that poem Marlowe has indulged himself in the conventional pastoral escapist fantasy, that the answer to man's problems is retreat from social complexity into a natural world whose beauty is self-justifying and transcendent of all the confusion and stress of life in the town. It is the attitude we now call "neo-primitivism" and is much in evidence in our own time, when many believe that life's challenges are best dealt with by moving to a cabin, studying *Mother Earth News*, and playing John Denver records without interruption. After this poem began to circulate in the early 1590s it began to be accompanied by its companion piece (usually though not always attributed to Raleigh). Raleigh's reply is from the viewpoint of the nymph, who has been around enough to know that Marlowe's shepherd, in assuming the permanence of youth and joy, is promising what no man can deliver. Raleigh's concluding stanza sums up the nymph's cautious and commonsensical position:

> But could youth last, and loue still breede,
> Had ioyes no date, nor age no neede,
> Then these delights my minde might moue,
> To liue with thee, and be thy loue.

There are around forty poems generally attributed to Raleigh, only about half of which can be claimed with any degree of certainty. The difficulty of attribution is partly owing to the social assumptions behind the role of the courtier/poet: poetry, as I said earlier, was an expected accomplishment of a courtly man, but it was also expected that this poetry would remain within the confines of its social milieu. To seek publication of one's poems would have been, for a courtier, to show too much concern for what one was supposed to treat with cultivated nonchalance. So Raleigh made no attempt to preserve his poems. Nor did his widow, although she allegedly preserved his head, embalmed in a velvet bag, until the end of her life. To add confusion, Raleigh was such a popular and controversial figure that many things he didn't write were ascribed to him by others.

With his prose works we are on firmer ground; a number of these were published with his own supervision, and they were widely disseminated in his own time. He was a magnificent prose stylist, and he wrote a great deal, especially during his long imprisonment after 1603—treatises on shipbuilding, agriculture and economics, royal marriages, the conduct of war, the nature of the soul, and the monumental *History of the World* which he published, incomplete, in 1614. During the reign of Elizabeth his major prose work had been *The Discovery of Guiana* (1596), which has been called one of the best true adventure stories ever written,[10] with its vivid narration of his journey up the Orinoco River, its detailed accounts of the land and the Indian inhabitants, and its lavish promise of what was to be gained by further investigation in the interest of a permanent English base in Spanish America.

What distinguishes almost all of Raleigh's prose is its vibrancy, immediacy, and closeness to actual experience—of which Raleigh of course had a great deal. Thoreau remarked, aptly, that he gives the impression of writing with a sword in one hand and a pen in the other. He always writes with a concrete purpose, and he always writes to persuade. He prefers the first person as a narrative stance, and the reader of his chief works is constantly aware of a unique, dominating personality behind the page. Ancient battles in *The History of the World* are illustrated with tactical details from his own military experience, and he tells us how this or that problem was handled when he met with it in France, or Ireland, or on the high seas. Biblical peoples are compared in various ways with the aborigines of Guiana and North Carolina. On the basis of personal study he concludes that the Tree of Life in the Garden of Eden must have been *ficus indica*, the Indian Fig Tree.

Given this sense of immediacy and individualism, it is tempting to conclude, as Thoreau seems to, that Raleigh was simply a natural stylist, and that his achievements in prose are the results of spontaneity and natural talent. Natural talent must have had a great deal to do with it; but it is not the whole story. For that we turn again to the education of the Renaissance man.

Having presumably been trained, like other Elizabethan pupils, on Aristotle's *Rhetoric*, Raleigh must have had drilled into him as a boy the three basic approaches of persuasive writing and oratory: *ethos, pathos,* and *logos*, or, the ethical, pathetic, and logical approaches. All three, Aristotle had written, must combine in an effective presentation.

The criterion of *ethos* refers to the speaker's establishment of his own authority to speak, his command of the facts, and the legitimacy of his purposes. He must gain the audience's confidence in his character. Notice how Raleigh does this in the following passage from *The Discovery of Guiana*, with its stress on the narrator's sober and competent possession of fact and detail. Surely this man can be trusted to get a traveler—and an investor's money—there and back:

> The great river of *Orinoco* or *Baraguan* hath nine branches which fall out on the north side of his own main mouth: on the south side it hath seven other fallings into the sea, so it disembogueth by 16 arms in all, between Islands and broken ground, but the Islands are very great, many of them as big as the Isle of *Wight* and bigger, and many less: from the first branch on the north to the last of the south it is at least 100 leagues, so as the river's mouth is no less than 300 miles wide at his entrance into the sea, which I take to be far bigger than that of *Amazones*: all those that inhabit in the mouth upon the several north branches are those *Tivitivas*, of which there are two chief Lords which have continual wars one with the other: the Islands which lie on the right hand are called *Pallamos*, and the land on the left *Hororotomaka*, and the river by which *John Douglas* returned within the land from *Amana* to *Capuri*, they call *Macuri*.[11]

Then follows the criterion of *pathos*, the writer's appeal to the emotions of his audience. This is Raleigh's goal in the most frequently quoted passage of the entire *Discovery*, a passage that evokes a pristine, Edenic beauty in the landscape and instills it with just enough danger to make it exciting:

> On both sides of this river, we passed the most beautiful country that ever mine eyes beheld: and whereas all that we had seen before was nothing but woods, prickles, bushes, and thorns, here we beheld plains of twenty miles in length, the grasses short and green, and in divers parts groves of trees by themselves, as if they had been by all the art and labour in the world so made of purpose: and still as we rowed, the Deer came down feeding by the water's side, as if they had been used to a keeper's call. Upon this river there were great store of fowl, and of many sorts: we saw in it divers sorts of strange fishes, and of marvelous bigness, but for *Lagartos* it exceeded, for there were thousands of those ugly serpents, and the people call it for the abundance of them the river of *Lagartos*, in their language. I had a *Negro* a very proper young fellow, that leaping out of the *Galley* to swim in the mouth of this river, was in all our sights taken and devoured with one of those *Lagartos*.

The criterion of *logos*, the logical approach, gets us to the purpose of it all. Having prepared us for the pitch, as it were, by eliciting our trust in the speaker and by making us participate in the emotional experience of the trip, Raleigh turns from time to time to the why and the how. The *why* is the need for development of Guiana as a hedge against Spanish power and as a source of national treasure:

> Now although these reports may seem stran͛   yet if we consider the
> many millions which are daily brought out of *Peru* into Spain, we may
> easily believe the same, for we find that by the abundant treasure of that
> country, the Spanish King vexeth all the Princes of Europe, and is become
> in a few years from a poor king of *Castile* the greatest monarch of this
> part of the world, and likely every day to increase, if other Princes foreslow
> the good occasions offered, and suffer him to add this Emprie to the
> rest, which by far exceedeth all the rest: if his gold now endanger us,
> he will then be unresistible.

The *how* is revealed in practical plans for fortification, military deployment, and provisioning of troops, plans laid out in the closing pages of the book.

As immediate propaganda, the *Discovery* did not succeed. It was twenty years later that Raleigh was able to return to South America, and then it was on the final, disastrous expedition that precipitated his execution. But its long-term effect in stimulating interest in the possibilities, and the romance, of the New World was immense. Among its abundant literary progeny, the works it influenced include Shakespeare's *The Tempest* and Defoe's *Robinson Crusoe*,[12] not to mention *Tarzan of the Apes*. It continues to attract readers for the best of all reasons: it is genuinely interesting to read.

I mentioned that all of Raleigh's prose writings had practical purpose and intent to persuade. How does this apply to *The History of the World*, whose title implies, at the least, a broad subject and a general approach? It does apply, for two reasons. Soon after Raleigh was imprisoned by King James in 1603, he began to perceive that his main hope for release and restoration to prominence lay in the young Prince Henry, who often visited Raleigh in the Tower and who, in modern psychological terms, had selected Raleigh as a mentor or father surrogate, a most attractive alternative to his own effeminate and neglectful father, the King.[13] It was for Prince Henry that *The History of the World* was written. When Henry died unexpectedly in 1612, Raleigh gave up the project, for Raleigh had intended to use the book as a means of molding and shaping the young heir to the throne in the concepts of enlightened sovereignty. This enlightenment would of course lead to Raleigh's release; but, beyond that, Raleigh hoped, through analysis of successes and failures among the rulers of the past, and by advice through historical example in the practical, political, and scientific spheres, to do in actuality what Shakespeare did fictively with the Prince Hal of his second tetralogy of history plays—to produce that Renaissance ideal of the perfect prince.

A second purpose had its roots in Raleigh's understandable bitterness toward King James. In the preface, especially, but also in the work at large, Raleigh develops a perspective by which James could be embarrassed if not instructed.

This perspective stresses the vanity of human pomp, the eternally fading glory of the kingdoms of the earth, and, especially, the principle that no monarch is above the law of God and none can expect to evade His justice. James *was* embarrassed: he remarked that Raleigh had been "too saucy in the censuring of princes," and ordered that Sir Walter's name and portrait be removed from all issues before further distribution. (Raleigh's triumph was, again, in the long run; except for the Bible itself, *The History of the World* was Oliver Cromwell's favorite book, and Cromwell's coreligionists, acting on the principle that no monarch was above the law of God, did unto a Stuart what a Stuart had done unto Raleigh.)[14]

Raleigh's dual purposes help account for the dual and in many ways contradictory approach to history evident in his book. The larger framework, and the one stressed in the preface, is the idea of Providential history, the medieval view formulated by Saint Augustine, that history is a record of God's will, that God intervenes in history to punish and reward the actions of human kings, either by direct action or by punishments deferred to later generations of the same line. God is the *first cause* in a history that ultimately conforms, in complex ways, to a plan laid down at the Creation and extending to Judgment Day. *Second causes* — human psychology, motivation, and behavior — are, in the purely Providential scheme, interesting only as examples of man's successes and failures at conforming to God's will.

But on the other hand, Raleigh was deeply interested in the newer theories of the so-called "politic" historians such as Machiavelli, Jean Bodin, and Francis Bacon, who concentrated on second causes, divorced history from theology, and studied it for practical, administrative lessons, believing, as they generally did, that man functions best as a political animal when unencumbered by an overactive sense of piety.[15]

Raleigh moves among, rather than assimilates, divergent approaches, and it is easy enough to complain about his lack of consistency. For example, as H.A. Kelly has pointed out, Raleigh generally maintains that God punishes kings by dealing harshly with their descendants, but in one theological digression he asserts that the dead have no knowledge of what happens on earth. How, then are the dead kings punished by the fates of their descendants?[16] But if Raleigh's approach is not consistent, his tone is: it is the somber, elegiac tone of those poems on mutability and time. Raleigh doubts that man can learn much from history, anyway; man's pride and his boneheadedness condemn him to repeat the errors of his forebears. The conclusion to his book, written after Prince Henry's death, extols the one great teacher whom no one refutes or ignores:

> We may add to that which hath been already said; That the Kings and Princes of the world have always laid before them, the actions, but not the ends, of those great Ones which preceded them. They are always transported with the glory of the one, but they never mind the misery

of the other, till they find the experience in themselves. They neglect the advice of God, while they enjoy life, or hope it; but they follow the counsel of Death, upon his first approach. It is he that puts into man all the wisdom of the world, without speaking a word. . . .

O eloquent, just and mighty Death! whom none could advise, thou hast persuaded; that none hath dared, thou hast done; and whom all the world hath flattered, thou only hath cast out of the world and despised: thou hast drawn together all the far stretched greatness, all the pride, cruelty, and ambition of man, and covered it all over with these two narrow words, *Hic jacet*.

Raleigh met the great instructor on 29 October 1618 with dignity and composure under two strokes of the axe.

Notes

*Jerry Mills was introduced by Stephen B. Baxter as follows: "Jerry Leith Mills was born in Burlington and took his B.A. at Chapel Hill in 1960 before going on to Harvard for graduate study. He joined the faculty of the Univeristy of North Carolina at Chapel Hill in 1965. A brilliant communicator, he has won two teaching awards and is currently Bowman and Gordon Gray professor of English. Outside the classroom he is equally skilled in his role as a Southern story-teller. His many publications have for the most part concentrated on Spenser, but there has been one excursus on Herbert, and his most recent book bears the title *Sir Walter Ralegh: A Reference Guide*.

"Dr. Mills was corresponding editor, 1970–74, and is now associate editor of the *Spenser Newsletter*, and since 1965 he has been associated with *Studies in Philology*, of which he has been editor for seven years. He has held a variety of administrative positions in the university, including secretary and vice-chairman of the Division of Humanities. His subject today is 'Raleigh as a Man of Letters.'"

[1]Frank Wilson Cheney Hersey, "Sir Walter Ralegh as a Man of Letters," in *Proceedings of the State Literary and Historical Association of North Carolina*, 25 (1918): 42–54.

[2]Pierre Lefranc, *Sir Walter Ralegh, écrivain: L'oeuvre et les idées*. Quebec: Presses de l'Université Laval, 1968.

[3]I have surveyed the recent writings on Raleigh, to many of which this paper owes a general debt, in my two bibliographical studies, "Recent Studies in Ralegh," *English Literary Renaissance*, 15 (1985): 225–44, and *Sir Walter Ralegh: A Reference Guide* (Boston: G.K. Hall & Co., 1986).

[4]Poems quoted in the text are from the edition of Agnes Latham, *The Poems of Sir Walter Ralegh* (Cambridge, Mass.: Harvard University Press, 1962).

[5]The phrase is that of A. D. Cousins, "Ralegh's 'A Vision upon this Conceipt of The Faery Queene,'" *Explicator*, 41 (1983): 14–16.

[6]Raleigh's poems to and about Queen Elizabeth are printed and discussed at length by Walter Oakeshott, *The Queen and the Poet* (London: Faber and Faber, 1960).

[7]Leonard Tennenhouse, "Sir Walter Ralegh and the Literature of Clientage," in *Patronage in the Renaissance*, edited by Guy Fitch Lytle and Stephen Orgel (Princeton: Princeton University Press, 1981), pp. 235–58.

[8]Henry David Thoreau, *Sir Walter Ralegh*, edited by Henry Aiken Metcalf (Boston: Bibliophile Society, 1905).

[9]Peter Ure, "The Poetry of Sir Walter Ralegh," *Review of English Literature*, 1 (1961): no. 3, 19–29. On this poem see also Cousins as cited above.

[10]Margaret Irwin, *That Great Lucifer: A Portrait of Sir Walter Ralegh* (New York: Harcourt, Brace, and World, 1960).

[11]Quotations of Raleigh's prose are from the edition of Gerald Hammond, *Sir Walter Ralegh: Selected Writings* (Harmondsworth: Penguin Books, 1984).

[12]See Uwe Böker, "Sir Walter Ralegh, Daniel Defoe und die Namengebung in Aphra Behns *Oroonoko*," *Anglia*, 90 (1972): 92–104.

[13]See J.W. Williamson, *The Myth of the Conqueror: Prince Henry Stuart. A Study of Seventeenth Century Personation* (New York: AMS Press, 1978).

[14]Christopher Hill, *Intellectual Origins of the English Revolution* (Oxford: The Clarendon Press, 1964), pp. 131–224.

[15]On these issues see F.J. Levy, *Tudor Historical Thought* (San Marino, Calif.: Huntington Library, 1967), and John Racin, *Sir Walter Ralegh as Historian: An Analysis of "The History of the World"* (Salzburg, Austria: Institute für englische Sprache und Literatur, 1974).

[16]H.A. Kelly, *Divine Providence in the England of Shakespeare's Histories* (Cambridge, Mass.: Harvard University Press, 1970).

Closing of the Conference

The conference was officially ended after a discussion period on Saturday afternoon. H. G. Jones, chairman of the conference, called attention to these lines from John Bain, Jr., *Tobacco in Song and Story* (New York: A. Gray and Company, 1896):

> SIR WALTER RALEIGH! name of worth,
>> How sweet for thee to know
> King James, who never smoked on earth,
>> Is smoking down below.

The North Caroliniana Gallery in Wilson Library was opened for the first time during the Raleigh Conference and featured selections from the Sir Walter Raleigh Collection, including the collotypes of the John White drawings.

A continuation of the exhibition of documents and artifacts from the Sir Walter Raleigh Collection. The door at right in lower photo leads into the Sir Walter Raleigh Rooms, paneled and furnished with period materials.

Professor Joyce Youings presents to Curator H. G. Jones a pitcher featuring Raleigh motifs and made by potter Harry Juniper of Devon. At bottom, former UNC chancellor N. Ferebee Taylor views a model of a Dutch galleon.

Among the participants in the Raleigh Conference were William P. Cumming, noted authority on Southern maps, and his wife Betty. At bottom is R. Neil Fulghum of the North Carolina Collection who prepared the special exhibition.

II

Proceedings of a Banquet
in honor of
David Beers Quinn
at the
University of North Carolina at Chapel Hill,
27 March 1987

Preliminary Remarks and Presentations

H. G. Jones
Master of Ceremonies

For the benefit of our guests from overseas, I should explain that the absence of an invocation before dinner results from the tendency of our American courts to declare unconstitutional any favorable—though not, strangely enough, *un*favorable—mention of the Almighty at functions carrying the imprimatur of a governmental agency such as the University of North Carolina. This double standard of our Orwellian legal minds, however, has not yet forbidden us from drawing upon other sources of inspiration, so I begin this affair by reading from the scripture according to Sir Walter Raleigh: "Whosoever shall follow truth too near the heels, it may haply strike out his teeth."

To emphasize the theme of this evening, let me repeat that verse: "Whosoever shall follow truth too near the heels, it may haply strike out his teeth."

Now, such a profound proverb may not impress some at this head table, but those of us with natural teeth find solace in anticipating an evening bereft of our usual Rankean obligation to the truth. After all, we have listened throughout the day to scholarly papers, and we deserve the escape provided by an evening of fiction.

The story line of tonight's novel is rather simple: Members of the Sir Walter Raleigh cult, holding a two-day conference in a university town and with nothing to do the night between, provide ourselves a bit of diversion by putting on display one of our members. The object of our attention is a member who has been longest associated with the courtier, who has done most to keep his memory alive, who has written and talked most about him, and who has traveled farthest and most often to the site of Raleigh's colonies, always accompanied by a little ball of energy who serves as his prompter, critic, researcher, indexer, and driver. For testimonial, we turn to a local dean who, having been his former student, has no reason whatever to be concerned about Rankean loyalty to the man who gave her so much grief. Finally, to heighten the fictional character of the evening, we have printed up a little certificate, which will be presented to him with the appearance of all pomp and seriousness.

Mercifully, however, we will be permitted to eat our dinner first. You may proceed to visit with your table mates and dine on, appropriately, Scallopini of Veal Elizabeth. We have been assured by the chef that, though the meal honors Elizabeth I, the veal was actually grown during the reign of Elizabeth II.

[Dinner followed.]

Now that you have, we hope, enjoyed your dinner and your table mates, I must put on another face and tell you that in reality we are here tonight for a serious purpose. Our focus is on David Beers Quinn, the man to whom I turned, as first chairman of America's Four Hundredth Anniversary Committee, to bring international credibility to what otherwise might have become an exercise in provincial chauvinism. I am convinced that it was in this very building, on a snowy weekend early in 1980, that credibility came to the commemoration, for at that time David and Alison Quinn, after a softening up process at professional gatherings such as the Sir Francis Drake Quadricentennial in California and the Organization of American Historians in New York, and through correspondence, became full partners with us. Not only did David agree to the republication of his *Virginia Voyages from Hakluyt* (under the new title *The First Colonists: Documents on the Planting of the First English Settlements in North America, 1584–1590*); he also committed himself to writing the centerpiece of a distinguished publications series, *Set Fair for Roanoke: Voyages and Colonies, 1584–1606*. And, of course, subsequently he wrote *The Lost Colonists: Their Fortune and Probable Fate*. Perhaps as important as his literary productions was David's influence in our enlistment of other British scholars like Paul Hulton, who produced *America 1585: The Complete Drawings of John White*; Helen Wallis, who sponsored the great British Library exhibition in London, Raleigh, and New York, and who, before she was assured that my intentions were honorable, sensed that I was "pursuing" her at the Drake Quadricentennial in California; and Joyce Youings, who wrote *Ralegh's Country; The South West of England in the Reign of Queen Elizabeth I*, and who was my gracious hostess during the Raleigh in Exeter Conference in 1985. No wonder, then, I gladly joined Karen Kupperman and Thad Tate three months ago in reading a paper on David Beers Quinn in Chicago as he was given the rare distinction of honorary membership in the American Historical Association.

But before we turn the spotlight on David Quinn, we want to remember three other friends from Britain who have become our associates and friends. The North Caroliniana Society demands service, not attention, and it seeks to express the appreciation of our fellow citizens to those who, with no thought of compensation or reward, share in promoting knowledge and appreciation of our state's heritage. We gladly do that tonight.

For the first of our recognitions, we turn to one of the three incorporators of the North Caroliniana Society a dozen years ago, our first president, and now our vice-president, who, in the face of publishers' deadlines for two textbooks on North Carolina history, the third volume of his monumental *Dictionary of North Carolina Biography,* a revision of *Paradise Preserved,* and only his wife Virginia knows how many other projects, always has time to recognize others who contribute to our common mission.

If Bill Powell is one of our first three members, Lindsay C. Warren, Jr., is our newest, and we are glad to announce his acceptance of election to the North Caroliniana Society within the past month. My first association with Lindsay Warren, Jr., came when I was director of the State Department of Archives and History and he was a state senator and member of the powerful Advisory Budget Commission. History has not since had a triumvirate of friends in high places to match senators Warren, Thomas J. White, and Ralph J. Scott, who invariably gave us courteous hearings and almost as consistently voted generous appropriations for our programs. It was his appreciation of history and the memory of his father's role in stimulating interest in the Roanoke colonies that led America's Four Hundredth Anniversary Committee to urge the governor in 1980 to consider Senator Warren for a vacant seat on the committee; and when it became painfully evident that I could not continue to devote the necessary time as committee chairman, we all urged his appointment to the chair, and Governor Hunt complied. The result has been a tasteful, dignified commemoration with an educational emphasis of which all North Carolinians can be proud.

I reserve for myself, however, the pleasure of presenting a certificate of appreciation to one of our friends from Great Britain. In all probability we would never have heard of David Beers Quinn except for two people. One was Sir Walter Raleigh, and we had hoped to have with us tonight a genuine Raleigh, but Dorothy W. Raleigh of Tunbridge Wells found it impossible to come to the States at this time. The other is a Scotswoman who helped save David from oblivion, for Alison Moffat Robertson Quinn has for a half century been more than a wife; she has been the other half of a remarkable professional couple, sharing his life and his career, always as a productive scholar in her own right. Alison, they're going to talk mostly about David tonight, but I want you always to be able to say, "I got mine first." [The certificate was accepted by Alison Quinn.]

Alison Moffat Robertson Quinn, wife and collaborator of David Quinn, accepts certificate of appreciation from H. G. Jones.

Lindsay C. Warren, Jr.
Chairman, America's Four Hundredth Anniversary Committee

In 1983, John Neville, Richardson Preyer, and I went to England to make plans for the April 1984 commemorative ceremonies in Plymouth. As you will recall, over two hundred North Carolinians journeyed to Devon and London, headed by then Governor Hunt, to commemorate the four hundredth anniversary of the departure of the first of the Roanoke voyages. While in London, we had occasion to visit Helen Wallis at the British Library to talk with her about the exhibition "Raleigh & Roanoke," which was to make its London debut while the North Carolinians were there. It was my first introduction to Dr. Wallis, and I remember the occasion vividly, for while we were there she did us the honor of bringing out for a private showing all of the famous John White watercolor drawings owned by the British Museum. It was a sight to behold. With security guards watching our every move, we gazed upon this remarkable collection for the first time. Fourteen of these paintings were later to come to North Carolina in January 1985 with the "Raleigh & Roanoke" exhibition. I want again to thank Dr. Wallis for that exciting opportunity. Now that she is with us on this occasion, I want to thank her also for participating in this conference and for the many other things she has done to contribute to the success of America's Four Hundredth Anniversary. And now I have the honor to present to Dr. Wallis this special certificate as a small token of North Carolina's appreciation for her role in the quadricentennial commemoration. [The certificate was accepted by Helen Wallis.]

Helen Wallis accepts certificate from Lindsay C. Warren, Jr. for her contributions to the quadricentennial.

William S. Powell
Emeritus Professor of History, UNC-CH

Professor Joyce Youings has virtually become North Carolina's chief booster in the West Country of England. As professor of history at the University of Exeter, she teaches English social history, but she has also become an authority on Elizabethan times, particularly with respect to Sir Walter Raleigh and his New World interests. She has often visited in North Carolina, and in her home district of Devon and Cornwall she has greeted numerous Tar Heels and shown them interesting places with Carolina associations.

Dr. Youings is a native of north Devon, and for the observance of the four hundredth anniversary of the Roanoke voyages she contributed one of the volumes in our series of publications. Entitled *Ralegh's Country: The South West of England in the Reign of Queen Elizabeth I*, it placed Sir Walter Raleigh in his native setting and characterized the people with whom he associated.

Professor Youings also planned and directed a two-day conference in May 1985 entitled "Raleigh in Exeter." The papers read on that occasion were published under her editorship by the University of Exeter Press, adding extensively to our understanding of the role played by Raleigh and by England in the early history of America.

Because of her scholarly research and publications and in gratitude for her continuing interest in the early history of North Carolina, the North Caroliniana Society is pleased to present this Certificate of Appreciation to Professor Joyce A. Youings. [The certificate was accepted by Dr. Youings.]

William S. Powell presents certificate to Joyce Youings for her work in connection with the four hundredth anniversary.

Tribute to David Beers Quinn

*Gillian T. Cell**

The relationship between a graduate student and an adviser is a very special and often a very complex one. The adviser can take on the role of the parent who is all powerful; the student the role of the child who has—sometimes painfully—to break away. Other times directors are so indifferent that one wonders whether they would recognize their students if they met them on the street. To me it is above all the relationship that David Quinn has with his students, and with the students of others whom he decides to "adopt," that best illustrates his extraordinary qualities both as a scholar and as a person.

I first met David in 1957 when he came to the University of Liverpool as Andrew Geddes and John Rankin professor of modern history and head of the Department of Modern History. Prior to that he had graduated with first class honours from the Queen's University at Belfast and done his graduate work at King's College, London, under the renowned A. P. Newton, Rhodes professor of imperial history. Newton, editor of the *Cambridge History of the British Empire*, was enough of an imperialist himself to wonder whether anyone schooled in Ireland could really be educated, and to insist that David take some undergraduate classes just to be sure. His doubts, I imagine, were soon put to rest, for after only two years David had completed his dissertation on "Early Tudor Rule in Ireland." In 1934 he took his first faculty position at University College, Southampton. There and throughout all the the years that have followed, David pursued his two linked interests—Tudor Ireland and the discovery and exploration of the New World—and began to explore the extent to which the English experience in Ireland would influence their later involvement in North America. That insight developed in David's work has, of course, become orthodoxy and a starting point for the work of many others. There, too, David met and married Alison Moffat Robertson, a Scot with an M.A. from the University of Edinburgh who was teaching in Southampton. In October of this year they will mark their fiftieth anniversary. But of that remarkable partnership more will need to be said later.

In 1939 David returned to Northern Ireland to teach Irish history at the Queen's University of Belfast. While spending many nights on duty as the casualty officer for South Belfast, which was of course heavily bombed, (and at least one convivial night with Professor Flynn, father of Errol Flynn, sheltering under a car with a bottle that had fortuitously survived when the window of a liquor store was blown out), David served as secretary of the Ulster Society for Historical Studies, as a member of the Irish Historical Society and the Irish Committee of Historical

Gillian T. Cell, dean of the College of Arts and Sciences and General College at UNC-CH, gave the main address at the banquet honoring David Beers Quinn.

Sciences, and was elected to the Royal Irish Academy. And during the years in Belfast the Hakluyt Society published his two-volume edition, *The Voyages and Colonising Enterprises of Sir Humphrey Gilbert*. His connection with the Hakluyt Society, begun in 1937, has continued with terms as vice-president and since 1982 as president.

Continuing his exploration of the Celtic fringe, in 1944 David moved to the University College of Swansea, a campus of the University of Wales, as professor and head of department. He remained there for thirteen years, including four years as dean of the Faculty of Arts. In 1948 he paid his first visit to the United States, based at the Institute of Early American History and Culture in Williamsburg, but coming down to Chapel Hill and to the Roanoke site — for by this time he was at work on *The Roanoke Voyages*, which the Hakluyt Society published in 1955. Those two volumes were described by the formidable English geographer E.G.R. Taylor as a fine work but "too bloody historical" and by the equally redoubtable Samuel Eliot Morison as a "monument to scholarship. Every possible document from every likely source is included, the notes on ethnology, botany, and the English background are informing and voluminous, and (most unusual for an historian) Professor Quinn twice visited and examined the area described in the narratives." Praise from the admiral is praise indeed, though he was less kind to David's later theories about pre-Cabot voyages, asserting that they put "Quinn as a dialectitian in a class with the Cortesão brothers."

In 1957 David left Swansea for what many people insist is the true capital of Wales, the city of Liverpool and its university. He remained there for the next nineteen years, until his so-called retirement in 1976. At Liverpool he was heavily involved in the expansion of the university and the building of the History Department which needed to be pulled together after some rather difficult years. Nevertheless the visits to the United States became more frequent (in 1963–64 after thirty years of teaching, he actually got the first research leave of his career), and conference papers and lectures were delivered as close at hand as Paris and as far away as New Zealand. Above all, the years of research, of vacation time regularly spent in the British Museum, the Public Record Office, and libraries and archives in Britain, the U.S. and continental Europe, began to bear fruit in an increasing volume of publications—many, many articles, the book *The Elizabethans and the Irish,* and the exquisite two-volume edition with Paul Hulton of *The American Drawings of John White,* which was published jointly by the British Museum and the University of North Carolina Press. A specially bound copy of those two volumes was presented to President Lyndon Johnson for the White House Library.

When David and Alison came to Liverpool, I was in the middle of my undergraduate degree. As students we were, of course, curious about this new head of department and mildly worried about how it would change things. I took a course from him in the history of the British constitution, read the required gobbets, wrote my required essays, did my required share of grumbling. But for my final year I had to choose a special subject—the area in which I would write my honors thesis. Somewhat sceptically I allowed myself to be persuaded by a friend that I should not do American history as I had always intended, but that we should take a chance on this new man and take his special subject on the discovery and exploration of North America. That did it! For someone who had been wandering through a degree, unsure of purpose, unsure of the future, it was a revelation. It was fun; it was hard work—very hard work; it was a fascinating mix of history, geography, cartography, ethnography, art, biology; but more than anything, it was my first real exposure to a scholar at work, totally engaged, totally involved. We sat in David's office and read the sources (always the sources)—Columbus, Cabot, Cartier, Champlain, De Soto, Gilbert, Raleigh, John Smith. We quickly learned to distinguish the excited "Yes, yes, yes" that greeted our more perceptive moments from the sceptical "well, well, well" that suggested we were just a little off the wall. Over Christmas vacation we were told we were all going to London; there we were personally introduced by David to the mysteries of the British Library and the Public Record Office and launched on the research for our theses. We were taken to see the originals of the White drawings; we were taken for coffee and introduced to the best of the inexpensive restaurants near the museum (there were some in those days). Above all we were taken seriously.

This, of course, goes back to my opening point about David and his students. I stayed on at Liverpool to do my Ph.D. with him—there was no point to going anywhere else—and from the beginning he put opportunities in my way. When, out of the blue, he was contacted about an unused collection of documents on the first Newfoundland colony, he responded that he was too busy to do anything with them himself, but he had this graduate student.... Those documents became the foundation of my dissertation and later publications. Through David came my contact with the Hakluyt Society, with the *Dictionary of Canadian Biography* and the University of Toronto Press, which would later ask for the manuscript of my dissertation. Even, you could say, through David came my husband and my reason for being in Chapel Hill, for David encouraged me to apply for a fellowship at the Institute of Historical Research where, following his example, I joined the seminar of the then Rhodes professor of imperial history, Gerald Graham. In that seminar I met my husband who teaches at Duke. David was one of the very few people in England in 1962 who had ever heard of Duke. "Yes," he said, "that's where my cousin Walter went at the age of fifteen before he went some place else to get an education." That story, I quickly learned, went down far better in Chapel Hill than in Durham.

When I first came to this country it was David who introduced me to Theodore Rabb; that introduction led to my giving a paper at the American Historical Association and helped convince the department here that I was respectable enough to be offered a one-year job, which they did in 1965. This is mentoring in the best sense of that now over-used word. His help, support, and friendship, as well as his intelligence and his knowledge, have been given generously to students and young colleagues from the beginning of his career to the present. And not insignificant to me is the fact that so many of David's successful students have been women.

David retired in 1976 and promptly became busier than ever. The list of appointments, publications, travels, and honors is exhausting simply to read. Suffice it to say that it includes teaching at St. Mary's College, Maryland, and pioneering work at the archaeological site there; an appointment at the University of Michigan at Ann Arbor; a fellowship at the National Humanities Center; conference papers around the world; four honorary degrees, including one from the University of North Carolina for which I had the honour and pleasure to present him; and publications such as *Set Fair for Roanoke* and *The First Colonists*. In 1984 he received the signal honour of being elected an honorary fellow of the British Academy; most recently in 1986 he was elected an honorary member of the American Historical Association and, in his own word "survived" a session in Chicago on "The Life and Work of David Beers Quinn." As a Fulbright 40th Anniversary Distinguished Fellow he lectured early this year in California, Florida, Tennessee, Connecticut, and Massachusetts. His plans for research and publication stretch into the 1990s. So much for retirement.

In the later part of David's career, as their three children grew up, Alison was more and more able to travel with him. Because David does not drive (for which pedestrians, other drivers, dogs, cats, and all living creatures should be profoundly grateful), Alison has driven him not only around Britain and Ireland, but from one end of North America to another. I recall their arrival in Durham in 1964, in a huge and ancient Oldsmobile which Alison had driven from the John Carter Brown to the Huntington and back again to the east coast. How she saw over the wheel I never quite knew. Increasingly they have worked together, and the publications that bear both names continue to appear. As an indexer not just of David's works but of such volumes as *The Complete Works of Captain John Smith*, Alison has gained an international reputation, the medal of the British Index Society—and the biggest collection of shoe boxes in the world. The Quinns are a formidable combination.

They are also great friends and great company. While the Quinns were at the National Humanities Center in 1983, it was a particular pleasure to see my own children, one of whom is named for David, listen with fascination to his talk about his work and to his stories, probable and improbable. The importance that David has had in my life—to a great extent to which I am what I am and where I am because of him—makes this opportunity to pay tribute to him one of the most enjoyable tasks I have ever been asked to perform.

Note

*Dean Cell was introduced as follows by H. G. Jones: "If this conference carries the tone of a Celebration of the British, it is not entirely accidental. After all, the subject of our discussion these two days makes it so. Beyond that, our conference reaffirms the ties between us and our Mother Country, a characterization not popular today but one that still accurately describes the language, traditions, laws, and institutions of the United States. Nor is it accidental that the dean of our College of Arts and Sciences and General College speaks with a non-Southern accent, for she too is a native of Great Britain. She came here as a history scholar, rising to chairman of our Department of History after holding several other positions of influence, some of them listed in the printed program of the conference.

"Gillian T. Cell is, I believe, unique in this room on several counts. The one that matters is that she received her doctorate under David Beers Quinn. Knowing the propensity of students to parody their professors, we thought she could add a light touch to our respite from our study of Sir Walter Raleigh. But, alas, we learn belatedly that she may be so beholden to him that she dare not tell all about the *real* David Beers Quinn, that gruffy old picky-picky professor, for who ever heard of such a bond that would not require the student to go back to Liverpool for her doctoral examination but instead would bring the professor to Chapel Hill? We await her tribute of truth—or fiction."

Presentation of Certificate of Appreciation to David Beers Quinn

Archie K. Davis*

To follow in the wake of Dean Cell's magnificent tribute to Dr. David Beers Quinn leaves me in an unenviable if not impossible position. For what more can one say about the life and works of this remarkable scholar whose accomplishments will forever shed a very special light on the Elizabethan era, and particularly on the four-hundredth anniversary of the first English settlement in America.

While the reading of his curriculum vitae leaves one almost breathless, it does confirm to our complete satisfaction that Professor Quinn's professional pursuits did bring him and his lovely wife Alison to North Carolina on many occasions, and that we may now be so bold as to claim them as fellow North Carolinians. In this sense, the use of the word "claim" is intended to convey a kindly attitude and one of affectionate goodwill, not one of demand or possessiveness.

This latter qualification of the word "claim" does apply, however, to a situation which the professor has undoubtedly observed. In the sixteenth century, well prior to the reign of Charles II, the use of the term Elizabethan "Virginia" applied to most of what we now know as North America. Neither Dr. Quinn nor others have ever questioned the fact that the first English settlement in America was on Roanoke Island in what would later become the proprietary colony of North Carolina, that the first *permanent* English settlement in America was founded at Jamestown on 26 April 1607, in what would later become the royal Colony of Virginia, and that the first child born of English parents in America was born on Roanoke Island. Surely, enough glory for all, but the commonwealth's penchant for primacy in all matters historical has never been stilled. To this day, there are those who answer our modest claim with this rhetorical flourish: "If the first English child to be born in America was born in North Carolina, why, then, did you name her *Virginia* Dare?"

If this comes as a matter of surprise to Professor Quinn, he should know that within recent years the work of North Carolina's Four Hundredth Anniversary Committee has occasioned untold anguish just north of the 36 degree, 30 minute parallel. Although Jamestown's four-hundredth anniversary was over twenty years away, the commonwealth could not let North Carolina go unchallenged. As we were building the *Elizabeth II*, a representation of a sixteenth-century vessel, the Jamestown-Yorktown Foundation was busily fabricating a reproduction of the *Godspeed* for a planned reenactment of the voyage to Virginia in 1607. This ship was afloat and making its way to our coastal waters in the spring of 1985, obviously not for the purpose of reenacting an event, whose four-hundredth anniversary will not take place until the year 2007, but presumably to divert world attention from this "vale of humility."

Happily this has not been the case. Just the reverse has been true, and to none are we more indebted than to our distinguished friend and scholarly patron, David Beers Quinn, whose active role as intermediary with other Elizabethan scholars, whose advice and support over the years, as well as the publication of his book entitled, *Set Fair for Roanoke: Voyages and Colonies, 1584–1606*, by the University of North Carolina Press in 1985, have added immeasurably to the historical credibility and world importance of North Carolina's claim.

But alas, our commonwealth friends have never been known to miss an opportunity for historical advantage. Obviously, Professor, you must be high on their list. I can even now picture a book by you entitled *Set Fair for Jamestown*. If that be the case, North Carolina will not be found wanting. Most assuredly, the *Elizabeth II*, bearing special greetings from Roanoke Island to her younger sister colony in Virginia, will heave to at Jamestown on 26 April 2007.

Dr. Quinn, we bask in your reflected glory this evening and shall be forever grateful for your friendship and support. On behalf of your many friends and admirers, it is my high privilege to present to you the North Caroliniana Society's Certificate of Appreciation, which reads,

The North Caroliniana Society,

in recognition of services to

North Carolina during the commemoration

of the Roanoke Voyages of 1584–1587,

is pleased to present this

Certificate of Appreciation

to

David Beers Quinn

27 March 1987

Note

*In introducing the president of the North Caroliniana Society, H. G. Jones said: "In the business world, Archie K. Davis is known as the only individual to have served as president of both the American Bankers Association and the United States Chamber of Commerce. In the cultural world he is known for his involvement in preservation activities, particularly as a leader in the historic Moravian town of Old Salem. In the academic world he is known for his role in bringing to North Carolina the National Humanities Center, whose headquarters building bears his name. In the literary world he is known for his graceful publications, including the book, *The Boy Colonel: Life and Times of Henry K. (Harry) Burgwyn*, soon to be followed by a study of North Carolina's international relations during the American Civil War. To me, he is known as the successful businessman and former senator who confided to me in Raleigh in 1972 that he had always wanted—even after forty years—to return to graduate school for an advanced degree in history, neither of us suspecting that we would meet again in Chapel Hill, I as his faculty advisor, he as my distinguished student. Never has a professor learned so much from his student; furthermore, and it is for me a signal honor to be working with him in his capacity as president of the North Caroliniana Society—an organization that embodies the interests, ideals, morals, and mission of Archie K. Davis who, burdened by all the recognitions a state can bestow upon a native son, remains a private in the Army of our Heritage."

In his best professorial posture, David Beers Quinn (left) describes his early expeditions to North Carolina's Outer Banks, then poses with his wife and colleague, Alison.

David Beers Quinn accepts certificate of appreciation from Archie K. Davis, president of the North Caroliniana Society, then (bottom) responds to remarks by his former student, Gillian T. Cell.

North Carolina: My First Contacts, 1948–1959

David B. Quinn*

North Carolina has been very kind to me for a very long time, and to Alison for a shorter but still considerable period. How many times have we been here together? How many of the people who are here have we known, some of them for a very long time, when we were here before? And how many of them are close and dear friends? Were we not involved quite early in the preparations for the 400th Anniversary and did we not contribute something, if only a little, to their fulfillment? The six months we spent at the Humanities Research Center remain with us as an exciting, unique, experience in our lives. The honor of an honorary degree from the University of North Carolina at Chapel Hill remains one of my proudest memories. But for this occasion I will try to leave the recollection of these more recent occasions and hark back to the first three visits I made, on my own, without Alison, in 1948, 1957, and 1959, all of which, but especially the first, have made a deep imprint on my mind and were reflected in so many ways in my subsequent lectures and writings.

While working on a small book, *Sir Walter Raleigh and the British Empire*, published in 1947, I had become deeply interested in the documentation of the first colonizing expeditions to what is now North Carolina and the splendid drawings of John White, which brought so much of the setting of the first colony to light. I decided to attempt to bring together all the materials, old and new, on what I was to name "the Roanoke voyages," and to explain as many aspects of them as could be traced. I was fortunately able, in the summer of 1948, with the aid of a grant from the Leverhulme Fellowships Committee, to make my first visit to North America, and to base myself at the Institute of Early American History and Culture, then recently established at Williamsburg under the directorship of the distinguished historian, Carl Bridenbaugh, with whom I had been in correspondence. Poring over the charts of the Carolina Outer Banks and sounds, the idea developed that it might be possible to mount a little expedition to the area. Carl was anxious to see it and so was a graduate student of his, John Gordon, who had later a career in the United States Navy and in education. Through his family's connections it was somehow arranged with Admiral J. F. Farley, who commanded the United States Coast Guard, that the three of us could spend a week in the care of the stations at that time liberally distributed along the coast, since there was no other way in which the then isolated and inaccessible region could be seen, unless with resources which were quite beyond our reach.

Accordingly, on 21 July 1948, the three of us set out from Williamsburg, through Norfolk, and across the area in which many of the Lost Colonists eventually met their end at Powhatan's hands, to the Outer Banks, our objective being Oregon Inlet Coast Guard Station, which was to be our base. Before we reached our destination I learned that I was financing an illegal operation, since there was a heavy suitcase of *Virginia Gentleman* on board, destined to ease our way from station to station, for the private use of the station chiefs, since the Coast Guard was then, and probably still is, as "dry" as Dare County then was. Perhaps this cache did serve us well, perhaps it had no influence whatsoever, as in any event the Coast Guard treated us with every possible consideration, and successive chiefs of station were intrigued to find that we were earnest students and not boondoggling fishermen, despatched at the whim of some senator or other.

I cannot say that any of us paid much attention to the upper part of the Outer Banks as we would have seen some fine forest remnants on the sound side of the banks, notably Kill Devil Woods, or remarked on the relatively few summer houses that lined a small part of the shore. Once settled, we had first to be reoriented to our new situation, which the men at Oregon Inlet proceeded to do almost at once, bringing the USC&GS charts to life with stories of the Outer Banks in times of storm and stress.

Our first expedition with them was by picket boat some little way offshore. We first coasted south of Oregon Inlet to see what must have looked very much like the Port Ferdinando named by Amadas and Barlowe in 1584, though not precisely at the same place. The Outer Banks, from the seaward approaches, were uniformly bare, nothing but beaches and, as we turned north again, the Coast Guard Station and then the scattered summer houses and beach hotel of Nags Head. We saw little change in the shoreline as we worked our way almost as far as Duck, none of the inlets of 1584–1590 then being open. Beyond that there was a restricted area used for naval gun practice, so we had to return without reaching Cape Henry. The stark bareness of the beaches was what struck us most: the luxuriant vegetation, which in the 1580s was evidently visible from the sea, had disappeared. As we passed through several shoals of fish the crew of the picket boat teased us lightly, saying that if we had been fishermen we might have had something to show for our journey.

Our next day's mission was to sail up Roanoke Sound, there then being no causeway to Roanoke Island from the Outer Banks. We sailed up the east shore of Roanoke Island, heavily wooded and with few houses visible except at Manteo. This was an experience I then appreciated strongly as for the first time I was able to get some slight impression of the island and of the waters where so much activity had taken place during those eventful years in the 1580s. We crossed the wide expanse of Albemarle Sound, and I remembered Ralph Lane's first description of it in September 1585, and its striking appearance on John White's map. We sailed up between wooded banks to Elizabeth City, small, compact, with attractive white houses and a number of small fishing vessels.

Once we arrived there we were shown the eighty-five-foot cutter, with her sleek lines, the pride of the Coast Guard, in which we were to journey south the next day, though we were to stay at a small hotel overnight.

We duly went on board the cutter next morning and were welcomed by the officer in command—names now escape me except that almost every second Coast Guardsman we met was a local man and bore the name of Midgett. Easing slowly out of the estuary, we soon saw the northeast tip of Roanoke Island ahead, near which I knew the fort and settlement of 1585–86 had been. We then cruised, with increasing speed, down Croatan Sound, long cleared of the

In July 1948, David B. Quinn was photographed during his first exploration of the Outer Banks aboard the Coast Guard Cutter 83493. *Photos furnished by Professor Quinn.*

obstructive islets which White's map had shown. Beyond that we were soon losing contact with the land, moving out into the wide stretches of Pamlico Sound, and with land receding rapidly out of sight. This gave me, for the first time, some sympathy with Verrazzano, who in 1524 had mistaken the Sound for the Pacific Ocean! It also gave me some sense of the range which the surveyors of the first colony, Thomas Harriot and John White, had traversed in their mapping and charting of the area, using ship's boats and at times their pinnace to cover what, for that time, were very considerable distances. The cutter made considerable speed across the sound, and there was enough motion to make some of us queasy when we had lunch below deck. However, I kept on the lookout as much as I could as we made our passage to Ocracoke, which took the greater part of the day. Eventually, the island came within view, its woods and houses standing out on the horizon. We drew in to the shore and soon entered the Silver Lake, the fine lagoon, on which the Coast Guard station stood.

As I walked out along the eastern shore near the Coast Guard Station with one of the men, I was soon put to a test. He stooped down, picked up a shellfish, flicked it open with his knife and offered it to me—my first clam—and as I swallowed it without obvious discomfort, I evidently passed. In the evening the chief, Carl, and I got down to study the charts—it appeared that the Wococon of 1584 might not have been the present Ocracoke but part of it only, joined to what is now Portsmouth Island. Meantime, it being Saturday, John Gordon had gone to a square dance in the town. But early next day we were on the move up the track northwards through the island. Vegetation was soon left behind: there was nothing but sand on either side, though the dunes gave us some shelter from the east. At Hatteras Inlet, a picket boat was waiting for us, and we crossed the inlet. It was well south of any that had been noted by White in 1585. Once on Hatteras Island we took to the beaches. We were travelling in a Coast Guard beach buggy, which swept along the shore at low tide with a pleasantly swaying motion as the wave troughs in the sand dictated. On the beach could be seen wrecks in all stages of decay, increasingly so as we went north—wooden remnants, substantial wooden vessels not entirely broken up, and very many steel Liberty Ships, victims of the U-Boat blitz of late 1942. I took some photographs and am now sorry I did not take more.

Eventually, some vegetation began to appear on the sound side and ultimately we reached Buxton, a fishing settlement then, but one retaining some substantial bushes and small trees, giving some impression of the earlier tree covering. This was very near where Manteo's village on Croatoan (as the island was then) had been between 1584 and 1590. Not long after we came to the knee bend in the Outer Banks, which marked the promontory of Cape Hatteras extending to the east. At Ocracoke there had been a chance, if we could have waited another day or so, of going on a cutter that was due to inspect the buoys off Cape Hatteras. It would have been a rough enough trip, and I was sorry not to have made it, but there was not enough time. But now standing guard on land was the Hatteras Lighthouse, still working and beaming its warning light down the dangerous shoals off the cape. It was a landmark that could be seen for many miles, even though it had already been threatened by erosion in the 1930s. Beyond it to the north there had been in 1585 the inlet, Chacandepeco, which marked the southern limit of the island of Croatamung of 1585, but had now become merely Pea Island. Here we left the beach and took the track up the island. At one point, we came to a marsh which was all that marked the place where an inlet had broken through some years before but had by then closed. I was wearing rather wide-legged baggy shorts (very British!) so that the mosquitoes that attacked us from the swamp had a fine meal, and I had very sore thighs for a few days. Finally we came to Oregon Inlet. Here another Coast Guard boat took us back to our base at Oregon Inlet Coast Guard station. The overland journey from Ocracoke to Oregon Inlet, which is now an easy run on a good road, had been something of an adventure. It had, above all, impressed me with the extent of the Banks and shown the great erosion (up to a mile or more) which had taken place since 1585, as well as the loss of vegetation.

Cape Hatteras Lighthouse appeared safe from the sea more than thirty years ago. At right, tire tracks nearby revealed the isolation of Hatteras Island in the early '50s. *Photos courtesy National Park Service.*

The final stage of our program was a visit to Roanoke Island. We were taken by picket boat to Manteo, then a very small town indeed, and I was able to set foot at last on Roanoke Island. We drove up to the almost uninhabited northeast end of the island and entered the area which the National Park Service had taken over—the Fort Raleigh site (the name, by the way, is their own). The excavations were virtually completed, and the bare sides of the reconstructed fort enclosure were in place. This, incidentally, was one of the very first authentic reconstructions to be made in North America, since the material for its banks had been taken from the fill in the original ditch, though, of course, sixteenth century illustrations were needed to ascertain the location of the firing step and other details. Unfortunately, the archaeologist, J. C. Harrington, universally known as "Pinky," was not at the site just then, but we were shown conscientiously round the site by the Park Service staff. We were also able to see the artefacts gleaned from the excavations—not as many as were expected—but the site had been combed over the years by curio hunters. However, the fort perimeter gave some idea of how small the colony had been (if indeed it was the sole defensive work of Lane's colony, which has been questioned). But for me it was a link with the documents and the people who were mentioned in them which, with the artefacts they had used, did much to enhance my understanding of the nature of the First Colony. We did not, however, gain any considerable knowledge of the Native Americans whom White had painted. We could also look over the sound across which the pinnaces and boats of the successive expeditions had plied, and could thus see in imagination, the vessels that White had so carefully depicted on his map.

This was the end of the line: we were conveyed back to Manteo and to Oregon Inlet and picked up Carl's car and set out on an uneventful return to Williamsburg. The whole experience was one that made a vivid impression on me at the time and one that I have not forgotten, and for which I am forever grateful to the United States Coast Guard. It enriched my understanding of how the first English explorers and colonists had chosen Roanoke Island as their base and how they had used the Outer Banks as their barrier from observation by sea, even if they had lost so much of their vegetation and had been shorn off by wind and tide over the 360 years or so that had passed. I cannot express how glad I am to have seen the Outer Banks and Roanoke Island also before the modern developments of the last forty years have taken place. Now there is little left for the imagination to work on.

Later that summer, fortified by work in Washington, during which I learned something, if not a great deal, about the Indians of coastal North Carolina and about Spanish concern at English activities on the coast north of Florida, I was able to return, by train and bus, to North Carolina, but this time, in the first place, to Raleigh. There I naturally stayed in the Sir Walter Hotel. This was a great chunk of a building, my room incredibly hot and stale with the tobacco smoke of years. My first impression of the main streets was not too favorable. Large buildings, stores and public buildings, were often islands in unbuilt lots or used car stands. Only when I penetrated the square in which the Capitol stood was there grace and elegance. The State Library contained many periodicals, some of which proved useful, but it was not specialized enough for me. The State Museum of Natural History was a very different proposition. There the director, Harry T. Davis, took me in hand and worked over with me, in a preliminary way, the identification of fauna and flora in Harriot's *Briefe and true report*, told me something of the geology of the coastal plain and had even news of a recent discovery of Indian artefacts on the Chowan River. I made my way next to the Department of Archives and History, already something of a museum as well as an archives. Christopher Crittenden (never called anything but Chris) did what he could for me and had to confess he had no documents which could help. There I met for the first time his young assistant, William S. Powell. An immense mural showed De Bry's version of Pomeioc, in color, and with a large mound on which the temple sat, to which I took some cautious exception. Chris took me under his wing and brought me, with his family, to a showing of "Gone with the Wind," without seeing which, he assured me, I would never understand the South. As I was at that time a devotee of French art films, I considered it wildly melodramatic, but something of it remained with me afterwards. Chris then directed my footsteps to Chapel Hill. Arriving there by bus, I went to lodge at the Carolina Inn, then a much more modest institution than it is now. However, when I got to know some graduate students—almost the only students left during the vacation—they assured me the $5 a night I was paying was outrageous and that I could have had better lodgings for $2 or $3 elsewhere. One of these young men had some money—most lived a very spartan life in dormitories—and a car and a girl friend. Before long a little group of us got together in the evenings fortified by beer and occasionally spirits brought by him from "wet" Durham to dry-as-dry Chapel Hill; I had already lived through a beerless ride down the Outer Banks and a dry one, as Coke disagreed with me very positively.

At Chapel Hill I was taken in hand by the formidable and very able Mary Thornton, who had built the North Carolina Collection in the Wilson Library. She showed me everything in print—history, myth, and fantasy—that had been written about the first colonists. Indeed she also gave me a file of cuttings, which told me something about the recent excavations on Roanoke Island but, more specifically, illustrated a casting counter, a German one of the mid-sixteenth century (a number were found at Fort Raleigh), which came from an Indian site (it never produced anything else except a little pottery) near Buxton and was quite likely the site of Manteo's village. This was an interesting and evocative find. From there she passed me on to the librarian, Charles Rush, who took a liking to me and went out of his way to help. First of all he set up a meeting at the Botany Department with Professor Henry Roland Totten, with whom I found the famous emeritus professor, W. C. Coker. They spent practically the whole day with me going over all the clues to flora contained in the Roanoke narratives. To hear them discussing where they had seen this or that plant or tree was fascinating. Finally, they took me to see the new arboretum, a standing memorial to W. C. Coker (as is the later Biology Department building named for him). This day's work was one of the most valuable I had so far had in clearing up one aspect of the annotation which I contemplated. Then Charles Rush suggested that we should make a visit to Davidson, where William P. Cumming, professor of English at Davidson College, had developed a special knowledge of early maps of North Carolina. Charles, his wife Lionne (whom I am amazed to hear is celebrating her 103rd birthday in 1987), and I drove to have lunch with the Cummings. This was my first contact with Bill and Betty Cumming, who have remained firm friends ever since, and occasional collaborators as well. At lunch Bill apologised for serving us fruit juice, explaining that it might not be a good thing if a professor at the so strictly dry college served anything so subversive as wine. What Bill did for me was to take me through his fine collection of photocopies of maps from the earliest times, revealing not only how the coastline had changed (the Cape Kenrick of John White's map of 1586 having been eliminated by the eighteenth century and was marked only as Wimble Shoals), but also how man's perception had altered between the mid-seventeenth century and the more or less correct charts of the early nineteenth century. From that point the accuracy of the White-Harriot map of 1585–1586 was brought home to me, and I was obliged to study its making much more closely than hitherto.

Back in Chapel Hill I was able to meet the doyen of Southern history, J. G. de Roulhac Hamilton, velvet-jacketed and serene (I only learned later of his extraordinary work in building the Southern Historical Collection), and I was able to talk directly about the early voyages with Professor Hugh Lefler. I may mention one other rather strange experience—nothing to do with the Roanoke voyages. Chris Crittenden had shown me the version of the 1663 charter which had then been offered for sale to the Archives, and I expressed some views on it. He had committed himself to talk about it to the Chamber of Commerce at Chapel Hill and wished me to come along and say something too. He arrived early and took me to meet R.D.W. Connor, who had written wisely on the early colonies before becoming first Archivist of the United States. He assured me that as fellow Irishmen we must have a drink together—his own Irish connections I later learned went back to the eighteenth century. He brought me a glass of the wine of the country, bourbon, which had, he assured me, plenty of branch water in it. However, there was much less water than whiskey and, though I got through the lunch and remember Chris speaking, I was well under the influence myself by this time and never to this day knew what I said about the charter, whether it made sense or nonsense. Chris was too kind to tell me, so I feared the worst.

Chapel Hill left me with the warmest of warm impressions. The university was most attractive—about 4,000 to 5,000 strong at that time. Its buildings formed a fine homogenous campus. The endless kindness I met with and the assistance I found there helped me along my way with the greatest of ease. I left with the impression that I might, after all, be able to achieve my aim of making something new out of the traditional documentation of the voyages.

Back in England I struggled with what became, with enormous help from Alison, *The Roanoke Voyages* (1955), helped also by R. A. Skelton, the then superintendent of the Map Room in the British Museum and secretary-editor of the Hakluyt Society. I had been corresponding vigorously with Pinky Harrington since 1948, and he generously let me use his then unpublished reports on Fort Raleigh, while I was able to meet him and his family when he was in England investigating glass smelting before his remarkable reconstruction of the 1608 glassworks at Jamestown. *Roanoke Voyages* was well received, and I had a characteristic laconic note from Miss Thornton in which she said she liked the book but didn't really know why she did so. After it was published, Bill and Virginia Powell came to England in 1956 to pursue his ambitious attempt to identify as many of the first colonists as he could, so we became friends, as he worked incredibly rapidly through published documents and some manuscripts in the short time he had to attempt such a large task. The result was that, besides correspondence with Bill Cumming, Charles Rush, and John Shirley, whom I had come to know earlier in London and had moved to the state, I was able to continue contact with North Carolina and especially with Chapel Hill.

It was 1957 before I had a chance to come to the United States again. By this time Pinky Harrington, now living at Richmond where I was able to visit him and his family, had become an administrator. He had been put in charge of the National Park Service's development of its sites in the southeast. He was especially concerned with Jamestown, and he took me round the newly installed tour route of the site and other improvements as a preliminary to a drive down the Carolina Banks to see what progress was being made there. This time we were able to drive down Route 158, and I was surprised to see so many of the Coast Guard stations abandoned (replaced as they were by a few highly manned stations, linked to the Loran radar and directional system which was then developed). We viewed the Wright Monument, by then complete, and crossed the new causeway to Roanoke Island. We stayed comfortably at what later came to be called the Elizabethan Inn but was somewhat more modest in size and name at that time. Then came the highlight of the tour, the full inspection of Fort Raleigh and of the restored fort perimeter, which was by now covered in grass and looked very effective. Having read the literature on its excavation, I was greatly impressed with the skill and effectiveness of the reconstruction and glad to have the recovered artefacts explained to me in detail. Pinky was pleased with what was being done: the Park Service personnel there were very cooperative and obviously thought the world of Pinky. He took the opportunity to introduce me to Horace Dough, who had helped to preserve the site and was the repository of much of the folklore of the district. Pinky's friendship with the local people was a factor of importance in making them accept the intrusion of the federal Park Service into their hitherto closed community. In the evening we sat through a performance of Paul Green's "Lost Colony," which was colorful and effective even if in places anachronistic. But we had a hard time keeping mosquitoes at bay.

We then drove down the Outer Banks. There was by now a remarkable road down to Oregon Inlet and a bridge across it. From Kitty Hawk southwards I had been able to see that development along the shore was going ahead, but I also saw on the shoreward side the Nags Head Woods, which gave me some impression of what the Outer Banks as a whole had looked like in 1584. By way of Pea Island we were able to drive rapidly down to Hatteras Inlet, where there was now a ferry, and to get quite quickly to Ocracoke, where the Park Service was busy establishing itself. On the way two things were noticeable. First, many, indeed most, of the wrecks had gone, the steel ones I suppose for scrap metal, some of the old wooden ones decayed or sandcovered. The other novel thing was the lighthouse at Hatteras. It was now out of service and had been handed over to the Park Service. Pinky had the idea it could hold a small museum, and I agreed. We made some plans about this, and I later sent over photographs of the Ralph Lane letters of 1585 which eventually formed part of the display. At Ocracoke we were able to rest overnight and walk around

Silver Lake and the village of Ocracoke (top) provided a placid scene in the 1950s. Pictured at bottom was one of the many shipwrecks inspected by Quinn on his peregrinations along the Outer Banks. *Photos courtesy National Park Service.*

the settlement, which was expanding but was still very attractive and under Park Service protection. Then we drove north once more. This time, with *Roanoke Voyages* behind me, I was able to review what I had said there and deepen my understanding of what had taken place in the sixteenth century.

This was not quite all I was able to do in North Carolina in 1957. I came down by rail to Raleigh and called on Chris Crittenden and his expanding empire and was able to see John and Jerry Shirley at their home in Raleigh before getting on the bus to Chapel Hill. There I was able to talk to Bill Powell, who was by then well established in the North Carolina Collection, having moved there in 1951. Miss Thornton was leaving an increasing amount of the planning to him, as she was herself about to retire. He showed me the Sir Walter Raleigh Rooms, plans for which Charles Rush and Mary Thornton discussed with me on my visit to the library nine years earlier. I was able chiefly to concern myself with social activities, but I was not without business commitments too. In England, Paul Hulton, of the British Museum's Prints and Drawings Department, and I were engaged in planning the production of a full collection of the John White drawings. This was far from clearly in prospect at the time, but I was able to talk to Lambert Davis at the UNC Press about it—and also his able lieutenant, Porter Cowles—and from that were to spring initiatives that helped to make the plan possible. Lambert Davis's intervention in obtaining a subsidy from the Old Dominion Foundation was, I believe, to be important, while in the end the University of North Carolina Press was to join with the British Museum in the publication and to arrange for the distribution of the 300 of the 600 copies in that very limited edition when they were finally published in 1964. This in turn led on to a reception in the White House for the presentation of a specially bound copy at which representatives of the university, the press, the Powells, the Leflers, and the Quinns were all to be present and to tie together many of the strings of earlier associations. Lady Bird Johnson and her daughters went through the pictures with me, and she picked out as her favorite the Sea Turtle—one of the finest drawings of all.

But to get back to 1957. Charles Rush was by now retired, and he and Lionne were kinder to me than ever, but his health was failing. The last outing I had with him was to the newly opened planetarium, when his weakness was already evident, and he was, much to my regret, to die shortly after my return to England. I was in touch too with the Cummings but only by phone and correspondence. Bill Cumming had by then brought out the first edition of his *The Southeast in Early Maps*, and I could congratulate him on this, a landmark in cartographic scholarship in the East. I was still unable to get any help with the coastal Indians whom White had drawn, as Joffre Coe was still involved in non-Carolinian studies (my efforts to reach him in 1948 had failed).

My third visit, the last I will attempt to say anything about now, was in 1959. This time I was at the Folger Library and working on the John White drawings and having been successful at long last in finding an anthropologist who knew enough about the Indians the colonists met to be able to help greatly with the analysis of the drawings. It is to him, William C. Sturtevant of the Department of Anthropology in the Smithsonian Institution, that I and Paul Hulton, my collaborator, owe much for our understanding of what the drawings portray. (Curiously the three of us are in 1987 collaborating again on a project which has a marginal association with the colonies, namely with Drake's call in June 1586 which led the first colony to return to England.) But to get back to North Carolina—I had a call from David Stick, to whom Pinky Harrington had introduced me in 1957, asking if I would come down to take part in a discussion on the Lost Colony on the stage before the Paul Green show. I was to fly to Norfolk where David would meet me, and which I duly did, the plane being late and David impatient that we would not get to Roanoke Island in time, even though I reckoned there was no need to hurry. We did in fact do so with plenty of time to spare and met with the rest of the panel—Chris Crittenden and Bill Powell—who were to be on stage with David Stick and myself. Quite abruptly David requested us to get our pieces together for an "interview session." This turned out to be a barrage of television lights and cameras tucked away out of our sight. It then became clear why David had been in such a rush to get me from Norfolk as he had laid this on to fit in before the stage show. It was the first time I had been subjected to TV in any shape or form. We were politely asked to say our pieces in two or three minutes each. Chris Crittenden and Bill Powell were very calm about the whole thing, but I was rather nervous, though I survived (I did not, however, see whatever was shown of the interview). David Stick wound up very coolly and we dispersed. But by now it was time for us to do our official piece on stage. There was a large audience, and the four of us said our pieces, mine being a very tentative version of my opinion that the majority of the Lost Colonists had survived for some time with the Chesapeake tribe. Of course it convinced no one, though I was to return to the matter later and remain reasonably certain that I am right. We had time only for a few discussion points to be raised, when we were shooed off the stage for the real performance to begin. It was on this occasion that I saw the Paul Green show for the second time, but I don't remember anything specific about it except that it had improved appreciably. David Stick had booked me in at the fine, old, summer hotel at Nags Head, and I was supposed to go off to Norfolk by bus in the morning, but I was too exhausted, and, attracted by a day on the beach, I booked myself in for another night so that I could enjoy a day lying on the beach and beachcombing. I was fortunate enough to find a virtually complete carapace of a spiny box-fish looking just like the one White had drawn in 1585. I managed to clean it up a bit, wrapped it well and eventually cured it. I got the bus next morning and returned to Norfolk and Washington.

My early connections with North Carolina were, therefore, very happy ones indeed. Almost everyone there—at Raleigh, Chapel Hill (especially), and at Roanoke Island—were almost invariably helpful. I am particularly glad that two people, Bill Cumming and Bill Powell, have remained close friends and, indeed, associates since those early days—and that I have been able for a long time after to cooperate closely with John Shirley. To them have been added many more in recent times, not least among them H. G. Jones, who took over the North Carolina Collection when Bill Powell succeeded Hugh Lefler as professor of North Carolina history at Chapel Hill. He has been our prop and stay in North Carolina for so many years as he has also been for so many others.

Those, then, are some memories of my early contacts with North Carolina and North Carolinians. Increasingly, as the numbers of my visits and friends have grown, I have come to feel at home among you, and no visit has been more enjoyable than the present one, during which you have honored Alison and me for roles that we gladly played in commemorating Sir Walter Raleigh's efforts to plant English colonies in North America. That we have joined hands across the Atlantic for this commemoration proves that Sir Walter's efforts were not entirely in vain.

III

Papers Read at a Session Titled
"The Life and Work of David Beers Quinn"
at a Meeting of the
American Historical Association,
Chicago, 29 December 1986

Presider's Remarks

Douglas E. Leach*

Presiding at this unusual session, my firm intention is to keep my own role close to an absolute minimum, so that we may have adequate time for all the good others. Like the little boy on the Fourth of July—or Guy Fawkes Day for that matter—I shall merely light the fuse and wait to see what happens. I predict that we shall not be disappointed.

We have assembled to hear and honor one of the world's great living historians, Emeritus Professor David Beers Quinn of the University of Liverpool. Many of you are also aware that Professor Quinn's wife Alison, a scholar in her own right, has contributed substantially to the lasting value of the immense corpus of publications for which her husband is so widely known and respected. So it is that we are doubly honored by Alison's presence this afternoon. I cannot let the occasion pass without remembering that it was Alison and David Quinn who were among the foremost in helping me and my young family integrate into English life and English ways in 1959 when I came to David's department at Liverpool as Fulbright Lecturer. We have been good friends ever since.

As all of you do know, David Quinn has been recognized and honored by many eminent institutions and organizations during his highly productive career extending over more than half a century. On this occasion we celebrate all of those well-earned honors plus two more, newly gained. First, honorary membership in the American Historical Association, a rare tribute reserved for especially distinguished foreign historians. Here David Quinn follows in the tracks of Leopold Von Ranke, among others. Second, David Quinn has been designated a Fulbright Fortieth Anniversary Distinguished Fellow. As such, in celebration of the fortieth anniversary of that magnificent program to which so many of us have reason to be grateful, he will undertake a three-week speaking tour from California to New England, under the sponsorship of the United States Information Agency and the Board of Foreign Scholarships. Our session this afternoon will serve as the launching pad for that tour. The itinerary is both extensive and complex. May the various airlines involved be on their best behavior!

So, let us proceed as follows. Three scholars who have been so fortunate as to work with David and Alison Quinn, and thereby savor not only the richness of their many contributions but also their personal graciousness and warmth, will come to the podium in succession to offer brief perceptions and tributes. These persons, in order of appearance, will be H. G. Jones, curator of the North Carolina Collection and adjunct professor of history at the University of North Carolina; Karen Ordahl Kupperman, professor of history at the University of Connecticut; and Thad W. Tate, director of the Institute of Early American

History and Culture at Williamsburg and William E. Pullen professor of history at the College of William and Mary. Then Lois Green Carr, historian, Historic St. Mary's City and Maryland State Archives, will introduce Professor Quinn. Accordingly, I now ask these four colleagues to perform their pleasant duties in succession, without further interruption by me.

Note

*Douglas E. Leach, who presided at the session titled "The Life and Work of David Beers Quinn" at the annual meeting of the American Historical Association in Chicago on 29 December 1987, is professor of history emeritus at Vanderbilt University. His most recent book is *Now Hear This: The Memoir of a Junior Naval Officer in the Great Pacific War*.

Bringing Credibility to a Commemoration: David Beers Quinn and the Quadricentennial of the Roanoke Voyages

*H. G. Jones**

For those of us accustomed for a third of a century to the confrontational traditions of AHA sessions, there is a bit of awkwardness in participating in a session whose description contains the words "distinguished" and "tributes." The three of us chosen to comment on David Beers Quinn, therefore, must wend our way between our Rankean obligation to tell the truth and our personal inclination to be civil—particularly with the subject, very much alive and with acute hearing—sitting in state before us.

In this quandary, I share with my fellow panelists a quotation nearly four centuries old: "Whosoever shall follow truth too near the heels, it may haply strike out his teeth." That caution is all the more appropriate today because had it not been for its author, Walter Raleigh, we probably would not be holding this session; in fact, we might never have heard of David Beers Quinn. It is of course possible that his wife and associate, Alison, might have saved him from obscurity, but we shall never know.

Now, David Quinn's career certainly has not been limited to interest in Sir Walter Raleigh and English exploration and settlement; indeed, one only has to scan his impressive bibliography to sense the breadth of his research and writing. Still, he himself traces his interest in "early English colonial expansion" back fifty-five years to his graduation from the Queen's University of Belfast, and the editors of the festshrift *The Westward Enterprise* ten years ago concluded that "David Quinn's contribution to what may be called the prehistory of British North America stands out as uniquely important in the historiography of the subject." The eventful voyage on the ship *Scholar* from his initial publication on his native Ireland to his mastery of the story of early American settlement is gracefully and modestly told in the preface to *Set Fair for Roanoke*, and it will be more explicitly described at the International Sir Walter Raleigh Conference in Chapel Hill on 27–28 March 1987.

David Quinn's relationship with Walter Raleigh accounts for my relationship with David Quinn, and these two relationships helped produce a substantive observance of an important episode in British and American history. My remarks are mercifully brief because the genesis of the quadricentennial observance is told more fully in my article in the September 1985 issue of *Carolina Comments*, published by the North Carolina Divison of Archives and History.

Immortality tends to crown success and spurn failure, so the very fact that Raleigh's North American colonies failed while later ones at Jamestown and Plymouth succeeded helps explain the scant attention given in the national literature to the activities on Roanoke Island in the 1580s. The voyages, however, have not gone unheralded in "Ould Virginia," as a seventeenth-century cartographer called North Carolina, for we are reminded of them through the name of our capital city and a lengthy list of towns, counties, lakes, streets, ships, organizations, businesses, and commercial products, not to mention America's pioneer outdoor symphonic drama, Paul Green's *The Lost Colony*, performed at the Fort Raleigh National Historic Site each summer.

Consequently, when Governor James B. Hunt, Jr., in 1977 asked me to organize and chair America's Four Hundredth Anniversary Committee (the statute for which I had written four years earlier while I was director of the State Department of Archives and History), I knew that our first goal must be the legitimation of the Roanoke voyages as a subject worthy of serious international study. Not being a specialist of the period, I viewed my tasks as chairman to be that of stocking the committee with professionals and laypeople knowledgeable of the subject and of enlisting the active participation of English and American scholars eminent in the field. We had not yet recovered from the subordination of history to politics and tacky frivolity during the bicentennial of the American Revolution, and state government reorganization had exposed my old department to the political patronage system. I was determined, therefore, to conduct a commemoration rather than a celebration, based on history rather than politics, directed toward education rather than fleeting amusement, emphasizing substance rather than minutae, and fostered by specialists of the period being honored. Above all, this was to be an international observance, not one hidden behind our own provincial borders.

That's why I began my courtship with David and Alison Quinn, and through them, with other Elizabethan scholars. I had known of Dr. Quinn through my predecessors, Christopher Crittenden and William S. Powell, and of course his two-volume *Roanoke Voyages* and other studies of English exploration and colonization were standard works in North Carolina history. It was not until November 1977, however, that I first met him and Alison on their trip to Raleigh to speak to the Roanoke Island Historical Association. From that first restaurant conversation mine was a soft-sell approach, but a persistent one, to involve him with the four-year observance, 1984–87.

At the meeting of the Organization of American Historians in New York the next April, Professor Quinn began to make suggestions for the quadricentennial. In May he formalized in a letter a particularly welcome recommendation, a major commemorative volume containing all of the John White drawings of the 1580s, supplemented by "the principal original documents." He added, ". . . a publication team consisting of Bill Powell, myself and Paul Hulton could do such a book . . . ," and he enclosed an outline. I was elated, and at the Sir Francis Drake quadricentennial in California in 1979, we discussed the proposed book during our amusing travels to the several places seeking academic endorsement as Drake's landfall.

My elation was premature, for as so often happens when a splendid idea is put in the hands of a subcommittee, an entirely different publications program was proposed. It eliminated the grand volume and proposed instead the reprinting of Quinn's *Roanoke Voyages* (with additions), the revision of a small collection of documents previously published by the Division of Archives and History, and an inexpensive (if there be such) edition of the White drawings relating only to the Roanoke enterprises. To this Quinn was predictably unenthusiastic, noting that the revision of *RV*, even with the willingness of the Hakluyt Society, would be enormously expensive, and that his contract with Oxford University Press, whose *Virginia Voyages from Hakluyt* was still in print, would preclude his participation in a competing book. He did, however, say that if Oxford would give the Division of Archives and History softcover rights to *Virginia Voyages*, he would prepare a new preface. This was promptly agreed to, and the book appeared in 1982 as *The First Colonists: Documents on the Planting of the First English Settlements in North America, 1584–1590*.

Determined that neither partisanship nor parochialism should characterize the quadricentennial, I took what I then thought was a gamble (but of course, I know now that it involved little chance): I invited David and Alison Quinn to come to Chapel Hill for a two-day series of meetings of America's Four Hundredth Anniversary Committee. They participated in the discussions, never proselyting but always expressing a "beyond-our-borders" professional view, and did much to stem accusations that my emphasis on substantive matters reflected elitism (an odd attribution for a boy brought up on a tenant farm). Dr. Quinn's dinner address cemented the respect of members, and before David and Alison left the village (two days late because of the snow, which Alison says she always brings with her), his new offer—to write for the anniversary committee a narrative summarizing the lessons learned from four decades of study of the Roanoke venture (a surprise to everyone but me)—was accepted. This major contribution appeared from the University of North Carolina Press in 1985 as *Set Fair for Roanoke: Voyages and Colonies, 1584–1606*. In the interim, David received an honorary doctorate from UNC in 1980, returned to research in the Triangle during his fellowship at the National Humanities Center, delivered the Brewster lecture at East Carolina University, and generally became a loyal if adopted Tar Heel. In fact, he was so much at home that at the inauguration of the four-year festivities on Roanoke Island, he and Alison were there to welcome their Princess Anne. There is a rumor that the princess asked him, "Why is the American flag flying over our island?"

David Quinn's role was not limited to his direct assistance; he opened doors for us and enlisted other scholars: Helen Wallis of the British Library, who produced the *Raleigh & Roanoke* exhibition in London, Raleigh, and New York; Paul Hulton of the British Museum, who produced a new edition of the complete drawings of John White; Joyce Youings of the University of Exeter, who sponsored the Raleigh Conference in Devon; and others. A veritable trans-Atlantic coterie was formed, with David and Alison Quinn at the center.

David Quinn's involvement gave me confidence in 1980 that AFHAC would be able to withstand the natural tendencies of politicians and promoters to trivialize the quadricentennial, and I stepped aside as chairman. Since that time, there have been a few activities little related to the subject, but more than any previous anniversary observance, this one has emphasized the historical events and personages being commemorated. Education, not hoopla, has set the tone. If the *Elizabeth II*, a credible representation of a sixteenth-century sailing vessel, drew the most visitors, and if public ceremonies in England and the United States drew more television and press coverage, the outstanding British Library exhibition *Raleigh & Roanoke* in England and the United States provided a lasting impression to hundreds of thousands. But above all, the real legacy of the quadricentennial will be its outstanding series of publications—books like David Quinn's *Set Fair for Roanoke*, Paul Hulton's *America 1585: The Complete Drawings of John White*, and David Stick's *Roanoke Island: The Beginnings of English America*; booklets such as Quinn's *The Lost Colonists: Their Fortune and Probable Fate*, Helen Hill Miller's *Passage to America*, and Joyce Youing's *Ralegh's Country: The South West of England in the Reign of Queen Elizabeth I*; and leaflets on the native Americans, prepared by David Stick. In addition, of course, are the fine books on the subject by Karen Kupperman, David Durant, and others, produced by commercial presses. About eighteen inches of shelf space is required for the new publications dealing directly with the Roanoke voyages, and more are on the way. In no small measure, these additions to the historical literature of English exploration and American settlement have been influenced by David Beers Quinn, who was trotted out every time politicians and vendors threatened to divert our attention from history.

David, I am pleased to join mutual friends as the American Historical Association recognizes you for your distinguished career, for it again gives me the opportunity to congratulate you on your good judgment in taking as your life's partner that little ball of energy and good humor, Alison, and to express my personal appreciation to both of you for helping bring credibility to the quadricentennial of the Roanoke ventures. If you find yourselves squirming during this afternoon's session, remember that someone—perhaps it was Evelyn Walsh—observed that "No good deed goes unpunished."

Note

*H. G. Jones is curator of the North Carolina Collection and adjunct professor of history at the University of North Carolina at Chapel Hill.

David Quinn as Historian's Historian

Karen Ordahl Kupperman*

In his 1637 book the *New English Canaan*, Thomas Morton described the feats of magic performed by Indian shamans. Though English colonists attested that they had seen powwows make a piece of ice appear in a bowl of water in the middle of the summer, or a fresh green leaf in winter, Morton drew the line at one shaman's claim that he could swim a river under water with a single breath. Morton said the man fooled the spectators by "casting a mist before their eies" so they could not see him as he came up for breath.[1]

As I began my graduate work at Cambridge University, it seemed to me that many historians of great reputation are like Morton's shaman; their energies and brilliance go into creating a smokescreen of words and theory that make it appear they are doing something they in fact cannot or will not do. The work of David Quinn came as a revelation to me; rather than attempting to dazzle the reader, to cast a mist, he actually invited one behind the scenes to see how the magic was performed. In reading his works the novice scholar is led step by step as Professor Quinn builds his case through painstaking reconstruction, finally allowing us to see and experience what John White and Thomas Hariot saw at Roanoke, or Bartholomew Gosnold on Cuttyhunk Island.

I remember saying to many people at Cambridge that I was reading a book (it was Professor Quinn's edition of the *Roanoke Voyages*) which had a footnote that filled more than half a page discussing the possible identification of a small red berry one colonist had remarked on. At first that was just a source of amusement, but as I read more, I began to derive what is possibly the most important lesson I learned in graduate school: everything that the people you study cared about should also be the object of your concern. They are trying to tell you something if only you are capable of hearing and using the information your sources offer. If you dismiss or condemn without following up what the historical actors said, you impoverish your own work. The smallest detail may be the key to choosing one interpretation of events over another.

This principle led David Quinn into new approaches before they became fashionable. He early on discovered the importance of anthropology and geography to historical reconstruction. He did not, as far as I know, read trendy theorists, but rather went into the field and walked over the ground with active practitioners. As a novice scholar, I learned from his works the importance of a sense of place; Professor Quinn knows not only the topography, but also the soil, weather, water patterns, and plants of the areas whose exploration and colonization he studies.

Moreover, having learned as much as he could about his subjects and their experiences, David Quinn never sat on his mound of material guarding it against all challengers. It is clear to anyone who reads his work that he is constantly re-thinking, seeking out new information, looking for further understanding. For his latest book on Roanoke, though he had been working on the topic for forty years or more, he went over the sites again, conferring with those younger scholars who were now working in the region, always open. One index of his openness and quest for knowledge is that fact that if you happen to come to a colony site or an archaeological dig before or after a Quinn visit, you will find everyone who works there in a state of high excitement. People are eager to tell him what they have found or their newest theory, knowing they will get a respectful hearing, though often they will be told reasons why a new idea cannot work. Through such visits, especially his investigation of the area where he believes the Lost Colonists lived in peace for two decades after they were abandoned, and through fresh archival work, Professor Quinn's new book on Roanoke contains much that did not appear in any of his earlier studies of the subject.

The most stunning thing I learned from reading David Quinn was that such painstaking reconstruction, important in itself, also sets the stage for imaginative leaps of theory. There is no antiquarian's interest in facts for facts' sake here. Once you have done the work and know all you can about your subjects' experience, then you have the foundation from which you can begin to think about what it means. It is this stage of the process that has produced Professor Quinn's most hotly debated articles. Of all his intriguing theories probably the most controversial is his argument that English fishermen from Bristol discovered America in the 1480s and that Columbus knew about their voyage before 1492.[2]

I am happy to be now in the position of introducing new novice historians to his books and articles and seeing them take in the combination of hard work and audacity that makes Professor Quinn's work so exciting. His lesson for them is the same as it was for me: you, too, can be such a historian if you treat your sources with respect, including the respect of believing that they know what they are saying and mean what they say, if you keep your antennae out so that no lead is passed up, and if you genuinely desire to understand. Finally, of course, you have to be prepared to think.

The keynote of Professor Quinn's approach to historical writing is generosity. I knew he was a generous man long before I ever met him; all his work is kind in the sense that he holds nothing back, never seeks to mystify or dazzle. Everything is laid out for the reader, all steps are made accessible. His personal generosity to me has been immense, from the fact that he took me seriously as a scholar when we first met, even though I was freshly out of graduate school. Later when we were writing books on the same subject, and I was thus in a minor way a competitor, he answered every question I asked him fully and frankly, sharing his latest thoughts and evidence with me.

His gift to all American scholars is more general and less personal. It is particularly appropriate that the American Historical Association should honor him in this way, because he more than any other scholar has made it possible for Americans to work on the history of exploration of early colonization of North America. Beginning with the *Gilbert Voyages* in 1940, David Quinn, often in partnership with Alison Quinn, invented a new style of historical editing. In this collection for the Hakluyt Society and its successor the *Roanoke Voyages*, published in 1955, the Quinns brought together every document that bore on the ventures, combing archives in Spain and throughout England, and wrote notes and introductions that allowed all readers to profit from the books at their own level. As David Quinn remarked mildly in his recent book *Set Fair for Roanoke* (1985), the two-volume *Roanoke Voyages* caused "some surprise that it ran to just over 1,000 pages" (xix). Their generosity can also be seen in the way they have acted to save ventures that might have foundered without their help. It was the Quinns who stepped in to finish the editing and index for Philip L. Barbour's edition of *The Complete Works of Captain John Smith* after Barbour's death.

It is only when using other collections that one realizes just how much effort David and Alison Quinn put into making the material they present accessible and understandable, especially in the presentation of a strong narrative line to weld the disparate and often confusing documents together. They make sure that the reader knows the outlines of what is going on in the venture under study at all times and how each document fits into that narrative. The Quinns' work, capped by the immensely useful five-volume collection the *New American World*, published in 1979, is literally the fountainhead of all work on American colonization in the sixteenth and early seventeenth centuries. Not every scholar may feel that he or she learned how to be a historian by reading Professor Quinn, but no one can work in this field without using their document collections constantly and compiling an enormous debt to them. They have made the modern field of early colonization and exploration of North America possible; they have certainly made it possible for American scholars to have equal access in this field. I am grateful to have been invited to participate in this occasion; there is no one for whom the honor bestowed today is more appropriate.

Notes

*Karen Ordahl Kupperman is professor of history at the University of Connecticut and a specialist in early American history.

[1]Thomas Morton, *New English Canaan* (1637), in Peter Force (comp.), *Tracts and Other Papers, Relating Principally to the Origin, Settlement, and Progress of the Colonies in North America*, 4 vols. (Originally published 1836; reprint Gloucester, Mass.: 1963), II, 25–26.

[2]See his *England and the Discovery of America, 1481–1620* (New York: 1974), Chapter 1, "The Argument for the English Discovery of America Between 1480 and 1494."

David Quinn as Historical Editor

Thad W. Tate*

David Quinn begins the foreword to the five-volume documentary collection, *New American World*, which he edited with his wife Alison and his student Susan Hillier, with the following one-sentence paragraph:

> The intention in this collection has been to enable the person who has a vital interest in the beginnings of European activity in any part of North America to build up for himself a picture of how it began, how it changed from a discovery of some islands off the supposed shore of Asia to the long-continued scraping of the outlines of an endless coastline, to the penetration of an apparently limitless interior, to the exploitation of its inshore waters for fish and its forest fringes for fur, to the tentative assessment of the quality of the land to support European life, to the first attempts to plant Europeans on North American soil, to the early failures and the first successes, to the beginning of what was to become, in spite of the claims of its natural inhabitants, a part of the European-speaking, European-living world.[1]

As Professor Quinn remarks in the succeeding paragraph, "This is a long sentence"—all 145 words of it, I might add. But is is also a remarkably good summary of the thrust of all of Quinn's remarkable body of editorial scholarship. Those contributions as historical editor are, of course, but one facet of a varied and productive scholarly career. Yet, I think that for a number of reasons it is a matter worth singling out for special comment.

The first reason is that several of Quinn's larger editorial projects, especially those pertaining to the voyages of Sir Humphrey Gilbert, the Roanoke Colony of Sir Walter Ralegh, and the English voyages to New England in the first decade of the seventeenth century, stand among the brightest beacons of his many accomplishments. The record is the more impressive when we recall that the two volumes on Gilbert's enterprises, published in 1940, were the Hakluyt Society volumes for 1938 and 1939, nos. 83 and 84 of its second series, while the New England volume appeared in 1983 as the one hundred and sixty-first volume of the same series. Thus, they frame a career of more than forty years duration, not that it appears in the least to be winding down.[2]

If I may, as an outsider, a dabbler at best in the subject of early European exploration and discovery, venture a judgment in the matter, it also strikes me that this is a field in which the edited and printed documentary record is unusually important to students and advanced scholars. The body of manuscripts and early printed works on which the field rests is not unlimited, although those sources are, in fact, unexpectedly rich because the discovery of the New World stirred the imagination of educated Europeans of the time. Yet, those sources also call for extensive compilation, interpretation, clarification, and annotation to be fully accessible to all but the most advanced scholar. Although the history of European exploration is a significant harbinger of the modern era, it is, in a sense, also a concluding phase of the medieval world. Rather like medieval history it presents an especially acute need for reliable printed and edited texts, and no one has supplied them in any greater quantity or with any higher quality than David Quinn.

The three Hakluyt Society editions on Gilbert, Roanoke, and New England to which I have already referred, plus his work on the *Hakluyt Handbook* and facsimile editions with introductions of major Richard Hakluyt writings, constitute Quinn's major corpus of editorial scholarship on early English exploration, but they do not exhaust his contributions.[3] The five-volume *New American World*, from which I quoted a moment ago, occupies what I think of as a distinctive niche. The texts are not annotated, although the very process of selection and organization of documents and the provision of introductory headnotes for a series as comprehensive as this one is in itself a task that demands an experienced, knowledgeable scholar. Spanning the whole of New World exploration and discovery from medieval antecedents to 1612 and including records of the Vikings, French, Spanish, and Dutch as well as the English, the volumes display an impressive comprehensiveness. At the same time Quinn and his collaborators provide a degree of accessibility to the record for non-scholars that admirably fulfills their stated intention.

Quinn's editorial scholarship likewise embraces a host of briefer publications. Some, like the handsome volume of accounts of Virginia voyages from Hakluyt that he and Alison Quinn prepared for an Oxford Press series in 1973 and a subsequent 1982 reprint, were readers' editions of significant but generally familiar texts.[4] In other instances—for example, an edition of *The Last Voyage of Thomas Cavendish, 1591–1592*, and another prepared with Neil M. Cheshire, of two poems of Stephen Parmenius, the Hungarian poet who drowned on a Newfoundland voyage in 1583—Quinn produced the first modern editions of less familiar parts of the record.[5]

You may also have detected by now a recurring note running through the editorial credits of a number of these works. I refer to the frequency with which his wife Alison appears as his collaborator in the preparation of a number of them, bringing her own skillful eye, enthusiasm, and insights to the scholarly enterprises in which the Quinns have shared. I have known them and watched them at work too long not to make a point of this collaboration. I especially have in mind, from my own personal knowledge, the extent to which the late Philip Barbour counted upon their advice in preparing his new edition of the writings of Captain John Smith and the significant contribution that both made to the final shape of the edition.[6]

Finally, I should like to return briefly to those major editorial works on Gilbert, Roanoke, the Hakluyts, and New England—plus his Virginia contributions—that, I think, define the parameters of Quinn's editorial scholarship and also inform much of his own historical writing. His contributions are too varied to identify exclusively with any single aspect or theme of his subject—he is simply *the* historian and editor of English exploration and discovery. But what he does catch particularly well, I think, is an all-important transition that he identifies clearly in the foreword to *New American World*, that is, the transition from the discovery of islands and coastline to assessment of the ability of the land to sustain European settlement and the first attempts to plant such settlements.

Quinn's particular genius lies, I think, precisely in looking toward this significant end result of exploration. Many scholars in the field choose to emphasize first discoveries, leaving the momentous shift to European colonization to others. Call it permanent settlement, call it colonization, or call it invasion, it is a critical transformation, marking a decisive shift in the character of European overseas activity. Virtually all of Quinn's editorial works make major contributions to our understanding of this transitional process. Richard Hakluyt was its chief theorist; some of the first glimmers of the possibility of European settlement loom up in Humphrey Gilbert's endeavors; Sir Walter Ralegh's Roanoke constitutes a major, if flawed, effort, to effect lasting English colonization; Virginia under John Smith's aegis achieved success, however narrowly it escaped failure; and, finally, weighing the possibilities for colonization became an increasingly dominant purpose of the post-1600 New England voyages that Quinn documents in his most recent editorial volume. What in the end is most impressive, then, about David Quinn as editor is not simply the quality and quantity of his editorial scholarship, but the extent to which that impressive body of work traces a clear, coherent line of development and thereby makes a major interpretative contribution to his chosen field of study.

Notes

*Thad W. Tate is director of the Institute of Early American History and Culture and William E. Pullen professor of history at the College of William and Mary.

[1]David B. Quinn (editor), *New American World: A Documentary History of North America to 1612* (New York: 1979; 5 vols.), I, v.

[2]David B. Quinn (editor), *The Voyages and Colonising Enterprises of Sir Humphrey Gilbert*, Hakluyt Soc., 2nd ser., nos. 83–84 (London: 1940; 2 vols.); David B. Quinn (editor), *The Roanoke Voyages, 1584–1590* ..., Hakluyt Soc., 2nd ser., no. 104 (London: 1955); David B. and Alison M. Quinn (editors), *The English New England Voyages, 1602–1608*, Hakluyt Soc., 2nd ser., no. 161 (London: 1983).

[3]David B. Quinn (editor), *The Hakluyt Handbook*, Hakluyt Soc., 2nd ser., nos. 144–145 (London: 1974: 2 vols.); Richard Hakluyt, *The principall navigations, voiages, and discoveries of the English nation,* edited by David B. Quinn, Hakluyt Soc., ex. ser., no. 39 (Cambridge: 1965; 2 vols.).

[4]David B. and Alison M. Quinn (editors), *Virginia Voyages from Hakluyt* (London and New York: 1973).

[5]David B. Quinn (editor), *The Last Voyage of Thomas Cavendish, 1591–1592* . . . (Chicago: 1975); David B. Quinn and Neil M. Cheshire (editors), *The New Found Land of Stephen Parmenius* . . . (Toronto: 1972).

[6]Philip L. Barbour (editor), *The Complete Works of Captain John Smith (1580–1631) in Three Volumes* (Chapel Hill: 1986).

Introduction of David Beers Quinn

*Lois Green Carr**

My predecessors here have outlined David Quinn's contributions as a scholar, an editor, a mentor for younger scholars, and a promoter of public interest in the history of exploration and colonization via recent celebrations of 400th anniversaries. This long career of major accomplishment began in Ireland, where he was born and was educated until he began studies at the University of London. There he received his Ph.D. in 1934. After teaching for several years at University College, Southampton, he returned in 1939 to Ireland to be senior lecturer in Irish History at Queens University, Belfast, where he had done his undergraduate work. In 1944 he moved on to University College, Swansea, as professor of history and head of the department until 1957, when he became Andrew Geddes and John Rankin professor of modern history and department head at the University of Liverpool. Upon his retirement in 1976 he came to St. Mary's College of Maryland to begin a new career as a teacher of American under-graduates. Here through 1984 he taught at least one semester of every year but two, at the same time carrying on his myriad activities as lecturer, editor, author, and adviser. During this period and since have appeared the five-volume *New American World* and the *English New England Voyages, 1602–1608*, both edited in collaboration with Alison Quinn; *Early Maryland in a Wider World*, a collection of essays that began as a lecture series David organized at St. Mary's College; his book about the Roanoke colony; and more than a dozen published articles and lectures on early discovery and colonization. At the same time he has been vice-president and then president of the Hakluyt Society. A more energetic and productive retirement can hardly be imagined.

I came to know David and Alison Quinn through their interest in what material artifacts can tell us, whether they be pictures, maps, objects, and structures still preserved or archaeological findings. David's work in cooperation with Paul Hulton on John White's watercolors is, of course, an outstanding contribution of this nature. He has followed and often been consulted on archaeological projects up and down the Atlantic Coast from Baffin Island, where Frobisher had planned to establish a colony, to Spanish St. Augustine in Florida. This part of his mental outlook has been especially important to those of us who have had the opportunity to work with him at St. Mary's City, where since 1968 the outdoor history museum, now called Historic St. Mary's City, has been excavating Maryland's seventeenth-century capital. David's enthusiasm for this work and what it can reveal about everyday life on an English seventeenth-century frontier has been stimulating and refreshing to all of us involved, historians and archaeologists alike. Real conversation between historians and archaeologist-anthropologists is beginning to enrich vastly our understanding of the past before us. Over his scholarly career, David's pioneering interest in archaeological projects has helped create such conversation.

I should like to add a comment on David's participation in historical anniversaries—those already discussed for North Carolina and others not touched on, such as Maryland's recent celebration of its 350th year. If more historians of his calibre would expend their talents on this method of exciting public interest in history, our profession in this country might not be in its present doldrums. I like to believe that the American Historical Association, in offering David Quinn honorary membership, is recognizing not only the value of his scholarship but this public-spirited use of it as well.

And now it is time to let David Quinn speak for himself.

Note

*Lois Green Carr is historian for Historic St. Mary's City and the Maryland State Archives.

Reflections

David Beers Quinn*

This occasion is the more gratifying to me because I have thought of myself very much as a historical work horse, clearing the way through documentary tangles for others to follow. This has certainly been both my endeavour and to some appreciable extent the result of what I have achieved within my rather limited field. But I have probably added something in perspective also to the general picture of the European penetration of North America as a whole during the early stages of white intervention. Exactly how much only time will tell. Whether I have made a more general impact on history, as seen by Americans, I am more doubtful.

It is very difficult to look back over fifty years of teaching and nearly fifty-five years of writing to summarize briefly one's career in a meaningful fashion.

First of all, though, just a little on my education. Brought up in an Irish country village (Clara, Kings County) in a one-teacher school (four teachers, in fact, successively) from age five to fourteen, I was lucky in my parents who, without having had the advantage of higher education, were intelligent and well-read. They gave me every incentive they could to develop my intellectual curiosity as well as my knowledge, as did my teachers, especially one of them. I got a little private teaching too before my family moved to Belfast in 1923, where I entered rather late a famous day school and enjoyed the association of a number of boys who were to become prominent in later life in many fields. There I was well taught, perhaps best in geography, which was my main love and in which I would have majored if I could. At Queen's University (1927–31) I had the good fortune to be taught history mainly by Professor James Eadie Todd, who had a formidable reputation for high standards and who drilled his students in them sternly if mercifully. His lectures were polished prose which one took down verbatim (not possible in these days), but his interests were wide and his instincts for novelty were very sharp. My most stimulating teacher was a young lecturer who had come to start the teaching of geography in the university. Estyn Evans is still alive and is revered as a man of extraordinary wide interests and achievement. He tried to cultivate a broad range of interests in his students, introducing me to archaeology and ethnology as well as the traditional aspects of his subject. When I got the chance to do graduate work I would like to have gone on to do so in geography or anthropology or even archaeology, but as this was not possible I went instead to King's College and the Institute of Historical Research in London, where my supervisor was A. P. Newton, Rhodes professor of imperial history (a Yale Ph.D., incidentally), who had drawn from the British empire and from the United States a remarkable seminar of talented men and women. Todd had taken a suggestion from something Newton wrote—that it would be worth following the careers of men who had been involved in projects for colonies both in Ireland and in America—and passed it on to me. That was indeed a fruitful starting point. Over the next few years I was well grounded in British colonial history, but Newton felt I should tackle a straight piece of Irish history, much neglected at the time, for my dissertation. Despite lack of encouragement from historians in Ireland, who did not think that much could be done as a result of the destruction of the main corpus of Irish records in 1922, I set to work. If my dissertation on early Tudor Ireland has now been superseded, working on it taught me how to search for material in unlikely sources and how to combine apparently discrete data into something of a coherent pattern. I also learned, I hope, never to take first impressions for granted but to look at every document as a challenge from which unexpected information could be extracted if it was examined time after time. Not, perhaps, that this is a very unusual process, but it proved invaluable to me later in my career.

It helps to explain how and why I have been able to make some sense of obscure happenings on both sides of the Atlantic (though no doubt some nonsense also). I need scarcely stress that early ventures into the Atlantic are very poorly documented and that to make a reasonable sequence out of them demands not only repeated attempts to extract every possible implication from each piece of evidence, but also willingness to recognise that if new scraps of evidence appear they must somehow be accommodated, even if it involves starting again and shaping an altered pattern and sequence. This kind of work teaches ingenuity, it is true, but it also teaches humility—knowledge that material for anything like a complete understanding of a series of such episodes may never be forthcoming and that any attempt at narrative, much less analysis, is bound to be ephemeral.

To return to my career. Newton fortunately recommended me at the beginning of 1934 to fill a post mainly concerned with British colonial history at University College, Southampton, then a small college, now a distinguished university. I was fortunate in my colleagues there—Reginald Betts, later Masaryk professor of Central European history in London, and Joel Hurstfield, later Astor professor of English history in London also. In spite of a heavy teaching load I was able to do some editing work on Southampton trade in the fifteenth century, valuable for my interest in later maritime history, and to take up the study of one of the personalities who had early connections with both Ireland and America, Sir Humphrey Gilbert. Edward Lynam, superintendent of the Map Room in the British Museum, then secretary-editor of the Hakluyt Society, an Irishman, was interested in the combination of Sir Humphrey Gilbert's interests in Ireland as well as America, and got the society to accept a collection of documents on Gilbert, with some reflection of his Irish as well as his American interests. This I was able to deliver to the British Museum on the day in August 1939 when it was packing its treasures to send them out of London for safety as war was threatening. The two volumes duly appeared in 1940 about the time the Battle of Britain was taking place.

I should interpolate here that in 1937 I was fortunate enough to meet Alison Moffat Robertson when we were both looking after Basque child refugees from the Spanish Civil War. We soon married and she proved willing to turn from teaching and to use her Edinburgh University degree in history and English to work at my side during vacations in the Public Record Office and British Museum. She thus became my—often unacknowledged—collaborator. In subsequent years the Quinn and Quinn names have appeared on several books, if not as many as there should have been, since her insights and her critical sense have made a contribution to my own work which it is difficult over forty-nine years to acknowledge at all adequately. I only hope that our collaboration will continue into our eighties.

It so happened that in August 1939 we were moving to Belfast. I had kept up my Irish history by a number of articles since 1934. Professor Todd had introduced the teaching of Irish history (then frowned on by the Northern Ireland government) both as a means, perhaps, of soothing a few quarrels as well as being a worthwhile subject in its own right. He appointed me to replace T. W. Moody who had moved to his outstanding career in Trinity College, Dublin. During the war years I was not only engaged in civil defense duties but also in learning to combine the teaching of Irish and early American history, publishing some papers stressing the colonial aspect of Irish history and its analogies in the sixteenth and early seventeenth centuries with colonial ventures in America. I think the high point here was getting a paper on Sir Thomas Smith and the beginnings of English colonial theory accepted by the American Philosophical Society in 1943. This was the year when I escaped from Belfast for six months to replace a colleague of Professor Betts's in the BBC European Service writing news bulletins for Czechoslovakia. At that time A. L. Rowse asked me if I would consider writing a little book on Sir Walter Ralegh for a new series. What convinced me that this might carry forward my linking of Irish and American and early colonial history a stage further was the chance to see the John White drawings in the British Museum, brought from their hiding place to be shown to Archibald MacLeish, then assistant secretary of state, who had some notion of having them published as a signal of English and American cultural interdependence. I was so taken by them as throwing a new light on Ralegh's colonial activities that I accepted the invitation to write what became *Raleigh and the British Empire*, a title which surprisingly survived from 1947, when it first came out, to 1973, its last appearance in paperback.

Before the war was over we had moved to Swansea, a small campus of the University of Wales, where I was professor and head of department. I was very busy there but began to teach both some American and early modern European expansion history, and continued my work on what had now become a real subject for me, the early American colonising attempts. I spent every moment I could in London, with the aid of my wife's fortitude in bringing up three young children in difficult postwar conditions, without much help from me.

I soon became convinced that uncritical reliance on what Hakluyt had published on the voyages of the 1580s to the newly named "Virginia" was inadequate. I kept finding things which added bits and pieces to the accepted story and accumulated unanswered questions about what I was to call "The Roanoke Voyages"—a term which now appears to have become established. I proposed (rashly) to the Hakluyt Society that I might edit for it all the documents on English connections with North America before 1607 which had not already appeared in their publications. Fortunately I did not press this at the time, but I did enough to get an article on the 1585 Virginia voyage accepted for the *William and Mary Quarterly*, which in turn brought me a grant of enough dollars from the Leverhulme Trust to spend ten weeks in America in 1948. During this time I ranged from Massachusetts to North Carolina, scouting out the land, as I was convinced that only seeing the terrain, and consulting with people who knew about ethnography, linguistics, botany, and zoology would enable me to comment adequately on the early voyages. The high point of this visit was a week spent in the Carolina Outer Banks under the auspices of the Coast Guard, in company with Professor Carl Bridenbaugh and John Gordon. This enabled me to see a good part of the banks and sounds from sea and land—a great good fortune as many parts of them have by now become unrecognisable. The reconstruction too of the outer works of the defences of 1585–86 on Roanoke Island was then going on, and, after seeing them, brought me into contact with America's leading historical archaeologist, J. C. (Pinky) Harrington, in whose honour an annual medal is being awarded by the Society for Historical Archaeology. I also met Professor William P. Cumming of Davidson College, who has long been recognised as the outstanding historical cartographer of eastern North America. With all these people, happily still with us, I have maintained contact and have had assistance from them and sometimes assisted them, in turn, over almost forty years. The making of *Roanoke Voyages* as a fully documented and annotated body of material would not have been possible but for two people in England—R. A. (Peter) Skelton, killed in a car crash in 1970, and Paul Hulton, who is very much alive. Skelton had just taken over the editorship of Hakluyt Society publications and with his encouragement and help we set out to shape the volumes, as it was now clear there would be two, into a new pattern, that would raise the level of detailed scholarship of the society's famous series and present it in a more attractive form. I think we did this, if comparison is made between publications before and after 1955. The other piece of good fortune was that after I had decided to use the John White drawings, as far as it was possible to do so, as historical documents, Paul Hulton joined the staff of the

British Museum's Prints and Drawings Department and became involved in their official catalogue of British drawings. Cooperation with him helped that part of my collections forward (and left both of us determined to get the White drawings published in full as soon as possible). Finally, Alison Quinn, besides helping with the documentary works, compiled a fine pair of indexes that helped greatly to make the volumes accessible. When the volumes appeared they were well received, but by then I was already branching out into other aspects of English activity in North America, being able in the summer of 1957 to spend some months in the great libraries in the East reading as much contemporary material as I could and widening the range of my inquiry, especially into Spanish concern with North America.

In the autumn of 1957 we moved to Liverpool, where I was to remain for the next nineteen years as professor of modern history. It was there that I was able for the first time to concentrate much of my teaching on the early expansion of Europe, on Tudor Ireland, and to do some concentrated work on early North America, being fortunate enough to have a small sequence of high quality graduate students to inspire me on my way. Some of them have gone far professionally since then: Gillian Cell is dean of the College of Arts and Sciences in the University of North Carolina at Chapel Hill; another, Colin Steele, is librarian of the Australian National University; another, Joyce Lorimer, is professor of history in Wilfred Laurier University, Ontario; and Susan Hillier is a highly regarded record agent. I mention them, apart from others, since each has made valuable contributions to the history of the Americas.

I may say that the decade from 1954 to 1964 was overshadowed by the problem of how to get the White drawings published, and then by getting it done. The history of this long drawn-out epic for Quinn and Hulton had best be told elsewhere, but it ended with two very finely produced volumes. Specially bound copies were presented, respectively, in 1964 to Queen Elizabeth II, and to Lady Bird Johnson—who with her daughters clearly enjoyed them. Many other things occurred during this decade. I was able to visit the United States and Canada in 1959, partly to work on White, and was especially fortunate to become acquainted with William C. Sturtevant, who became our invaluable adviser on the ethnography of the John White Indian, and with whom, I may say, I am at present collaborating on another project. I was able to work up material on a number of specialised topics through this visit. However, already R. A. Skelton and I had decided to collaborate on a facsimile editon of Richard Hakluyt's first great voyage collection, *The principall navigations* of 1589, hitherto neglected. We worked on an extended introduction, where Skelton's bibliographical skills proved invaluable, and got the facsimile into order. Alison took on the difficult job of preparing a full index to this Black Letter text. Technically a very difficult thing to do, she eventually completed it with such success that she was awarded the Wheatley Medal of the Library Association and Society of Indexers for 1965 when the two volumes appeared as Extra Series volumes for the Hakluyt Society.

So far my experience of America had been for summer vacations only, but in 1963–64 I got my first sabbatical in twenty years of teaching and this enabled both of us to work in American libraries for some fourteen months. The research we managed to do there (and Alison did as much as I did to cover every possible piece of ground and each piece of literature) was partly directed to continuing the Roanoke voyages by a comparable volume or volumes on New England and perhaps Newfoundland. This took us to Newfoundland, often to Maine, to much of Massachusetts, and to use libraries across North America, especially the John Carter Brown, the Henry E. Huntington (for which Alison drove across America, following parts of Soto's and Coronado's routes), the Houghton and Widener libraries, the Folger, and the Library of Congress. Under Louis Wright's guidance in the Folger I wrote a short book, *The Elizabethans and the Irish*, which came out in 1966 and was mainly intended to help literary students to understand Tudor Ireland and to record a few links between Ireland and America.

After our return I got involved, on the margins, with the fine editions of Captain Cook's journal, which John Beaglehole was editing for the Hakluyt Society of which I was by now a council member. Alison was responsible for indexing the two vast volumes on the third voyage, and I became interested too. In 1967 the British Council, through John Beaglehole, arranged that we should go to New Zealand to tour the four old universities and the two new ones. I found a very considerable response in all the universities to early American history, especially to the establishment of New England, and interest too in parallels between John White's American drawings and those made on Cook's voyages. Alison had the job of talking to librarians and others on indexing Cook. The glimpses we had of the Pacific going and coming home certainly enlarged our range of interests.

The American interlude of 1963–64 had been followed in successive vacations by continued searches of local archives and private collections over most of the west and southwest of England (greatly helped by former students who had become archivists) for manuscript material on North America in the sixteenth and early seventeenth century, especially on the New England enterprises before 1609. We had little success in the latter quest, but an unexpected find helped to draw us back to Sir Humphrey Gilbert—the discovery of some personal letters on his preparations for the 1583 voyage at Longleat. This, in turn, enabled us to follow up an associate of Gilbert through a proposal for a translation of Stephen Parmenius's poem on Gilbert by a classically minded psychologist, Neil Cheshire. Our collaboration on *The new found land of Stephen Parmenius*, finely produced for us by Toronto University Press in 1973, brought invitations to both of us in turn to visit Hungary, since Paremenius was the first Hungarian to write on a North American theme and to be drowned on Sable Island before he had composed his planned epic on an American voyage. We each duly lectured at the Academy of Sciences in Budapest on this unusual subject.

In the late 1960s and early 1970s I had an opportunity to collaborate in a small way with Professor William P. Cumming in the volume *The Discovery of North America* (1971), for whose fine maps and annotations Peter Skelton was responsible just before his death, and also in the later *The Exploration of North America, 1634–1776* (1974), in which Susan Hillier also took part. Both these volumes proved very popular, but my personal part in them was limited; however, they taught me much about the appeal of highly illustrated books with a straightforward narrative and some documents attached.

In 1965 Harper and Row asked me to contribute a volume on the early discovery period in North America to the New American Nation Series. This forced me to work over the whole field from the Norse voyages down to the early settlements (and I was able to include something on the L'Anse aux Meadows discovery of a Norse site) as far as 1612 in Florida, Virginia, Canada, and Newfoundland. This was done in intervals in other work, especially when I was Harrison visiting professor of history at the College of William and Mary in 1969–70, another enjoyable and productive year off. It was completed only in 1976 as I was about to retire from my Liverpool chair. In this I tried to give a balanced view of the activity of the various European powers in North America, sticking mainly to narrative to bring out the relative importance of the various countries involved, but with some degree of assessment of their achievements. The most original part was probably on the Newfoundland fisheries, which I stressed as being the major economic motive for European concern with North America. Thanks to Mrs. Selma Barkham, I was able to say a little about her astonishing revelation of the extent of the Basque whale fishery on the Gulf of St. Lawrence. Alison and I were able to see relics of this at Red Bay in Labrador in 1979. (These researches have been carried much further since, though not by us.)

In 1975, when my retirement from Liverpool was approaching, I was honoured by being asked to give the annual Prothero Lecture for the Royal Historical Society, and in "Renaissance Influences in English Colonisation" I tried to give some indication of the range of my North American interests. I did not know that at that time some of my friends in England, Ireland, and America were preparing a *festschrift* for me—*The Westward Enterprise*, which came out in 1978. I was able to retire, however, knowing that there was still much to be done. In fact I was already doing it.

In 1974 Robert Hector, a New York publisher, asked me if I would compile a comprehensive reprint (with introductions) of all the major narratives which had been published in English, for the use of smaller colleges and high school libraries that might not have been able to get out-of-print materials. I started on this innocently enough before I retired, with Alison's and Susan Hillier's help, and had collected a substantial amount of material by 1976. I had insisted on adding a few translations and was getting ahead with them through the assistance of colleagues in Liverpool. About halfway through the whole project I was suddenly confronted with the demand on the part of the co-publisher, Arno Press, that I must add a substantial amount of hitherto unpublished material and much more in the way of translations to lend more originality to the project. The former request I could only respond to by throwing into the collection many of the manuscript materials on English enterprises I had been assembling for future Hakluyt Society volumes without, of course, the annotation that was being planned for them. I did not have time or money to have very many further translations made. This gave the collection a somewhat uneven character, though I tried to balance the extra English documents with some French, Spanish, and a little Portuguese material. We had almost finished when I was instructed to delete some one hundred pages from the fifth volume, which was about Spanish Florida and Virginia, so that I had to discard some of our hard-won translations on Florida as well as a good deal on Virginia. By the time the title was ready for the press, Alison and I were already in America. To reach deadlines all three of us had to stretch ourselves to the limit, so that if mistakes continue to be found it is because the pressure was so great we could do no more proofreading than we did. However, in the general introduction, I did try to give some perspective to the documentation of early European involvement in America and to indicate directions for further research which perhaps are beginning to bear some fruit.

New American World as it appeared in five volumes in 1979 is scarcely what I envisaged when I first suggested a project of this sort as a member of the council of the Institute of Early American History in 1969. The suggestion that it might need twenty volumes to complete the documentation of the pre-Jamestown period and take many years of research shocked that eighteenth-century centered body to the core and was turned down out of hand, so that *New American World* was the best I and my collaborators could do in the circumstances.

In 1970, too, when we were visiting Harvard, Bernard Bailyn suggested to me that I should attempt to put what I had already written, and whatever additional material I had in hand, into a book, and introduced me to Jane Garret, an editor at Alfred Knopf. With her help and the devoted labour of one of her subeditors, my book, *England and the Discovery of America, 1481–1620*, was published in 1974. This contained a certain amount of controversial material about the beginnings of English enterprise in the fifteenth century and on the Vinland Map, but it also collected my more specialised studies on the later sixteenth century and the opening of the seventeenth, which have stood up better to later scrutiny. The experience of working with such an enlightened editor and publisher was exciting.

The development of scholarly interest in Thomas Harriot led, from 1969 onwards, to a series of seminars at Oxford, Newark (Delaware), and Durham (England), intended to elucidate his significance as a Renaissance scholar and scientist—the first to come to North America. John W. Shirley and I collaborated in a paper on him in 1969, and I published several more later, including "Thomas Harriot and the New World" in Shirley's edited volume, *Thomas Harriot, Renaissance Scientist* (1974). Studies are still being made of his mathematical works for which he left many rough notes, but unfortunately almost all his manuscript materials on North America have been lost. His surviving papers have been assembled by a committee of which I was chairman, and photocopies have been placed in repositories in England and the United States.

Several other interesting projects had been completed in the early 1970s. One was *The Hakluyt Handbook* (1974), which Peter Skelton and I had planned in the sixties. Unfortunately he died before he had made more than one contribution to it. It involved getting a team of contributors together, with the help of Terence Armstrong, who had succeeded Skelton in the Hakluyt Society. Alison and I were left with most of the bibliographical work to do, and we missed Peter Skelton's expertise in this field very greatly, while we had to rove over eastern England to trace his movements and summarize the facts of Hakluyt's career. It was a rush job but nonetheless, with Alison's two fine indexes, it has proved very useful.

The other task was a fascinating one. Among the Phillipps Manuscripts, Philip Robinson had found a small handwritten book, which eventually passed into the possession of Paul Mellon, and which appeared to be the last testament of Thomas Cavendish on his fatal last voyage, written at the point of death in the Atlantic in 1593. I was able to publish this in 1975 in facsimile and a line-by-line transcript and with an adequate editorial apparatus. (Recently some doubt has been cast on whether the writing is Cavendish's or not, or whether it is a duplicate, imitating Cavendish's hand; my own conviction is still that the manuscript or at least the signed conclusion is Cavendish's own.) The task was a most exciting one as it revealed the personality of its author, ill and paranoic, in a way that few documents of the time do.

If I may, I will interpolate still another phase of activity. I had not abandoned Irish history. I have been associated since 1969 with the preparation, under the auspices of the Royal Irish Academy, of which I have been a member since 1942, of *A New History of Ireland*. Like many collaborative works it has been slow to appear. With Kenneth Nicholls, I contributed a chapter to the early modern volume (III) in 1977 and four to the late medieval one (II) which has recently appeared. I number young Irish historians among my friends and have encouraged them to carry on work which I may have started but which they are now bringing to a much higher level of expertise and understanding.

Over the years I had gradually to pick up what could be learned about the Native Americans of eastern North America, though my knowledge has still remained very much that of the amateur. I knew nothing of the Eskimos (or Inuit). In Canada, briefly in 1959 and 1963, and later in 1970, I learned much about them from Jacques Rousseau, head of the Institute of Northern Studies at Laval University and collaborated with him on a few small papers. I was also in touch with Gordon Day at the Museum of Man, who persuaded me to put together a *Guide to Sources for the Ethnography of Northeastern North America to 1611*. This was very good for me, as it made me go over the sources for the area between the Hudson River and Montreal with a new care for detail. This was a long time in typescript—indeed it was lost for several years—but it eventually appeared in 1981, though I still think it was a rash thing to attempt, given my limited background in this area. Visits to Canada included several to Newfoundland between 1963 and 1979. Having at least seen the Maritimes, the Saguenay, and the St. Lawrence Valley, I felt not too far from home when writing about the French in Canada and the fishermen in Newfoundland, where in 1963 I was able to see the workings of the inshore fishery in its old form, little changed from the sixteenth century, before the great changes which had taken place by 1979, when it had almost disappeared.

When I was about to retire I had intended to continue my work mainly in Liverpool with occasional visits to the United States, but in 1975, when we were briefly in Washington, I had an opportunity to meet (through an old friend, Wilcomb Washburn) President Renwick Jackson of St. Mary's College of Maryland. He told me he wished to have a senior visiting professor at the college to develop American colonial history in view of the important excavations taking place of the first Maryland settlement, St. Mary's City, founded in 1634, and to coordinate undergraduate teaching to some extent with the archaeological work being done by the St. Mary's City Commission. I agreed to go there for the session 1976–77. In the end, Alison and I went to St. Mary's City for seven years for one or two semesters a year if not every year. This involved me in teaching American undergraduates American colonial history, the early expansion of Europe, and some early modern British history. It also involved close but informal cooperation with Lois Green Carr, historian of the commission, and Gary Stone, the chief archaeologist. This continued from 1976 to 1984. At St. Mary's City we were able to attract distinguished lecturers to visit us from time to time, and with President Jackson's assistance, and in order to contribute to the approaching 350th anniversary of Maryland, I was able to get the lectures with some additional material published as *Early Maryland in a Wider World*, which came out in 1982 and has been well received. This sequence was broken in 1979 by a semester teaching at Ann Arbor, where I had an enjoyable few months, especially with an outstanding graduate seminar and the use of the resources of the William L. Clements Library. From 1980 onward, too,

I was involved in the preliminary preparations in North Carolina for the 400th anniversary of the Roanoke Colonies, timed to last from 1984 to 1987. It was finally decided I should contribute a general book on the Roanoke voyages; in 1983 I was able to spend six months at the National Humanities Center in North Carolina, during which I drafted, and Alison helped revise, a book eventually called *Set Fair for Roanoke*. It needed a good deal of improvement and was not finally published until 1985. It was my first attempt to write something accessible to the nonspecialist reader since 1947, but it seems to have served its purpose. Needless to say, I was involved in a good many lectures and other engagements in the state during the celebrations, which end in 1987.

Ever since my first visit to Martha's Vineyard in 1948 and the coaching of the Gosnold enthusiast Warner Gookin, I had intended to collect and annotate all the earliest writings about the English in New England. They had come marginally into my Gilbert volumes in 1940. In later visits, notably in 1959, I went sailing along the Maine coast with Samuel E. Morison and visited Monhegan as well. Alison and I visited Maine together in 1963–64, but it was in 1969–70 that we seriously got down to work on the details of such narratives as we had been able to collect. The late Wendell Hadlock with Lawrence and Eleanor Smith especially helped us in Maine. Alison worked particularly on the botany and other aspects of natural history. I mainly concentrated on the native peoples and both of us on the topography. Good friends made it possible for us to follow the route taken by Waymouth in 1605 to the tidal head of the St. George River, and we also got to Monhegan (in 1959 I had left hurriedly, having contracted pneumonia). Flying along the coast several times at no great altitude we were able to see a great deal of the incredibly indented coast of Maine. Our second son, Rory, worked for a time with the Park Service excavation (frustratingly unsuccessful) on the site of the 1607 Sagadahoc colony. But we were never able to get much satisfaction from our own examination of the 1607 site, concluding in the end that most of it had been removed for material to build Fort Popham in the late 1850s.

However, after we got *New American World* off our hands, we did make a determined effort to get our thousands of New England notes in order. As St. Mary's College completed its year in May we were able to get a month or two in various libraries, in Washington mainly, but also in the Huntington and John Carter Brown, while we managed in our intervals in England to spend a certain amount of time in the renamed British Library and the Public Record Office. Eventually we got out *The English New England Voyages, 1602–1608* in 1983 with only 2,000 footnotes instead of about 4,000 we had collected—though enough to give most publishers the horrors. It will be a useful volume but lacking such originality as the Gilbert and Roanoke collections had. But it did bring our documentary work on pre-Jamestown North America to an end, except for one thing, Hakluyt's "Discourse of Western Planting" for which an elaborate edition has been planned, if we could ever pull the bits and pieces of the commentary together. Somehow during odd vacations, too, I managed to write half of an introductory book on *England's Sea Empire, 1550–1640*, the original parts of which on the navy were the work of my Liverpool colleague and naval historian, Anthony N. Ryan.

History has, I think, to be told in relatively simple, straightforward terms and with due consciousness of its imperfection and incompleteness. It can never do more than make a few boreholes into the human past. At the same time, where materials are scanty, it should use every feasible method of exploiting them. Perhaps nowadays, with technical devices, more can be done in certain areas, but in all the areas with which I have been concerned in research broad theoretical approaches tend to founder from lack of sufficient data to go beyond the most tentative generalizations. This does not mean that the historian of the fifteenth to the seventeenth century in these areas cannot make any generalizations, but they should, I believe very firmly, be such as can tentatively, and not dogmatically, link disparate data, without fitting or attempting to fit them into any all-encompassing categories of thought or action.

It is a matter of good fortune to find intimate data about individuals in these fields, and when it is found it should be nourished and set out with all possible attention to detail. Similarly, in dealing with voyages or colonizing enterprises, which have formed the staple of my own work in the American field, it is the detail which is worth finding and commenting on, because the better known narrative data will in a sense not reveal as much, anything like as much, as the fully researched and annotated texts, not only of what was done but what was the context in which it took place. I have, as it happened, concentrated very much on English contacts across the Atlantic, but if I had another life to live I would like to have done as much for Spain. Even now the vast area of the North American fishery remains largely unresearched in detail, even though new sources are fairly rapidly being opened up.

Considerations such as these explain why I have allowed my natural curiosity to range so widely over the areas of human activity and their geographic background in the period in which I have been most concerned (though I have been greatly helped by Alison's perceptions and work).

Historical archaeologists and ethnographers will still need to have historians to enable them to follow up the more elementary clues which we have tried as far as we could—even if we are very conscious that others can, and we hope will, take them very much farther. Reading through considerable numbers of manuscripts and books in several languages has gradually brought me to see—if still dimly—patterns of activity engaged in by the various European peoples concerned with North America in the very limited period with which we have concerned ourselves. These will have become apparent in the rather stark outline of my New American Nation textbook, though after a decade since it was written

I would like to restate some of them. I think I may have got the English aspects nearly right, if there is any such thing to be said. I cannot pretend that for Spain, France, and Portugal—let alone the Dutch who peer in at the end of it—my views as expressed then have the best obtainable perspective. But in the past decade enough work has been done or published on Spanish Florida, for example, as to make my formulations appear rather limited in scope and probably inaccurate in substantial part. I may not have got the French so far wrong, but I would like to see more of their maritime activities brought to light before I would be dogmatic about this. So far as the Portuguese are concerned the absence of data so far discovered puts a block, almost a complete one, on my general picture of their significance in the general picture. I am inclined to observe that it was greater than we know. But at the end of each project I have undertaken, there remains the question, "Have I gone as far as possible with the information at my disposal?" Sometimes this is an incentive to Alison or myself to hunt a little further. But continuously I have been more and more aware as I passed towards the limits of my effective contribution to American studies that the early story is still incomplete, that the data may very well not exist to make many aspects of it fully intelligible, so that any generalizations which take the perception of what happened further must depend more on speculation than information. Gradually improved formulation of what has happened can develop, but it has its dangers. Such progress can very well wean a scholar from history to mythology—to belief in all the hare-brained theories about European, African, or Asian contacts with America in the centuries before the late fifteenth, but on the other hand cautious extrapolation from fully authenticated data may not wholly be worth condemnation. I have tried it out to some extent in *Set Fair for Roanoke* and, at least, it tends to provoke counterspeculation which may (or may not) carry our understanding a few tiny stages forward.

I have long been certain that early American history can only properly be seen in a wide Atlantic context and must take in Europe and Africa in a western Atlantic history which will enable us to assess the precise nature of the European impact on the new lands in their early stages. This must involve not only strictly colonial history but maritime history and even the tremendous problem of categorising in relevant terms the organisation of society in the eastern Atlantic as well. The traditional concentration on the East, the growing point it is true for the later United States, but not of the beginnings of European intervention in the landmass as a whole, must end.

We cannot eliminate the Spanish penetration of the interior—if only because it provided one main incentive for the exploration of the east. And further, it is vital for the understanding of European cartographical concepts of North America as a whole. Was there a way round it by the north? Was there a narrow waist (as Verrazzano thought and some Englishmen believed until the end of the sixteenth century)? Or was there a mountain range which, when reached, would provide rivers flowing to the Pacific? The Atlantic indeed cannot be understood unless we see it not only as a route to North America for its own sake, but also as a halfway stage towards the Orient. I have therefore been determined to try to assert the unity of European efforts to explore and understand the whole of North America and not confine my view to what small parts of it the Europeans came to dominate in the early seventeenth century.

One of the problems about *New American World* was that a good deal of material had to be put in without footnotes or full explanations, though it was not left entirely bare. But whatever weaknesses the collection has, it does, I think, take the study of American history in this period a stage further in that it tries to present the process of European activity for North America as a whole from east to west, from north to south. There is, however, a problem with the southern limit. Geography stresses that North America begins at the Yucatan peninsula, not at the artificial 1849 frontier. But in defining North America in this way how can Mexico, its exploration and history into the seventeenth century, be split in a documentary collection? It is simply impossible. Mexico has had to await John Parry's *New Iberian World* (5 volumes, 1985), which we arranged should not overlap with our North America. Unfortunately John Parry did not live to see his fine collection brought to its final conclusion, though when we spoke to him about it only a few weeks before his sudden death in 1982 he was, he assured me, very nearly at the end, and fortunately his friends have been able to round it off for publication.

One of the most valuable growing points in the study of the early history of North America is the increasing convergence of history, anthropology, and archaeology, each discipline retaining its autonomy. The anthropologists have reinforced the historical study of early contacts between European and Native Americans besides providing a basis for the study of man in North America before 1492. Archaeologists have developed ever more sophisticated techniques for the interpretation of the material remains which men, both before and after 1492, have left behind them in the ground. They too have learned that, where it exists, documentary evidence is essential in planning and interpreting excavations. The work of the St. Mary's City Commission (now renamed), which I was fortunate enough to see at close quarters for some years, profited enormously from the cooperation of historians, more particularly social historians, with archaeologists, even if in the end some vital issues had to be resolved by repeated reevaluations of their work by the archaeologists themselves, which threw new light on problems not capable of solution by the immediate correlation of historical materials and archaeological finds.

The Society for Historical Archaeology has attracted a number of historians of early North American history, and no wonder. At their 1987 annual meeting, archaeology, anthropology, and historical research combined produced some remarkable results. Among them was the creation of a picture of St. Augustine in the sixteenth century which could not have been attained by any one discipline in isolation; excavations at a mission site on St. Catherine's Island which reinforced the considerable existing documentation with fresh insights into the relations between Franciscan friars and Guale Indians; a Smithsonian team consisting of an anthropologist, an archaeologist, and, not least, a historian, was able to report on the first major European mining venture in North America (in Baffin Island in 1578) with significant results. These examples show that the effective study of the early contact period, at least, can make its perhaps most spectacular progress by this alliance of hitherto separate disciplines, even if there are still many documents to be explored in Spain, France, and other parts of Europe, which can advance our knowledge and understanding. But, of course, what happened in North America in the period down, say, to 1630, still depends on increased understanding of the economic, social, and political objectives of western Europeans and the character of the societies in which they lived, an area where research and interpretation are still bringing novel information and viewpoints to light and where there is no consensus in sight. However, there is gradually emerging (most recently in D. W. Meinig's *Atlantic America, 1492–1800* [1986]), a new synthesis on the convergence of Europe and North America in this early period. If this is so, and if I have played some small part in bringing it about, I am very glad to have been able to assist in a process that is still far from being complete.

It is now, perhaps, possible to see a pattern emerging in the earliest relations of European powers with North America in the sixteenth and early seventeenth centuries. Despite a considerable amount of discovery and an appreciable degree of exploration, no state was willing to take on responsibility for the penetration of North America and the establishment of a permanent hold on the mainland, as it had not been established that such action would repay the effort and expenditure involved in it. The exception, the Spanish occupation of Florida, a limited occupation only, was done primarily for strategic reasons rather than because Florida offered, it was soon found, any appreciable resources of its own. Consequently, it was left to private or corporate risk capital to develop slowly the conviction that direct exploitation of America would pay its way and make profits. The first and most significant factor in this was the growth of the cod fishery, into which France, England, and the Iberian countries poured increasing amounts of capital and human resources and made considerable profits. The growth of the fishery and its ramifications in western Europe is an important indicator of how the proto-capitalism of these countries was developing. But it did not involve either capitalists or fishermen with more than peripheral contacts with the land surface of any part of North America. The Basque whale fishery on a limited section of the Labrador coast required some degree of continuity, if not year-round occupation, but the installations on the coasts of Newfoundland and the Maritimes were transitory and European occupation lasted for only a few months in the year. But the scale of the fishery made it possible for those with money to invest to consider North America as a possible source of profits. This, in turn, led to investment of French capital in the fur trade, which, if it was also seasonal, brought traders into close contact with the interior in the St. Lawrence valley and in the Maritimes. It was clear that precious metals were not very likely to be found—the mining venture of 1577–78 in Baffin Island having proved a fiasco—though their existence could not be ruled out, while iron, copper, and other non-precious metals were at least possible resources which might be developed (traces were discovered in Newfoundland in 1583 by Sir Humphrey Gilbert). But it was the fur trade, as much as anything else, which led on to experiments in a wider range of exploitation, the implantation of agricultural settlements, under corporate management and control, on the assumption that subtropical products could be obtained in latitudes comparable with those in the Old World if such settlements were established. The attempt to do so in 1585–86 by the colonists sent by Sir Walter Ralegh to Roanoke Island proved inconclusive. After the return of the colonists in 1586 Ralegh became skeptical about the possibility of profits to be made from continuing such an enterprise. Had it then been pursued, private capital would have had to be raised over a period of years and land acquired from its inhabitants, involving direct penetration of the mainland territory for the first time by Englishmen. The venture of 1587, in which a small band of colonists, in family units, proposed to live on a more or less self-supporting basis, was an aberration, if a significant one, in the process which had hitherto been developing. As it was, the sixteenth century ended without a single English or French colony (apart from a few convicts on Sable Island) being established in North America. The conditions for profitable investment had not yet become clear, even though France and England had mapped out paper spheres of influence which they might eventually wish to exploit.

Even in the early seventeenth century no attempts at systematic occupation under state auspices were made until private capital had established advance trading stations on the mainland. The Virginia Company of 1607 was a trading company, chartered by the Crown, and Jamestown was founded and supplied on the assumption that exotic products could be grown there which would aid England's trade balance as well as to exploit timber and other natural resources, though after 1609 it operated as a national rather than a sectional corporation through many vicissitudes. But it was not until 1618 that most of those in employment there ceased to be servants of the company and small-scale enterpreneurial efforts were added to the corporation's own activities. Only the bankruptcy of the corporation forced the Crown to take direct responsibility for the government of Virginia, when colonial penetration began in earnest. Similarly, the fur trade on the St. Lawrence was managed as a trading venture by the port towns of Normandy and Brittany, the establishment of Québec as a permanent trading post being financed by private capital. Only gradually down to 1627 was the French state involved to any significant extent in the trading operations, nor was there any colonisation. Private enterprise, too, began the creation of fishing stations in what was known from 1616 as New England; the Pilgrims of 1620 were essentially a group of persons operating without any measure of control from England in creating what was intended to be a self-supporting settlement — but based on London-raised finance. Even in the late 1620s it was private, not state, enterprise that laid foundations for other settlements in New England.

What has been said is not to attempt to give a summary history of English and French involvement apart from making the point that only when North America was thought to be able to pay its own way and make profits (whether it did or not is irrelevant in this context) was the land penetrated, and that the means for doing so was provided by private individuals or corporations. The state became involved only in setting out formal terms under which commercial corporations could operate. If this had not been the case settlements might have been deferred indefinitely, unless strategic issues were at stake. Indeed, in the case of New France, colonization was long delayed, and only the profits to be made by private individuals from tobacco and furs on the Chesapeake and by farming and fishing in New England brought English settlers to these areas ahead of any systematic state involvement in colonization.

Considerations of this character have, I believe, informed my work on North America. Whether they make any long term contribution, apart from the documentary work I have done, remains for others to judge.

My approach has almost certainly been too European-centered. It is necessary to balance the generalizations I have attempted by revealing what Europeans were doing to Native American society by their invasive character, first of their commerce and later — and more radically — of their physical penetration. Just as much of the commercial propaganda about the resources of North America was false, so also was the view dominating most contemporary documents that the "savages" had little in the way of a mature social organization and a coherent body of concepts, and that they had not appropriated in their own fashion land of which Europeans were gradually, once settlement of any sort began, to deprive them. Europeans arrived and continued with the twin assumptions that they could bring to Native Americans both Christianity and European civilization as bounteous gifts, while at the same time depriving them of their traditional social cohesion and their territory. The drive for gain was overlaid by partly unconscious beliefs that they could improve indigenous society at the same time as they were exploiting it. This context is now being explored by such leading scholars as James Axtell and Calvin Martin with results which compel much revision of views I have expressed in my writings.

But I must leave the problems the early arrival of the Europeans created to say that I have been especially happy and lucky with my collaborators. As far as Alison is concerned, what she has done and what I have done have been so mixed that we can scarcely sort them out, but I could not possibly have covered so much ground without her constant help. But Peter Skelton, Paul Hulton, Bill Cumming, John Shirley, Neil Cheshire, Gillian Cell, Susan Hillier, Jacques Rousseau, Tony Ryan, Selma Barkham, and Bill Sturtevant, among others, have all enabled me to do things I could not otherwise have completed on my own. What I can look back on is a series of happy collaborations and the making of lasting friendships. I should also mention Kenneth Andrews, who has been a constant associate, sharing documents and ideas, even if we have not formally collaborated; while the same may be said of Lois Carr, with whom I have worked so closely in Maryland, even if I have not contributed anything directly to her remarkable original work on the social history of the colony.

The welcome and exciting invitation to become an Honorary Member of the American Historical Association, together with an appointment as Distinguished Fulbright Fellow, was a complete surprise to me. I am glad to have been able to come to Chicago to meet this audience and convey something of my thanks for all the kindness and hospitality and assistance I have received in the United States since 1948 and which I am to attempt to repay in some small part by a long run of visits to universities and learned institutions over the next three weeks. This will take me to campuses I have never visited before, such as Stanford, Tallahassee, Knoxville, and Boston University. If we survive this I hope that this will not be our last visit to the United States. Indeed we are already bidden to a farewell to the 400th anniversary of North Carolina in March 1987. Thank you all for your tributes and for your patience in listening to an account of what has been in essence not a very exciting career, but a very enjoyable one in the company of past propagandists, explorers, and colonizers, good and bad, crazy or farsighted, whose thoughts and actions were to have an influence, fortunate or unfortunate, seminal or anachronistic, on the fortunes of Europe's early impact on North America.

Note

*A shorter oral version of this paper was delivered by Professor Quinn during a session titled "The Life and Work of David Beers Quinn" at the annual meeting of the American Historical Association in Chicago on 29 December 1986, at which time he was inducted into the AHA as an honorary member. A somewhat different version is scheduled in the July 1988 issue of the *William and Mary Quarterly*.

IV

The Publications of David Beers Quinn
for the Years 1932–1987

The Publications of David Beers Quinn for the Years 1932–1987*

1932

"Descriptions of Ards Peninsula by William Montgomery of Rosemount in 1683 and 1701." *Irish Booklover* 20 (1932): 28–32.

"An Early Irish Settlement at Malone, Belfast." *Proceedings and Reports of the Belfast Natural History and Philosophical Society, 1930–1931* (1932): 46–49.

1933

"Irish Records, 1920–1933: A Survey." *Bulletin of the Institute of Historical Research* 11 (1933): 99–104.

"MSS in Lough Fea Library Catalogue of 1872." *Irish Booklover* 21 (1933): 12–13.

1935

"Anglo-Irish Ulster in the Early Sixteenth Century." *Proceedings and Reports of the Belfast Natural History and Philosophical Society, 1933–1934* (1935): 28–42; reprinted as *Ulster, 1460–1550*. Belfast, 1935.

"Edward IV and Exploration." *Mariner's Mirror* 21 (1935): 275–84.

"Henry, Duke of Richmond and His Connexion with Ireland, 1529–1530." *Bulletin of the Institute of Historical Research* 12 (1935): 175–77.

"The Irish Parliamentary Subsidy in the Fifteenth and Sixteenth Centuries." *Proceedings of the Royal Irish Academy* 42, sect. C, no. 11 (1935): 219–46.

1937

"Ormond Papers, 1480–1535." In *Calendar of Ormond Deeds*, edited by E. Curtis, vol. 4, Dublin, 1937: 307–80.

The Port Books or Local Customs Accounts of Southampton, 1468–1481. 2 vols. Southampton Record Society, nos. 37–38 (1937, 1938).

1939

"Anglo-Irish Local Government, 1484–1534." *Irish Historical Studies* I (1939): 354–81.

"Revolutionary Army." review of *Puritanism and Liberty*, by A.S.P. Woodhouse. *Modern Quarterly* 2/2 (April 1939): 205–11.

1940

The Voyages and Colonising Enterprises of Sir Humphrey Gilbert. 2 vols. Hakluyt Society, 2nd series, nos. 83–84. London, 1940; Nendeln, 1967. (Index by Alison Quinn).

1941

"Bills and Statutes of the Irish Parliaments of Henry VII and Henry VIII." *Analecta Hibernica* 10 (1941): 71–169.

"The Early Interpretation of Poyning's Law, 1494–1534." *Irish Historical Studies* 2 (1941): 241–54.

"Guide to English Financial Records for Irish History, 1461–1558." *Analecta Hibernica* 10 (1941): 1–69.

(With Oliver Davies). "The Irish Pipe Roll of 14 John, 1211–1212." *Ulster Journal of Archaeology,* 3rd ser., IV (1941): supplement, 1–76.

1942

"'A Discourse of Ireland' (*circa* 1599): A Sidelight on English Colonial Policy." *Proceedings of the Royal Irish Academy* 47, sect. C, no. 3 (1942): 151–66.

"Information about Dublin Printers, 1556–1573, in English Financial Records." *Irish Booklover* 28 (1942): 112–14.

"Parliaments and Great Councils in Ireland, 1461–1586." *Irish Historical Studies* 3 (1942): 60–77.

1943

"Government Printing and the Publication of the Irish Statutes in the Sixteenth Century." *Proceedings of the Royal Irish Academy* 49, sect. C, no. 2 (1943): 45–129.

1945

"Agenda for Irish History: Ireland from 1461 to 1603." *Irish Historical Studies* 4 (1945): 258–69.

"Sir Thomas Smith (1513–1577) and the Beginnings of English Colonial Theory." *Proceedings of the American Philosophical Society* 89 (1945): 543–60.

1947

"Edward Walshe's 'Conjectures' Concerning the State of Ireland, [1552]." *Irish Historical Studies* 5 (1947): 303–22.

Raleigh and the British Empire. London, 1947, 1962, 1973; New York, 1949, enlarged 1962).

1949

"The Failure of Raleigh's American Colonies." In *Essays in British and Irish History in Honour of J.E. Todd*, edited by H.A. Cronne, T.W. Moody, and D.B. Quinn. London, 1949: 61–85.

"Preparations for the 1585 Virginia Voyage." *William and Mary Quarterly*, 3rd ser., 6 (1949): 208–36.

1950

"The Expansion of Europe to 1783." *Annual Bulletin of Historical Literature*. London: Historical Association, 1950 and annually to 1959, and 1960 with A.N. Ryan.

"Ireland, History [from 1171]." *Chamber's Encyclopedia*. London, 1950, and subsequent editions.

1951

"Some Spanish Reactions to Elizabethan Colonial Enterprises." *Transactions of the Royal Historical Society*, 5th ser., 1 (1951): 1–23.

1952

"Christopher Newport in 1590." *North Carolina Historical Review* 29 (1952): 305–16.

1954

Preface to *Black Gown and Redskins: Adventures and Travels of the Early Jesuit Missionaries in North America (1610–1791)*, edited by E. Kenton. New York, 1954; London, 1956, iii-xi.

1955

The Roanoke Voyages, 1584–1590: Documents to Illustrate the English Voyages to North America under the Patent Granted to Walter Raleigh in 1584. 2 vols. Hakluyt Society, 2nd ser., nos. 104–05. London, 1955; Nendeln, 1967. (Index by Alison Quinn).

1956

"The Library as the Arts Faculty's Laboratory." *23rd Conference of Library Authorities in Wales and Monmouthshire, Newport, 1956*. Swansea, 1956: 14–18.

"A Merchant's Long Memory." *Gower* 9 (1956): 8–11.

1958

"Ireland and Sixteenth Century European Expansion." In *Historical Studies: I: Papers Read before the Second Irish Conference of Historians,* edited by T. Desmond Williams. London, 1958: 22–32; reprinted with corrections, Tralee, 1959.

"Local History in Perspective." *Morgannwg* 2 (1958): 3–8.

1959

"Die Anfänge des Britischen Weltreiches bis zum Ende der Napoleonischen Kriege." In *Historia Mundi: Eine Handbuch der Weltgeschichte* 8 (1959): 455–95.

"Notes by a Pious Colonial Investor, 1608–1610." *William and Mary Quarterly,* 3rd ser., 16 (1959): 551–55.

(With Jacques Rousseau). "Hakluyt et le Mot 'Esquimau.'" *Revue de l'Historie de l'Amérique Française* 12 (1959): 597–601.

1960

"Edward Hayes, Liverpool Colonial Pioneer." *Transactions of the Historic Society of Lancashire and Cheshire* 111 (1960): 25–45.

"Henry the Navigator." *Listener* (27 October 1960): 736–738.

1961

"The Argument for the English Discovery of America between 1480 and 1494." *Geographical Journal* 127 (1961): 277–85.

"Henry VIII and Ireland, 1509–1534." *Irish Historical Studies* 12 (1961): 318–44.

"Simão Fernandes, a Portuguese Pilot in the English Service, circa 1573–1588." In *Actas, Congresso Internacional de História dos Descobrimentos,* 3 (Lisbon, 1961): 449–65.

1962

"The Voyage of Étienne Bellenger to the Maritimes in 1584; a New Document." *Canadian Historical Review* 43 (1962): 328–43.

1963

(With Paul Hulton). "John White and the English Naturalists." *History Today* 13 (1963): 310–20.

1964

(With Paul Hulton). *The American Drawings of John White.* 2 vols. London and Chapel Hill, 1964.

The New Found Land: The English Contribution to the Discovery and Settlement of North America, An Address . . . Together with a Catalogue of the Exhibition. Providence, R.I.: John Carter Brown Library, 1964.

"Sailors and the Sea." In *Shakespeare Survey 17,* edited by Allardyce Nicoll. Cambridge, 1964; reprinted 1976: 21–36, 242–45.

1965

"Elizabethan Birdman." *Times Literary Supplement* (1 April 1965): 250.

"England and the St. Lawrence, 1577 to 1602." In *Merchants and Scholars,* edited by John Parker. Minneapolis, 1965: 117–44.

"Étienne Bellenger," "Thomas Bradley," "Richard Clarke," "Thomas Croft," "Sir Bernard Drake," "Hugh Eliot," "Richard Fisher," "Sir Humphrey Gilbert," "Edward Hayes," "Richard Hore," "David Ingram," "John Jay," "George Johnson," "La Court de Pré-Ravillon et de Grandpré," "Charles Leigh," "Madoc," "Anthony Parkhurst," "Stephanus Parmenius," "John Rastell," "John Rut," "Lancelot Thirkill," "Robert Thorne," "Silvester Wyet." In *Dictionary of Canadian Biography/Dictionnaire Biographique du Canada, 1, 1000–1700,* edited by G.W. Brown, Marcel Trudel, and André Vachon. Toronto and Quebec, 1965.

"Exploration and the Expansion of Europe." *Rapports, 1, Comité International des Sciences Historiques, XIIᵉ Congrès International des Sciences Historiques.* Vienna, 1965: 45–60.

(With R.A. Skelton). *Richard Hakluyt, The Principall Navigations, Voiages and Discoveries of the English Nation: A Facsimile of the Edition of 1589, with an Introduction by D.B. Quinn and R.A. Skelton and with an Index by Alison Quinn.* 2 vols. Hakluyt Society, Extra Series, 39. Cambridge, 1965.

1966

"Advice for Investors in Virginia, Bermuda, and Newfoundland, 1611." *William and Mary Quarterly,* 3rd ser., 23 (1966): 136–45.

The Elizabethans and the Irish. Ithaca, N.Y.: Folger Monographs on Tudor and Stuart Civilization, 1966. (Index by Alison Quinn).

"État Présent des Études sur la Découverte de l'Amérique au XVᵉ Siècle." *Journal de la Société des Américanistes* 55 (1966): 343–82.

"The First Pilgrims." *William and Mary Quarterly,* 3rd ser., 23 (1966): 359–90.

"The Munster Plantation: Problems and Opportunities." *Journal of the Cork Historical and Archaeological Society* 71 (1966): 19–40.

(With Jacques Rousseau). "Les Toponymes Amérindiens du Canada Chez les Anciens Voyageurs Anglais, 1591–1602." *Cahiers de Géographie de Québec* 10 (1966): 263–78.

"The Road to Jamestown." In *Shakespeare Celebrated*, edited by Louis B. Wright. Ithaca, N.Y.: Folger Library Publications, 1966: 31–60.

(With P.G. Foote). "The Vinland Map." *Saga Book, Viking Society for Northern Research* 17 (1966): 63–89.

1967

"Calendar of the Irish Council Book, 1 March 1581 to 1 July 1586." *Analecta Hibernica* 24 (1967): 93–180.

"The English Discovery of America." In *The Expansion of Europe*, edited by DeLamar Jensen. Boston, 1967: 47–51.

"John Cabot's *Matthew*." In *Times Literary Supplement* (8 June 1967): 517.

"John Day and Columbus." *Geographical Journal* 133 (1967): 205–09.

(With Warner F. Gookin). "Martin Pring at Provincetown in 1603?" *New England Quarterly* 40 (1967): 79–91.

(Editor). *Observations Gathered out of 'A Discourse of the Plantation of the Southern Colony in Virginia by the English, 1606.' Written by That Honorable Gentleman, Master George Percy.* Charlottesville, 1967.

Richard Hakluyt, Editor: With Facsimiles of Richard Hakluyt, Divers Voyages Touching the Discoverie of America (1582), and A Journal of Several Voyages into New France (1580). 2 vols. Amsterdam, 1967. (Index by Alison Quinn).

1968

"La Contribution des Anglais à la Dècouverte de l'Amérique du Nord au XVIᵉ Siècle." In Manuel Ballesteros-Gaibrois *et al.*, *La Découverte de L'Amérique: Esquisse d'une Synthèse: Conditions Historiques et Conséquences Culturelles.* Paris, 1968: 61–76.

Sebastian Cabot and Bristol Exploration. Bristol Branch of the Historical Association, Local History Pamphlets, 21, Bristol, 1968: 30.

(With R. Dudley Edwards). "Thirty Years' Work in Irish History (ii); Sixteenth Century Ireland, 1485–1603." *Irish Historical Studies* 16 (1968): 15–32.

1969

(With John W. Shirley). "A Contemporary List of Hariot References." *Renaissance Quarterly* 22 (1969): 9–26.

Jamestown Day Address, May 11, 1969. Richmond: Association for the Preservation of Virginia Antiquities, 1969.

"Josias Crowe," "Archibald Cumings," "Samuel Gledhill," "Arthur Holdsworth," "Thomas Lloyd," "William Pynne," "James Smith." In *Dictionary of Canadian Biography/ Dictionnaire Biographique du Canada, 2, 1701–1740*, edited by David M. Hayne and André Vachon. Toronto and Quebec, 1969.

"A List of Books Purchased for the Virginia Company." *Virginia Magazine of History and Biography* 77 (1969): 347–60.

(With A.C. Crombie, J.V. Pepper, J.W. Shirley, and R.C.H. Tanner). "Thomas Harriot (1560–1621): An Original Practitioner in the Scientific Art." *Times Literary Supplement* (23 October 1969): 1237–38.

1970

"Additional Sidney State Papers, 1566–1570." *Analecta Hibernica* 26 (1970): 89–98.

"Thomas Hariot and the Virginia Voyages of 1602." *William and Mary Quarterly*, 3rd series, 27 (1970): 268–81.

"'Virginians' on the Thames in 1603." *Terrae Incognitae* 2 (1970): 7–14.

1971

(With W.P. Cumming and R.A. Skelton). *The Discovery of North America*. London and New York, 1971. (Index by Mollie Skelton and Alison Quinn).

North American Discovery, Circa 1000–1612. New York and Columbia, S.C., 1971.

"Raleigh Ashlin Skelton: His Contributions to the History of Discovery." *Imago Mundi* 25 (1971): 13–15.

(With R. Dudley Edwards). "Sixteenth Century Ireland." In *Irish Historiography*, edited by T.W. Moody, Dublin, 1971: 23–42.

"A Tempest Allusion?" *Shakespeare Quarterly* 22 (1971): 78.

"The Voyage of *Triall*, 1606–1607: An Abortive Virginia Venture." *American Neptune* 31 (1971): 85–103.

1972

(With Neil M. Cheshire). *The New Found Land of Stephen Parmenius*. Toronto, 1972. (Index by Alison Quinn).

"Richard Hakluyt and His Successors." *Annual Report of the Hakluyt Society* (1972): 1–11.

"William Montgomery and the Description of the Ards." *Irish Booklore* 2 (1972): 29–43.

1973

(With Alison M. Quinn). *Virginia Voyages from Hakluyt*. London, 1973.

1974

"Budai Parmenius István: Az Elsö Magyarutazó Eszak-Amerikában." *Irodalomtörteneti Közlemenyek* 2 (1974): 203–10.

England and the Discovery of America, 1481–1620. London and New York, 1974. (Index by Alison Quinn).

(With W.P. Cumming *et al*). *The Exploration of North America, 1630–1776.* London, 1974.

(Editor). *The Hakluyt Handbook.* 2 vols, Hakluyt Society, 2nd series, nos. 144 and 145, London, 1974. (Index by Alison Quinn).

"James I and the Beginnings of Empire in America." *Journal of Imperial and Commonwealth History* 2 (1974): 135–52.

"Stephen Parmenius of Buda: The First Hungarian in North America." *New Hungarian Quarterly* 14 (1974): 152–57.

"Thomas Harriot and the New World." In *Thomas Harriot, Renaissance Scientist*, edited by John W. Shirley. Oxford, 1974: 36–53.

"The Vinland Map and the Historian." *Geographical Journal* 140 (1974): 194–99.

"William Taverner." In *Dictionary of Canadian Biography/Dictionnaire Biographique du Canada, 3, 1740–1770*, edited by F.G. Halpenny *et al*. Toronto and Quebec, 1974.

1975

"An Anglo-French 'Voyage of Discovery' to North America in 1604-05, and Its Sequel." In *Miscellanea Offerts à Charles Verlinden à l'Occasion de Ses Trente ans de Professorat*, 2 vols, Ghent, 1975: 513–34; also in *Bulletin de l'Institut Historique Belge de Rome* 14 (1974): 513–34.

The Last Voyage of Thomas Cavendish, 1591–1592. Chicago and London, 1975. (Index by Alison Quinn).

(With Selma Barkham). "Privateering: The North American Dimension (to 1625)." In *Course et Piraterie*, edited by M. Mollat, 2 vols., Paris, 1975: 360–86.

1976

"The Attempted Colonization of Florida by the French, 1562–1565." In Paul Hulton, *The Work of Jacques Le Moyne de Morgues, A Huguenot Artist in France, Florida and England* (1976): 17–44.

"Did Bristol Sailors Discover America?" *The Times* (30 April 1976): 17.

"Edward Walshe's *The Office and Duety in Fightyng for Our Countrey* (1545)." *Irish Booklore* 3 (1976): 28–31.

"The English Contribution to Early Overseas Discovery." *Terrae Incognitae* 8 (1976): 91–97.

"Hungary's First American." In *Mulberry Tree Papers*. St. Mary's College of Maryland (Fall 1976): 3–9.

(With K.W. Nicholls). "Ireland in 1534." In *A New History of Ireland*, edited by T.W. Moody, F.X. Martin, and F.J. Byrne, 3 (1976): 1–38. (Index by Alison Quinn).

"New Geographical Horizons: Literature." In *First Images of America*, edited by F. Chiapelli. 2 vols. Los Angeles, 1976, 2, 635–58.

"Renaissance Influences in English Colonization." *Transactions of the Royal Historical Society*, 5th ser., 25 (1976): 73–93.

1977

"The Attempted Colonisation of Florida by the French, 1562–1565." In P. Hulton, *The Work of Jacques Le Moyne de Morgues*, Vol. I. London, 1977: 18–40.

(With H.A. Cronne, T.W. Moody, eds.). *Essays in British and Irish History in Honour of J.E. Todd*. New York, 1977. Reprint.

"John Denton Desires William Kearney to Print Books for Use in Down, *circa* 1588: A Sidelight on Printing in Ireland." *Irish Booklore* 3 (1977): 87–90.

North America from First Discovery to Early Settlements: The Norse Voyages to 1612. New York, 1977.

1978

"A Chance Rag-Bag of Survivals: The Archives of Early American History." *Library Journal* 103 (1978): 2305–09.

"Documenting Canada's White History." *Archivaria* 7 (1978): 86–93.

"The Preliminaries to New France: Site Selection for the Fur Trade by the French, 1604–1608." In *Festschrift für Hermann Kellenbenz*, edited by Jürgen Schneider. West Germany, 1978.

1979

"England and the Azores, 1581–1583: Three Letters." Lisbon: Centro de Estudos de Cartografia Antigo. Seccão de Lisboa. Série Separatas 123. 1979.

(With Alison M. Quinn and Susan Hillier, eds.) *New American World: A Documentary History of North America from the Earliest Times to 1612*. 5 vols. New York and London, 1979.

"Spaniards at Sea." *Times Literary Supplement* (16 December 1981): 1473–74.

1980

(With N. Cheshire, T. Waldron, and Alison M. Quinn). "Frobisher's Eskimos in England." *Archivaria* 10 (1980): 23–50.

1981

Contributions on the Americas in Jan Rotz, *The Boke of Idrography*, edited by Helen Wallis. Roxburghe Club, 1981.

Drake's Circumnavigation of the Globe: A Review. Harte Lecture. Exeter, 1981.

"La Femme et l'Enfant Inuit de Nuremberg, 1566." *Récherches-Amérindiennes de Quebec* 11 (1981): 311–13.

"The Myriad Cities of the West: A Review Article." *Town Planning Review* 56 (1981): 325–34.

Sources for the Ethnography of Northeastern North America to 1611. Museum of Man Mercury Series No. 76. Ottawa, 1981.

1982

"   ." In G.M. Story, ed. *Early English Settlement and Exploitation in Eastern Canada*. St. Johns, 1982: 9–30.

(Editor). *Early Maryland in a Wider World*. Detroit, 1982.

(With Alison M. Quinn, eds.). *The First Colonists: Documents on the Planting of the First English Settlements in North America, 1584–1590*. Raleigh, 1982; reprinted 1985. (Reprinted from *Virginia Voyages from Hakluyt*, London, 1973, with a new Preface by D.B. Quinn.

"Turks, Moors, Blacks and Others in Drake's West Indian Voyage." *Terrae Incognitae* 14 (1982): 97–104.

1983

(With A.N. Ryan). *England's Sea Empire, 1550–1640*. London, 1983.

(With Alison M. Quinn). *The English New England Voyages, 1602–1608*. Hakluyt Society, 1983.

"Foreword." S.E. Morrison, *Admiral of the Ocean Sea: A Life of Christopher Columbus*. Paperback ed. Boston, 1983: xvii–xix.

Sir Humphrey Gilbert and Newfoundland. St. Johns, 1983.

1984

"American Students and British Students." *Precinct* (Dec. 1984), University of Liverpool.

"Early Accounts of the Famous Voyage." In *Sir Francis Drake and the Famous Voyage, 1577–1580*, edited by Norman J.W. Thrower. Berkeley, 1984: 33–48.

The Lost Colonists: Their Fortune and Probable Fate. Raleigh, 1984.

"John Horace Parry (1914–1982)." American Philosophical Society *Yearbook, 1983*, Philadelphia, 1984: 421–25.

"Spanish Armada Prisoners' Escape from Ireland." *Mariner's Mirror* 70 (1984): 117–18.

"Wales and the West." In *Welsh Society and Nationhood: Essays Presented to Glanmor Williams*, edited by R.R. Davies, R.A. Griffiths, I.G. Jones, K.O. Morgan. Cardiff, 1984: 90–107.

1985

(With Alison M. Quinn, eds.) Derricke, John. *The Image of Ireland, 1581*. Belfast, 1985 (1986).

"The Lost Colony." In *Raleigh in Exeter, 1985: Privateering and Colonisation in the Reign of Elizabeth I*. Exeter, 1985: 59–72.

Set Fair for Roanoke: Voyages and Colonies, 1584–1606. Chapel Hill, 1985.

"Travel by Sea and Land." In *William Shakespeare: His World, His Work, His Influence*, edited by John F. Andrews. 3 vols. New York, 1985: vol. 1, 195–200.

1986

"Artists and Illustrators in the Early Mapping of North America." *Mariner's Mirror* 72 (1986): 244–72. (E.G.R. Taylor Lecture, 1982).

(With Alison M. Quinn). Contributions to *The Complete Works of Captain John Smith*, edited by P.L. Barbour. 3 vols. Chapel Hill, 1986.

"Ireland, 1460–1534." *A New History of Ireland*, edited by T.W. Moody, F.X. Martin, F.J. Byrne. Oxford, 1986: 591–687.

Theory and Practice: Roanoke and Jamestown. Greenville, N.C., 1986. (Lawrence F. Brewster Lecture).

1987

(With William C. Sturtevant). "The New Prey: Eskimos in Europe in 1567, 1576, and 1577." In *Indians and Europe*, edited by Christian Feest. Aachen, 1987.

"Visions, 1567." *Album Kenneth Muir 80*. Liverpool, 1987.

In press

"Colonies in the Beginning: Some Examples from North America." In *Essays on the History of North American History and Exploration.* Texas A.&M. at Arlington University Press. (Walter Prescott Webb Lecture at University of Texas).

"La Connaissance des peuples et Sociéties exotiques." *Histoire Comparée des Littératures en Langues Européennes. L'Époque de la Renaissance.* 4. Crises et essors nouveaux, 1560–1600.

"Edmund Spenser's 'View of the State of Ireland.' " In *The Spenser Encyclopaedia,* edited by A.C. Hamilton. Toronto University Press.

The Elizabethans and the Irish. Reissue, with new preface. Dublin.

"North America, the Circumnavigations." In *The Purchas Handbook,* edited by Loren Pennington. Hakluyt Society.

"North Carolina, My First Contacts, 1948–1959," and "Reflections." In *Raleigh and Quinn: The Explorer and His Boswell,* edited by H.G. Jones. *North Caroliniana Society Imprints,* No. 14 (1987).

*Adapted by Robert G. Anthony, Jr., from Alison M. Quinn and P.E.H. Hair (compilers), "The Writings of D.B. Quinn," in K.R. Andrews, N.P. Canny, and P.E.H. Hair (editors), *The Westward Enterprise: English Activities in Ireland, the Atlantic, and America, 1480–1650* (Liverpool, 1978), with typescript additions furnished by David B. Quinn, 1987.

V

Sir Walter's Surname

Sir Walter's Surname

Compiled by H. G. Jones

The spelling of Sir Walter's surname has long been debated by his biographers, some belligerently claiming only one correct spelling, others granting license to inconsistency. William Stebbing, in his *Sir Walter Ralegh, A Biography* (Oxford: Clarendon Press, 1891), p. 30, put the issue in perspective: "There was no standard of orthography for surnames till the latter part of the seventeenth century. Neither the owners, nor others were slaves to uniformity. Posterity has used its own liberty of selection, often very arbitrarily.... For Ralegh's name his contemporaries never had a fixed rule to the end of him. Transcribers with the signature before them would not copy it; they could not keep to one form of their own. His correspondents and friends followed the idea of the moment."

Willard M. Wallace, in his *Sir Walter Raleigh* (Princeton: Princeton University Press, 1959), pp. 319-320, counted more than seventy contemporary spellings of the courtier's name: Raleigh, Ralegh, Rawley, Raweley, Raulie, Rawlegh, Rawleigh, Rawleighe, Raleghe, Rawlye, Rawleie, Rawligh, Raileigh, Raughlie, Rauleigh, Raleighe, Raylie, Raghley, Raghlie, Rawleygh, Rawleyghe, Rawely, Ralighe, Raule, Rawlee, Rauley, Rawleye, Raulyghe, Rawlyghe, Ralleigh, Rawlighe, Rawleighe, Rauleighe, Raughlie, Rallegh, Rawlei, Rauly, Raughley, Raughly, Raylye, Rolye, Rolle, Raughleigh, Raleikk, Rale, Real, Reali, Ralego, Rahlegh, Raley, Raleye, Raleagh, Raleygh, Raleyghe, Ralli, Raughleye, Rauleghe, Raulghe, Raweleigh, Raylygh, Reigley, Rhaleigh, Rhaly, Wrawly, Wrawley, Raleich, Ralo, Ralle, Halley, Raulaeus, and Raleghus. The Spanish often used his first name — Gualtero, Guatteral, or Gualteral.

To King James, he was Raleigh and Raulie; to Henry Howard, Ralegh and Rawlie; to Cecil, Raleigh, Ralegh, and Rawley; and to his wife he was usually Ralegh but on at least one occasion Raleigh. Sir Walter himself used three spellings in a single deed dated 1578 — Rawleyghe, Rawlygh, and Ralegh. In later life he preferred Ralegh.

Stebbing, however, may have stubbed his pencil when he wrote (p. 31), "Of the one fact there is no doubt. The spelling Raleigh, which posterity has preferred, happens to be one he is not known to have every employed."

No doubt? Ever? We leave the debate to others, but with considerable mischievousness we toss into the controversy the indenture from Walter Raleigh to Phillip Haywood and Johanne Haywood Somers, the original of which is in the Sir Walter Raleigh Collection, a part of the University of North Carolina Library's North Carolina Collection. Dated 4 December 1583, the document spells the name with an "i" throughout, including the steel-stamped signature. To those who argue that the stamp may not have been made from a genuine

Raleigh signature, we point out that if that be the case, the legality of the license may be in doubt. If so, such a technicality appears to have bothered neither the father-daughter vintners, who gladly practiced their trade, nor Walter Raleigh, who just as gladly accepted his handsome fee for the grant of the license.

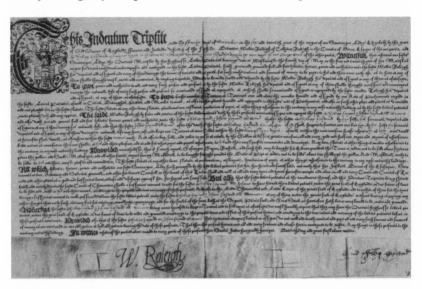

Walter Raleigh's license, 4 December 1583, authorizing Phillip Haywood and his daughter Johanne Haywood Somers to keep a tavern in Lyme Regis. Throughout, Raleigh's name is spelled with an "i". The original is in the North Carolina Collection's Sir Walter Raleigh Collection.